THE FOUNDATIONS OF
Religious Life

Essay collections rarely mark an intellectual turning point. This volume is a notable exception to that rule. In large ways and small ways, the authors show just how profoundly Pope John Paul II's theology of the body has revitalized Catholic thinking about religious life, while putting the spousal love of which St. Paul spoke to the Ephesians at the heart of the vocation to religious life. Mind-opening, challenging, and essential reading for all those, whatever their vocation, who take seriously the universal call to holiness.

George Weigel
Author of *Witness to Hope: The Biography of Pope John Paul II*

The five authors coming from different religious congregations sing an admirable quintet. They find poignant words to highlight the beauty of a total self donation to God as a key to finding oneself and to true communion with others. Though living a different calling, married people would greatly benefit by reading this book; it is a clarion call for them to re-discover the beauty of their own vocation. Supernature does not eliminate nature: it fulfills it. This is why the words of these Brides of Christ will superabundantly fecundate those of us living in the world.

Alice Von Hildebrand
Author of *The Privilege of Being a Woman*

At exactly the right moment, this marvelous new book on religious life, written by women from five different and thriving religious communities, offers a vision of the religious vocation for today—and into the future—that is fresh, authentic, compelling and true. I highly recommend it.

†Charles J. Chaput, O.F.M. Cap.
Archbishop of Denver

The Foundations of Religious Life is an extraordinary synthesis of ecclesial documents, delineating what it means to be a religious woman and why she needs to live in a special way to be fulfilled in her self-gift. This brilliant work will add to the rediscovery of religious life for active religious women and be a foundation for future novices to come, even of the cloistered communities.

Fr. Basil Cole, O.P., S.T.D,
The Dominican House of Studies, Washington, D.C..

The Council of Major Superiors of Women Religious is one of the most positive and encouraging signs in the renewal of the Church. Anyone reading this book will find a great deal of encouragement and even new insights.

Fr. Benedict Groeschel, C.F.R.

THE FOUNDATIONS OF

Religious Life

Revisting the Vision

COUNCIL OF

Major Superiors of Women Religious

ave maria press AmP notre dame, indiana

Nihil Obstat:
Rev. Gabriel P. O'Donnell, O.P.
Censor Librorum

Imprimatur:
Most Rev. Barry C. Knestout
Vicar General
Archdiocese of Washington

February 9, 2009

The *nihil obstat* and *imprimatur* are official declarations that a book or pamphlet is free of doctrinal or moral error. There is no implication that those who granted the *nihil obstat* and the *imprimatur* agree with the content, opinions or statements therein.

Founded in 1865, Ave Maria Press is a ministry of the Indiana Province of Holy Cross.

www.avemariapress.com

ISBN-10 1-59471-198-4   ISBN-13 978-1-59471-198-5

Cover image©Phillippe Lissac/Godlong/Corbis.

Cover and text design by Katherine Robinson Coleman.

Printed and bound in the United States of America.

Library of Congress Cataloging-in-Publication Data

   The foundations of religious life : revisiting the vision / Council of Major Superiors of Women Religious.
      p. cm.
   Includes bibliographical references.
   ISBN-13: 978-1-59471-198-5
   ISBN-10: 1-59471-198-4
1. Monastic and religious life of women. I. Council of Major Superiors of Women Religious.
   BX4210.F68 2009
   255'.9—dc22

                              2009004038

We publish this book under

the patronage

of Our Lady of Guadalupe

and dedicate it to the

memory of

James Cardinal Hickey.

CONTENTS

FOREWORD

M any works have been undertaken with regard to the consecrated religious life since the reforms of the Second Vatican Council, as elucidated particularly in the Decree on Religious Life.[1] Books and articles have been written on various aspects of religious life, such as the evangelical counsels, community life, authority, communal and private prayer, religious presence, community and apostolic mission.

Under the auspices of the Council of Major Superiors of Women Religious in the United States (CMSWR), six religious representing five religious institutes of consecrated life have collaborated in producing a multifaceted work, focusing upon the topics of religious consecration, the spousal bond, the three-fold response to the vows, communion in community, and mission. Their reflections present the reader with a developed exposé of the consecrated religious life, as they attempt to show the relevancy of this unique form of consecrated life in the Church and the world today. These reflections of Mother Agnes Mary Donovan, S.V., and her co-authors present the reader with a thorough description of the consecrated religious life, particularly in areas which many authors treat in a cursory manner. The consecrated religious life, as a vocation that originates in the primary consecration of every Christian to Jesus Christ through Baptism, is properly highlighted throughout this inspiring work, which I am pleased and honored to present to all who will be its readers.

In the most recent document on religious life from the Apostolic See, the Instruction of the Congregation for Institutes of Consecrated Life and Societies of Apostolic Life, titled "The Service of Authority and Obedience," it is stated in clear terms how the consecrated life is a witness of the search for God, expressed in sentiments found in Psalm 27.[2] This thought recurs throughout *The Foundations of Religious Life: Revisiting the Vision*. Some of the principal notions of the Instruction are beautifully developed in the chapters of this new work, namely, ". . . the coming to awareness of the value of the individual person with his or her vocation, and intellectual, affective and spiritual gifts, with his or her freedom and rational abilities; the centrality of the spirituality of communion, with the valuing of the instruments that help one to live it; a different and less individualistic way of understanding mission, in the sharing of all members of the People of God, with the resulting form of concrete collaboration."[3]

In his Address on the twelfth World Day for Consecrated Life, February 2, 2008, our Holy Father Pope Benedict XVI told the religious assembled in Saint Peter's Basilica at Rome that ". . . the following of Christ without compromise, as it is presented to us in the Gospel . . . constitute[s] the ultimate and supreme rule for religious life." I am confident that this new work will greatly assist consecrated religious in returning to the life-giving source of their vocation, which is Jesus Christ, and in reanimating that vocation in joy by "starting afresh" from Him.

Cardinal Justin Rigali
Archbishop of Philadelphia

INTRODUCTION

Much has been done in recent times to adapt religious life to the changed circumstances of today, and the benefit of this can be seen in the lives of very many men and women religious. But there is need for a renewed appreciation of the deeper theological reasons for this special form of consecration. We still await a full flowering of the teaching of the Second Vatican Council on the transcendent value of that special love of God and others which leads to the vowed life of poverty, chastity, and obedience.[1]

In this excerpt from his homily for the beatification of Sister Maria Adeodata Pisani in 2001, Pope John Paul II expressed the need for a deeper reflection on the transcendent value of religious life in the light of the documents of the Second Vatican Council. This request might seem unusual, for often the Conciliar teachings are given as the reason for the rapid exodus of religious from their convents, schools, and hospitals. Moreover, with the growth of secular institutes and lay movements in the Church, many ask if there still is a place for religious in the Church. Are religious institutes needed in today's society?

By revisiting the vision of religious life, this book seeks to answer that question and to contribute to a renewed understanding of religious life rooted in the firm tradition of the Church and recognized in its ecclesial dimension in the documents of the Second Vatican Council. It will perhaps be surprising to learn that the Second Vatican Council returned to the vision of Saint Thomas Aquinas and affirmed religious life as essential for the life and holiness of the Church. The following chapters were chosen to reflect some of the essential components of religious life: the meaning of consecrated life, the reality of the spousal bond this life embraces, the necessity of the vows to live out this spousal bond, the call to be a witness to communion in the Church, and the resulting mission that springs from this communion. Each chapter is written by a member of a different institute of women religious in the United States and for that reason only addresses active female religious institutes.

There is a remarkable difference in the approach taken by each author. While this reflects the differences in the professional background of each author, it is not the main reason this compilation was chosen. Each author is a member of a religious institute that belongs to the Council of Major Superiors of Women Religious, which was created in 1992 as a second organization of women religious in the United States for those institutes who hold "a shared commitment to consecrated life as set forth by Vatican II." The different theological and philosophical approaches of the chapters reflect the richness of the various charisms, or unique gifts of the Holy Spirit, granted to each religious institute. A religious institute which follows the mandates of the Church does not lose its distinctiveness as, unfortunately, some falsely claim.

To understand why the authors cite ecclesial documents primarily from the twentieth century will require some historical background. Active religious institutes for women were only approved by the Church in 1900. Prior to that time, there were strictly enclosed orders of women religious and pious sodalities; the latter groups were private societies with no canonical status. Over the next sixty-five years there was an evolution in the Church's understanding of religious life leading up to the documents of the Second Vatican Council that clarified and affirmed the ecclesial dimension of religious life. To place this evolution in context it will be helpful to look at a brief description of the history of religious life for both male and female institutes.

HISTORICAL CONTEXT

In the early centuries of the Church, many of the first Christians desired to follow the life of Christ more closely and professed a life of continence and sometimes poverty. Saint Paul refers to widows (1 Tim 5:9) and virgins (1 Cor 7) devoted to the Lord. By the third century there is mention of hermits and monks; unlike the early ascetics, they were characterized by seclusion from the world. These first virgins and confessors led solitary lives of sanctity and austerity. Their way of life soon attracted disciples eager to imitate their example, which led to the formation of the first monastic communities. Saint Pachomius was followed by Saint Basil and Saint Benedict, who was to be named the Father of Monasticism. The sisters of these great saints followed their brothers into the desert and became the leaders of small female communities. Usually monasteries of women were located a distance from that of the monks.

Having attracted large numbers of followers, many of these early abbots drew up rules in order to establish peace and order within their monasteries. Their followers committed themselves by vowing *a life* which included virginity and following the rule as a way to sanctification. The disciple was to offer himself in an act of self-donation, a *traditio* in the manner of Roman law. The person entered into a bi-lateral contract or an associative pact with the superior, who was then empowered to command the subject and to dispose of his/her activities according to the proper rule.

This contract gave the abbot or superior a form of private power, which was later called *dominative*. In these formative centuries of the Church, the first monastic abbots were laymen seeking to live as Christ. In ecclesiastical matters they were subject to the jurisdiction of the bishop, as were all Christians. Often they sought the bishop's guidance and protection. At first there were few conflicts between these founding abbots and their local bishops, but as monastic communities prospered and spread, episcopal involvement increased. The bishops sought both to protect the dedication of these early religious and to correct any aberrations that may have entered into their way of life.

Decisions of the early Church councils reflect this increasing involvement. Certain groups, such as the followers of Eutyches and the Waldensians, withdrew themselves from the jurisdiction of the bishop. Eutyches and his followers charged the bishops with heresy; the Waldensians insisted their obedience was due to God and not man. In the fifth century, these actions resulted in norms requiring episcopal approbation before the establishment of any religious house. In the thirteenth century, papal approbation was necessary for any new religious institute.

While affirming the jurisdiction of the bishops, the Holy See also recognized that some bishops treated monasteries with undue harshness. This oppression led to the practice of exemption, a privilege by which persons or places are withdrawn from the jurisdiction of bishops and made subject to the supreme pontiff or another ecclesiastical authority. By the end of the eleventh century, whole orders were exempted from episcopal jurisdiction; by the twelfth century, exemption became the rule.

With exemption, certain powers were given to the religious superiors; for men's religious institutes this often included juris-dictional power, a power that was considered to be united with sacred orders. Pope Eugene II in 826 ordered the ordination of all abbots, but this regulation was not rigidly enforced until the same injunction was made by the Council of Poitiers (1078). By requiring ordination, abbots became capable of exercising the power of jurisdiction. By no longer permitting lay abbots with the power of jurisdiction, the Church was restoring the unity between jurisdiction and sacred orders. At the same time, the Church was also drawing the institute into a closer identifica-tion with its ecclesial mission. This will be discussed more extensively in the conclusion.

The early monasteries for women followed the rule of life of their brother monasteries. When in the eighth and ninth cen-turies a number of clergy of a particular church chose to live in community and observe a rule, some women also followed this canonical way of life. They professed a vow of chastity but not of poverty. In the East a strict enclosure was demanded for all women's communities. In the West, on the other hand, at least until the thirteenth century, nuns could catechize and take care of orphans. Sometimes young girls were offered by their par-ents to the monasteries. It became the custom that anyone who wore the habit and lived with the professed sisters was consid-ered a professed religious herself. Thus profession at that time was seen as an individual decision; no liturgical ceremony was strictly necessary.

The thirteenth century saw the advent of the mendicant orders. Saint Clare founded the Second Order of Franciscans in 1212; Saint Dominic wrote a constitution for nuns even prior to founding the Friars Preachers. Monasteries for nuns, however, were ordered to observe a strict enclosure. This regulation was confirmed by Boniface VII in his constitution *Periculoso* (1582) and further mandated by the Council of Trent. All bishops were ordered "under threat of eternal malediction," to restore the enclosure of nuns wherever it was violated and to preserve it everywhere,

> restraining with ecclesiastical censures and other penalties, every appeal being set aside, the disobedient and gainsayers, even summoning for this purpose, if need be the aid of the

secular arm. . . . No nun shall after her profession be permitted to go out of the monastery except for a lawful reason approved by the bishop.[2]

The apostolate of these nuns, who professed what was historically referred to as *solemn* vows, was limited to the education of young girls if that did not require leaving the enclosure.

In 1566 Pius V compelled tertiaries, or those women who were ministering to the needy with what were called *simple* vows, to be bound by the obligation of solemn vows with papal enclosure. Therefore, those women who desired to serve the poor and the sick or to educate the young outside of their convents could not be considered religious. Although in 1727 Benedict XIII said he did not wish to prohibit tertiaries, this period of tolerance was short-lived. In 1732 Clement XII, in *Romanus pontifex,* revoked all privileges and favors granted to institutes with simple vows. Even as late as 1864 the Congregation of Bishops and Regulars said that vows of a congregation without solemn vows could not be called religious vows. Moreover, the members could not be called religious but rather *sodalitates piae* or pious sodalities; they were totally under the jurisdiction of the local bishop, with no autonomy of their own.

Most of these congregations of women, established to serve those in need, lived a way of life similar to that of religious. They lived the evangelical counsels of poverty, chastity, and obedience in a form of common life under a superior, but the power of the superior was restricted to matters of minor importance, such as the supervision of the education of those under the care of the institute. The power of the bishop was absolute. So important were the services rendered by these congregations that the Holy See confirmed several of their constitutions but with the reservation, *citra tamen approbationem conservatorii.* The constitutions were approved but the congregations were not!

The apostolic constitution by Leo XIII, *Conditae a Christo,* called the *magna charta* for religious institutes, initiated a new era for religious life in the Church. The significance of this constitution cannot be overstated. It gave canonical existence to active religious congregations and norms to govern the relationship of religious orders with their local ordinary as well as with the Holy See. The Church took to herself the apostolic mission of institutes of simple vows, blessing them with the title and privileges of *religious.* The legitimately elected authority assumed those powers granted to the superior of the institute; the bishop could neither appoint a superior nor assume those powers himself. Shortly after the promulgation of *Conditae a Christo, Normae,* issued by the Sacred Congregation for Bishops and Regulars, listed those elements essential for religious life and outlined the ideal government and structure of a religious institute. Noteworthy is the fact that religious profession, according to the *Normae,* was seen as a pact between the person and the institute; it was accepted by the superior *in the name of the Institute.*[3] (This profession did not consist of vows taken to God and received by the superior *in the name of the Church,* which would be the case in just sixteen years.) In 1901, although non-ordained religious congregations received a certain autonomy and a closer relationship with the Church, they were still considered to be private societies.

The first codification of canon law in 1917 introduced a new understanding of active religious life. C. 488 of *The Code of Canon Law, 1917,* described a religious institute as:

> a society approved by legitimate authority, the members of which strive after evangelical perfection according to the laws proper to their society, by the profession of public vows, either perpetual or temporary (c. 488,1˚).

The introduction of the word *public* was extremely significant. Public vows are accepted *in the name of the Church* by a legitimate ecclesiastical superior (see c. 1308§1 CIC 17). For the first time in history, by profession a religious was seen to be bound to the Church.

The recognition of the public character of the religious institute was not consistent, however. For one to accept public vows in the name of the Church, one would expect to have public power. The use of the terms *public* and *private* in relation to power in the Church has a long history. In essence, private power is that which can arise naturally, as that of the head of a family, or through an agreement of members in a social grouping. Public power, on the other hand, is power exercised over an independent and autonomous society, as was the power of jurisdiction exercised by superiors of clerical religious institutes. The power granted to non-ordained religious superiors by the Code of 1917 was called *dominative,* a private power. Could someone with a private power accept public vows in the name of the Church? Many argued that this canon codified a great confusion.

A. Vermeersch, S.J., a prominent moral theologian and canonist at the time, recognized that if one was to call the power of religious superiors *dominative,* there had to be a public aspect to dominative power. If religious vows were merely personal, according to Vermeersch, they would be rendered in the individual's own name; then "his homage and his holocaust are private."[4] But, in reality, Vermeersch pointed out, the Church allows the religious to profess in its own name, for it is the Church that ratifies and accepts the vows. It did not take long after the promulgation of the Code of 1917 for many to agree with Vermeersch. Were not religious institutes living parts of the institutional Church, rather than private entities?

The first official document that seemed to be based on Vermeersch's theory of the public character of religious institutes was the *Normae* promulgated by the Sacred Congregation for Religious in 1921. These *Normae* include explicit requirements for the establishment of a religious institute. Only after a Bishop submitted a detailed report including the life and motive of the founder/foundress, the name of the institute, the scope of the work, the means of support, and even the style and color of the habit, would the Congregation issue a *nihil obstat.* Then the Bishop could erect the institute and accord it juridic personality. While the *Normae* elucidated a close link between the religious institute and the universal Church, as yet there was no definition of that bond.

Pope Pius XII's teachings on religious life affirmed its public nature and laid the groundwork for the profound reflections and observations of the Second Vatican Council. In his apostolic constitution *Provida mater ecclesia,* Pius XII called religious life "the *public* state of perfection" created "for no other reason than that it is closely identified with the essential purpose of the Church" (9). In his subsequent address to the members of the First Congress of the States of Perfection, Pius XII defined in greater detail how this identification takes place. Religious life, he said, "draws its existence and its worth from the fact that it is closely bound to the proper end of the Church, namely, to lead men to sanctity."[5] Finally in his 1954 encyclical *Sacra virginitas,* Pius XII called the state of consecrated virginity, "the most precious treasure which the Founder of the Church has left in heritage to the society which he established" (1). Then in an allocution to Superiors General of Religious Orders and Congregations, Pius XII offered a simple, concise, and memorable explanation of the power granted to religious superiors. He stated:

> We have taken you as associates of our supreme office, either directly by delegating to you through the Code of Canon Law some share of Our supreme jurisdiction, or by laying the foundations of your so-called *dominative* power by Our approval of your rules and Constitutions.[6]

The Holy Father declared that all religious institutes have a public power of governing that partakes of the supreme office of the Supreme Pontiff, and that power is delegated either through the Code of Canon Law or by the approval of the rules and Constitutions. Pius XII's insights regarding religious life would be developed by the Second Vatican Council, while the nature of the power with which lay religious superiors govern still awaits clarification by the Church.

From this very brief history of the development of religious institutes prior to the Second Vatican Council, it can be seen that there was an evolution of the understanding of religious life throughout the centuries of the Church. While clerical religious orders were more easily identified with the mission of the hierarchy, the place of non-ordained religious, and particularly active religious, was more difficult to define. Although the vows of religious were considered to be *public,* the power of the non-ordained religious superior was called *dominative,* a private power. While Pope Pius XII assured superiors general that they had a public power of governing which was delegated, the bond that united non-ordained religious institutes with the ecclesial structure of the Church was not yet defined.

In clarifying the nature of the Church itself, the Second Vatican Council described religious life in its ecclesial dimension. It is this dimension that is most reflected throughout the chapters of this book, while many of the authors indicate the foundation for this ecclesiology in the rich tradition of religious life. After delving into the essential nature of religious life through the various chapters that follow, the conclusion indicates certain areas that were not completely resolved during the Second Vatican Council and that bear further clarification in order for religious life to assume its unique role within the ecclesiology of the twenty-first century.

ACKNOWLEDGMENTS

The timing of this publication is to commemorate the twenty-fifth anniversary of an instruction that expressed the essentials of religious life and was written precisely for religious in the United States. Written at the request of certain bishops unsure of how to implement the provisions of the *Code of Canon Law, 1983, Essential Elements in the Church's Teaching on Religious Life as Applied to Institutes Dedicated to Works of the Apostolate* was sent to each bishop in the United States with a personal letter of endorsement by Pope John Paul II, dated April 3, 1983. The Holy Father expresses the deep concern of the Church for the proper renewal of religious life requested by the Second Vatican Council. Unfortunately *Essential Elements* was not well-received by many religious institutes in the States, but that does not diminish its critical importance as providing the foundations for the future of religious consecration.

This book is the contribution of the Council of Major Superiors of Women Religious (CMSWR) in the United States and expresses the belief in the essential elements of religious life based in the ecclesial documents and held and lived by the member institutes. The CMSWR desires that this book nurture "a renewed appreciation of the deeper theological reasons for this special form of consecrated life,"[1] requested by Pope John Paul II and provide a stimulus for further discussion for those religious who may have chosen a more radical form of renewal after the Second Vatican Council and were not able to respond to the direction offered by *The Code of Canon Law* and *Essential Elements*. The CMSWR offers these reflections from its understanding of the ecclesial meaning of religious life and in support of continuing suitable renewal, according to the spirit and charism of each religious institute.

The member communities of the CMSWR express their gratitude posthumously to Cardinal James Hickey, who worked tirelessly on behalf of women religious, being one of their most faithful admirers from his early boyhood. Also gratitude is expressed to Bishop William Lori, who, as friend and secretary of Cardinal Hickey, practically supported the emergence of the Council of Major Superiors of Women Religious.

This book is published within the year commemorating the 150th anniversary of the apparitions of Our Lady at Lourdes. May Our Lady, Health of the Sick and Mother of us all, guide each of us in living our vocations fruitfully in the service of truth in love.

Chapter 1

RELIGIOUS CONSECRATION— A PARTICULAR FORM OF CONSECRATED LIFE

Mother Agnes Mary Donovan, S.V.

Sister Mary Elizabeth Wusinich, S.V.

Catholics are most familiar with the term consecration through their participation in the Holy Sacrifice of the Mass during which ordinary bread and wine are consecrated and become the Body and Blood of the Lord. To consecrate is to "set apart for the sacred." Every baptized person is consecrated to God through baptism, a "setting apart" which is confirmed and deepened in the sacrament of confirmation.

Consecration entails the total dedication of a person or thing to God and to his service; it is far more than a blessing that may be transient. Through the act of consecration, a state or stable condition is created in which a person or thing belongs exclusively to God and is therefore separated from ordinary or irreligious use. Things or places, such as consecrated churches, altars, sacred vessels, and cemeteries, are to be used for no other purpose than the specific use for which they have been dedicated in service of the people of God. The consecration carries a characteristic of permanence and obliges the most reverent care.

For those who are baptized, consecration brings with it a call to holiness, a call to embrace the gift given and to live in a manner in keeping with the dignity to which one has been raised. This includes following the commandments of the Lord. From among those consecrated in baptism, the Father calls some to a more radical consecration, rooted in baptismal consecration yet distinct from that gift. This total dedication—born of love—obliges not only following the commandments but also the counsels of Jesus, thus conforming one's life to the poor, chaste, and obedient life of the Son of God. This way of life is known as the vocation to consecrated life.

Among other forms of consecrated life within the Church, religious life is a particular and time-honored form, with distinguishing characteristics. Contemporary articulation of religious life found in the *Code of Canon Law*, the *Catechism of the Catholic Church*, and post-Conciliar magisterial and papal documents reflects the development of the theology of religious life in the Church. Throughout the centuries, the Church has provided structures and guidance that serve to authenticate and support the action of the Holy Spirit in raising up new charisms and in guiding existing institutes as they respond to the needs of the day. It is not the purpose of this chapter to trace the history of religious life within the Church. However, the reader may find a synopsis of this history helpful background.[1]

This chapter initially looks at the foundational grace of baptism, from which comes the universal call to holiness, then examines the specific grace of a vocation to consecrated life, and specifically to religious consecration, the origins and experience of the call and the form and fruit of assent. Lastly, it considers those distinctive components essential to an authentic living of religious life.

BAPTISM:

A CALL TO HOLINESS

> Truly you have formed my inmost being; you knit me in my mother's womb. I give thanks that I am fearfully, wonderfully made; wonderful are your works. My soul also you knew full well; nor was my frame unknown to you when I was being made in secret, when I was being fashioned in the depths of the earth. Your eyes have seen my actions; in your book they are all written; my days were limited before one of them existed. How weighty are your designs, O God; how vast the sum of them! Were I to recount them, they would outnumber the sands; did I reach the end of them, I should still be with you. (Ps 139:13–18)

As the psalmist proclaims, every human being is an intricate wonder, carefully and deliberately fashioned by Almighty God, bearing an unrepeatable reflection of divinity. Every human being, created out of the life-giving love of the Holy Trinity, has a unique role to play in the Father's plan of salvation. All are called to holiness. As we journey with God through life, we are led to discover our specific vocation, the particular way in which the Lord calls us to be united with him and to participate in his work of redemption.

The journey of faith begins with baptism when one promises (directly or through his or her parents) to renounce the world and Satan, its "prince." One professes faith in the eternal triune God and is marked with the sign of the cross. Pope John Paul II, in his post-synodal apostolic exhortation, *Christifideles laici*, highlights the central and defining grace of baptism for the Christian:

> It is no exaggeration to say that the entire existence of the lay faithful has as its purpose to lead a person to a knowledge of the radical newness of the Christian life that comes from baptism, the sacrament of faith, so that this knowledge can help that person live the responsibilities which arise from that vocation received by God. . . . Baptism regenerates us in the life of the Son of God; unites us to Christ and his Body, the Church; and anoints us in the Holy Spirit, making us spiritual temples.[2]

Through the divine action of this sacrament, the baptized person receives a fundamental consecration. Through the initial gift of forgiveness of original sin, each of the baptized becomes an adopted child of God. Baptism is a rebirth in the state of grace, a regeneration in which a person is incorporated into God's family:

> We become children of God in his only-begotten Son, Jesus Christ. Rising from the waters of the baptismal font, every Christian hears again the voice that was once heard on the banks of the Jordan River: "You are my beloved Son; with you I am well pleased" (Lk 3:22).[3]

The newness effected by baptismal grace also results from one's entrance into Christ's Paschal mystery, signified by the triple immersion in the baptismal rite.

> Baptism symbolizes and brings about a mystical but real incorporation into the crucified and glorious body of Christ. Through the sacrament, Jesus unites the baptized to his death so as to unite the recipient to his resurrection (cf. Rom 6:3–5). The "old man" is stripped away for a reclothing with the "new man," that is, with Jesus himself: "For as many of you as were baptized into Christ have put on Christ" (Gal 3:27; cf. Eph 4:22–24; Col 3:9–1).[4]

In the extravagance of his love, God the Father introduces men and women into his own transcendent universe, the universe of Trinitarian life, which would otherwise be completely

inaccessible. Through the Incarnation, Jesus, who as God pertains to the divine world of holiness, has united to himself an
individual human nature. In Christ, humanity has penetrated
into the world of God.

> [Jesus] sanctifies his humanity, then, not merely on the moral
> level (how often Christian holiness is limited to this!) but essen-
> tially and primarily on the profoundest level, the ontological
> one. . . . He is . . . the Holy One, precisely because this human-
> ity itself (hence everything in him that pertains to the world of
> creation) is immersed in the very heart of the mystery of God.[5]

This image of communion between divinity and humanity,
between God and man, made manifest in Jesus Christ becomes
the model for the divine plan of salvation. Saint Augustine succinctly summarizes this mystery in a Christmas homily: "Of his
own will he was born for us today, in time, so that he could lead
us to his Father's eternity. God became man so that man might
become God."[6]

The mission of the baptized is to allow the Father to form
them more and more in the likeness of his Son so that their
light may shine forth in a world grown dim by sin. "In this the
eternal plan of the Father for each person is realized in history:
'For those whom he foreknew he also predestined to be conformed to the image of his Son, in order that he might be the
first-born among many brethren' (Rom 8:29)."[7] The Father
desires all believers to be introduced into the intimacy of his
own divine life through baptism. However, all too often this
grace, when given, lies dormant like a buried treasure hidden
within or like a gift that remains unopened whose content is
unknown to the recipient. Baptized as infants, the sacramental
grace remains largely unreleased in the lives of many because
they have not made a mature personal commitment to the
Lord.[8] Some have been raised with an understanding of the faith
primarily as a restrictive list of commands and prohibitions and
have not experienced for themselves the transforming power of
the life, death, and resurrection of the Lord Jesus. Lacking a
personal encounter with the living God, people's lives are often
reduced to an existence focused entirely on the present and
devoid of the transcendent. It is not enough to have been made
holy by God through baptism; it is also necessary to live in

accord with that root holiness and strive toward a more perfect response to God's gift.

One's fundamental baptismal consecration is not only a grace for the individual but is also a grace for the entire Church, incorporating a new member into the Mystical Body of Christ, the community of believers. As a member, one becomes an active participant in building the Kingdom of God. This missionary mandate is lived out according to one's state in life and vocation. The laity seek to order family life and temporal affairs according to the plan of God, and in this way partake in his work of creation.[9] Those called to the consecrated life live out this mandate in and through their dedicated union with Jesus poor, chaste, and obedient.

BUILDING UPON BAPTISM: CONSECRATED LIFE

The term *consecration* refers to various forms of commitment in which there exists the dedication of a person to God in a Spirit-filled life given specifically to the honor of God, the upbuilding of the Church, and the salvation of the world. The desire to make a gift of one's life to the Lord by way of the evangelical counsels is a human response to the divine initiative of love in a call to consecration. Of themselves, the profession of chastity, poverty, and obedience by way of the evangelical counsels does not yet distinguish the way of life in which a particular call to consecration is meant to be lived. For consecrated life may be lived in the lay state as an individual or within a secular institute, or as a vowed religious. In the lay state, a call to consecration is expressed by the life of a virgin who consecrates her virginity as a self-gift to God through the profession of a vow of virginity received by a bishop, by a hermit dedicated to prayer in radical solitude, or by a lay man or woman who professes promises in a secular institute and remains in the world as a hidden leaven through a discreet witness to the gospel of Jesus Christ. Consecrated life is also lived by those called to public vows and public witness to Christ and to the Church according to a specific charism in religious life characterized by a separation from the world (proper to the institute) and a stable, visible form of life lived in common with one's brothers or sisters. In accordance with the particular way of life,

> it is the duty of the consecrated life to show that the Incarnate Son of God is the eschatological goal towards which all things tend, the splendour before which every other light pales and the infinite beauty which alone can fully satisfy the human heart. In the consecrated life, then, it is not only a matter of following Christ with one's whole heart, of loving him "more than father or mother, more than son or daughter" (cf. Mt 10:37)—for this is required of every disciple—but of living and expressing this by conforming one's whole existence to Christ in an all-encompassing commitment which foreshadows the eschatological perfection, to the extent that this is possible in time and in accordance with the different charisms.[10]

In the *Code of Canon Law*, the canons dealing with Institutes of Consecrated Life and Societies of Apostolic Life are divided into two sections: one concerning institutes of consecrated life, and a second section of law governing societies of apostolic life (which are not a form of consecrated life per se). Those canons governing Institutes of Consecrated Life are further partitioned: Title I contains norms common to all institutes of consecrated life (Canons 573–606); Title II contains canons specific to religious institutes (Canons 607–709); Title III refers to the canons regulating secular institutes (Canons 710–730). The general description of consecrated life states:

> Life consecrated by the profession of the evangelical counsels is a stable form of living by which the faithful, following Christ more closely under the action of the Holy Spirit, are totally dedicated to God who is loved most of all, so that, having dedicated themselves to his honor, the upbuilding of the Church and the salvation of the world by a new and special title, they strive for the perfection of charity in the service to the Kingdom of God and, having become an outstanding sign in the Church, they may foretell the heavenly glory.[11]

It is beneficial to consider the means by which persons in consecrated life serve the mission of the Church. Virgins offer their own chastity as a gift to God, expressing an individual offering in prayer. Hermits embrace a life of seclusion in prayer attesting to the primacy of God. Members of secular institutes strive to imbue all things in the world with the spirit of the gospel for the growth and strengthening of the Body of Christ.[12]

The life of members of religious institutes are distinguished by their "liturgical character, public profession of the evangelical counsels, fraternal life led in common, and witness given to the union of Christ with the Church,"[13] and are, thereby, an eschatological sign of the great hope to which all are invited. It is to the total consecration given in religious life that we now turn our attention.

Religious Consecration:
A New and Special Bond

Baptismal consecration, in which Christ takes "possession of a person from within,"[14] is the foundation for religious consecration, the purpose of which

> is to scale the heights of love: a complete love, dedicated to Christ under the impulse of the Holy Spirit and, through Christ, offered to the Father: hence the value of the oblation and consecration of religious profession, which in Eastern and Western Christian tradition is considered as a *baptismus flaminis,* "inasmuch as a person's heart is moved by the Holy Spirit to believe in and love God, and to repent of his sins" (ST, III, q. 66, a. 11).[15]

While religious consecration is a flowering of baptismal consecration, it is also a new and distinct bond, which cannot be considered an implication of or a logical consequence of baptism. "Religious consecration, instead, means the call to a new life that implies the gift of an original charism not granted to everyone, as Jesus states when he speaks of voluntary celibacy (Mt 19:10–12). Hence, it is a sovereign act of God, who freely chooses, calls, opens a way that is certainly connected with the baptismal consecration, but is distinct from it."[16] *Vita consecrata* considers religious profession in the Church's tradition as a "special and fruitful deepening of the consecration received in baptism," by which one's union with Christ develops into a "fuller, more explicit and authentic configuration to him." This call entails a development and maturation of baptismal consecration to which not all the faithful are called.

> This further consecration, however, differs in a special way from baptismal consecration, of which it is not a necessary consequence. In fact, all those reborn in Christ are called to live out, with the strength that is the Spirit's gift, the chastity appropriate

to their state in life, obedience to God and to the Church, and a reasonable detachment from material possessions: for all are called to live in holiness, which consists in the perfection of love. But baptism in itself does not include the call to celibacy or virginity, the renunciation of possessions, or obedience to a superior, in the form proper to the evangelical counsels. The profession of the evangelical counsels thus presupposes a particular gift of God not given to everyone, as Jesus himself emphasizes with respect to voluntary celibacy.[17]

Being set apart for the sacred through religious consecration is different from the renunciation of the world promised at baptism. While baptism separates Christians from moral evil in the world, religious profession of the evangelical counsels separates the one called to such profession from many of the good things of the world for the sake of the Kingdom. This illustrates the difference between commandments (which oblige one to avoid sin) and counsels (which provide the means to overcome the obstacles to the attainment of the good, that is, the perfection of charity). This new title of belonging to God "entails a sacrifice of joys and legitimate goods, a sacrifice which the consecrated person accepts willingly to give witness to the supreme rights of God and his own adherence to him as his only love, in imitation of Jesus chaste, poor, and obedient."[18]

In his apostolic exhortation to religious, *Redemptionis donum*, John Paul II describes the specific way in which the religious is more closely conformed to Christ through a "new" bond by uniting the complete oblation of their lives with his Paschal sacrifice: "Religious profession is a new 'burial in the death of Christ': new, because it is made with awareness and choice; new, because of love and vocation; new, by reason of unceasing 'conversion.' This 'burial in death' causes the person 'buried together with Christ' to 'walk like Christ in newness of life.'"

As the act of prostration in the rite of perpetual profession suggests, the vows affect a certain death in the person. The religious is laying down her life, in order to enter as fully as possible into the Paschal mystery, to arise a new creation in Christ. John Paul II in *Redemptionis donum*, within the section titled "Religious Profession as a 'Fuller Expression' of Baptismal Consecration," proclaims:

The depth and power of being rooted in Christ is decided precisely by religious profession. Religious profession creates a new bond between the person and the One Triune God, in Jesus Christ. This bond develops on the foundation of the original bond that is contained in the sacrament of baptism. Religious profession is "deeply rooted in baptismal consecration and is a fuller expression of it." In this way religious profession, in its constitutive content, becomes a new consecration: the consecration and giving of the human person to God, loved above all else.[19]

The religious desires to live a eucharistic life. Participation in the Holy Sacrifice of the Mass becomes the daily focal point in which one renews the gift and sacrifice of self, made on the day of profession, uniting oneself to Christ's self-offering along with the particular joys and sorrows of the day. Seeking to imitate the self-emptying of Christ (see Philippians 2:5–8), the religious is molded by the Lord's Pasch so that she may abide in Christ and Christ in her for the redemption of the world.[20] It is in and through her humanity that the invisible reality of God is made visible in the world today.

Through the total gift of self of the religious, Jesus again finds a dwelling place on earth, and seeks to *assimilate* the one consecrated to himself. "Consecrated persons make visible, in their consecration and total dedication, the loving and saving presence of Christ, the One consecrated by the Father, sent in mission. Allowing themselves to be won over by him (see Philippians 3:12), they prepare to become, in a certain way, a prolongation of his humanity."[21] The love, mercy, and providence of God are made tangible and real to people of every age through the religious who becomes a sign and vehicle of his presence and action in the world today. It is through this entrance into the Paschal mystery that a religious is conformed to Christ and discovers her deepest identity: "And I have given them the glory you gave me, so that they may be one as we are one, I in them and you in me, that they may be brought to perfection as one, that the world may know that you sent me, and that you loved them even as you loved me" (Jn 17:22–23).

ORIGINS OF RELIGIOUS CONSECRATION:
THE CALL

Throughout sacred scripture, there are numerous stories of individuals called out of the ordinary circumstances of their lives to place themselves totally and unreservedly at the service of Almighty God as instruments of his plan of salvation. The Old Testament recounts the stories of Abraham (Gn 12), Moses (Ex 3), and Jeremiah (Jer 1) to name a few. In the New Testament, the annunciation of the Lord (Lk 1:26–38) and the calling of the apostles (e.g., Jn 1:35–51) can be seen as paradigms of the call to religious consecration.

In the annunciation we see the basic structure of the call: divine initiative in inviting an individual to place her life at the service of God's plan; and human response, accepting the call and all that it entails (often unknown at the time) with loving trust in the providence of God, through a total surrender of one's life. By responding to this divine initiative, a person discovers the particular role for which he or she has been created and called to participate in the mission of the redemption of the world. The fulfillment of this vocation is beyond human ability and thus it is accompanied by God's promise of grace. Within the call, the person experiences being prized by the Lord and known in a personal way that calms fear and doubt. In response, she engages her whole self: intellect, will, and emotions in order to effectively accomplish the mission entrusted to her. *Redemptionis donum* describes the structure of a vocation as springing

> from the interior encounter with the love of Christ. . . . Christ calls precisely through this love of His. . . . The encounter with this love becomes something specifically personal . . . It [takes] on a spousal character; it [becomes] a love of choice. This love embraces the whole person, soul and body, whether man or woman, in that person's unique and unrepeatable personal "I."[22]

The structure of a vocation to religious life is illustrated in the special relationship Jesus established with some of his disciples during his earthly life. "He called them not only to welcome the Kingdom of God into their own lives, but also to put their lives at its service, leaving everything behind and closely imitating his own way of life."[23] The call begins through an encounter with the Lord in which the person is drawn to know Jesus more fully. In this deepening relationship, the individual experiences an invitation to "come and see," that is, to take on Jesus' way of living, to dwell with him and to make him the center of his or her life. While every vocation story or journey is unique, each has the encounter with Jesus Christ as its cornerstone.[24]

Eventually, the search for fulfillment of God's call leads the person to make a definitive commitment to the Lord, realizing that Christ has become all for her. Like Peter, she recognizes that the path has both narrowed and become more intense: "Master, to whom shall we go? You have the words of everlasting life" (Jn 6:68). "In them burns a unique thirst for love that can only be quenched by the Eternal One alone."[25]

The experience of living with Jesus effects a reordering of one's whole life. What once seemed important, the center and driving force in one's life, that is, education, career, personal relationships of choice, possessions, a comfortable way of life, now pale in comparison to this new love, which has seized one's heart.[26] The person desires the infinite and senses that nothing short of God will be enough. Saint Paul expressed it in this way: "But whatever gain I had, I counted as loss for the sake of Christ. Indeed I count everything as loss because of the surpassing worth of knowing Christ Jesus my Lord. For His sake I have suffered the loss of all things, and count them as refuse, in order that I may gain Christ and be found in Him" (Phil 3:7–9).

This interior experience of willingly and joyfully surrendering all to seek the pearl of great price has no explanation except in the divine encounter. This can seem irrational or irresponsible to those standing outside the mystery, but to those who have known the irresistible attraction of divine beauty, the supernatural workings of grace in the soul are recognizable. They understand that "when men have a longing so great that it surpasses human nature . . . it is the Bridegroom who has smitten them with this longing. It is he who has sent a ray of his beauty into their eyes. The greatness of the wound already shows the arrow which has struck home, the longing indicates who has inflicted the wound."[27]

The call to consecration is not the result of personal achievement; it is a gift that is "freely given and unmerited,"[28] always finding its source in God: "You did not choose me, but I chose you and appointed you that you should go and bear fruit and that your fruit should abide" (Jn 15:16). The human person who is the subject of such a divine calling,

> and the interior attraction which accompanies it . . . senses the need to respond by unconditionally dedicating his or her life to God, consecrating to him all things present and future, and placing them in his hands. This is why, with Saint Thomas, we come to understand the identity of the consecrated person, beginning with his or her complete self-offering, as being comparable to a genuine holocaust.[29]

THE PARADOX OF THE GIFT: FREEDOM THROUGH COMMITMENT

Responding to this divine calling involves renunciation. Paradoxically, personal dignity and freedom are served by a total, complete, and irrevocable gift of self to God. The one captivated by love and therefore willing to give herself completely, can appreciate the freedom that lies behind her choice, understanding that any positive choice rejects alternatives, even though they be good in themselves. Through religious consecration, the person presents her whole self to the Father as a gift, freely and joyfully given, relinquished as a sacrifice comparable to that of a holocaust—a whole burnt offering—to use as he wishes. She seeks to entrust herself into the hands of the Father in a radical state of availability, in love and without fear. She trusts with Christ that her holocaust of self, the suffering of which she will endure at times in her life, is not a rejection of her humanity but rather elevates and enhances her human nature, and fills her with a capacity to respond in ever greater measure to the grace of God. John Paul II explains:

> The sovereign power exercised by the grace of Christ in consecration does not at all diminish the freedom of the response to the call, nor the value or importance of human effort. This is made particularly clear in the call and practice of the evangelical counsels. Christ's call is accompanied by a grace that elevates the human person and gives him abilities of a higher

order to follow these counsels. This means that in consecrated
life there is a development of the human personality itself,
which is not frustrated but elevated and enhanced by the divine
gift.[30]

Far from being a destruction of anything truly human, it is
precisely within this context that the consecrated religious finds
liberation from the egotism and restless self-seeking that so
characterize our times and much more: the joy of a deep and
true relationship of spousal love with God. Pope Benedict XVI,
speaking to the youth of the world, proclaimed: "If we let Christ
into our lives, we lose nothing, nothing, absolutely nothing of
what makes life free, beautiful and great. . . . Be completely con-
vinced of this: Christ takes nothing that is beautiful and great,
but brings everything to perfection for the glory of God, the
happiness of men and women, and the salvation of the world."[31]
These words find a parallel in the 1983 document on religious
life, *Essential Elements*, which states:

> God calls a person whom he sets apart for a particular dedication
> to himself. At the same time, he offers the grace to respond so
> that consecration is expressed on the human side by a profound
> and free self-surrender. The resulting relationship is pure gift. It
> is a covenant of mutual love and fidelity, of communion and
> mission, established for God's glory, the joy of the person conse-
> crated and the salvation of the world.[32]

Touched by God's love, called into a deep, personal relationship with him alone as the source, center, and goal of one's life,
the person who hands her life completely over to the Lord to be
set apart for him alone gives up worldly riches, the possibility of
exclusive affection with another human being, and makes the
supreme sacrifice of his or her own will. What is left is the person—stripped of any status gained from family background,
education, worldly achievements, or possessions acquired.
Admittedly, the renunciation of many natural human goods can
be the source of personal suffering, but a suffering offered for
the world in union with Christ, and a sacrifice that does not
overwhelm hope. This very renunciation of temporal goods,
made in freedom for the sake of the eternal, gives moral authority to the witness of hope offered by religious to the world.

If religious life is engaged fully and authentically, the joy
and freedom found in the midst of obvious renunciations is

itself a powerful witness to the world. How is such joy and freedom possible? It is precisely through this letting go, and in the purification of heart that follows, that the deepest yearnings of the human heart are awakened: infinite love enduring beyond death, mercy that heals all wounds, and certain hope in eternal life. By embracing the evangelical counsels, religious discover the meaning and direction of life: Jesus, the wellspring of life and love. "Life in its true sense is not something we have exclusively in or from ourselves: It is a relationship. And life in its totality is a relationship with him who is the source of life. If we are in relation with him who does not die, who is Life itself and Love itself, then we are in life. Then we 'live.'"[33]

ESPOUSED TO CHRIST THE LORD

In their text on the theology of the consecrated life, *Christian Totality*, Basil Cole, O.P., and Paul Conner, O.P., make the important distinction between the divine and human action in consecration by examining the terms used by the council:

> The Latin terms used by Vatican II, *consecrare* and *consecratio*, make it clear that consecration is exclusively an action of God. The very root of these terms is the word *sacrum*, "sacred," holy or God-like. Hence these terms are not used to describe a human action. The Council designates the human element by words such as *se devovere* (LG 43c), *mancipare* (PC 5a) and *dedicare* (PC 11). Clearly, the Council meant to distinguish the radical dedication of oneself (a human act) from consecration (an act of God).[34]

By professing the evangelical counsels, the religious translates her call into practice; her "yes" is a response to God's love and binds her exclusively to the Lord. The human response to the divine invitation to consecration for religious is total and irreversible, generous, and without reservation,[35] unconditional, absolute, definitive, and exclusive.[36]

Rev. Elio Gambari describes the relationship between consecration and the profession of the evangelical counsels in this way: "Consecration is not the result of the three counsels; rather, it is the consecration that leads to the profession of the vows. . . . It could be said that spiritually and interiorly it is the call of God that consecrates, but juridically and ecclesiastically this comes about by profession."[37] In answer to the question of when exactly religious consecration occurs, the Sacred Congregation of Divine Worship stated that consecration occurs with the religious profession itself. "Consecration by profession of the counsels is affirmed as a definitive response to God in a public commitment taken before the Church. . . . It is the Church which authenticates the gift and which mediates the consecration."[38]

The profession of public vows received by the Church establishes the religious in a distinct state of life that is perpetual in nature and frees her to love God with an undivided heart. It is the pursuit of this *undividedness* that has led religious institutes to create concrete structures that foster poverty of spirit and detachment in order to free their members from the innumerable distractions of the world. Thus they can more securely seek the face of the Lord and entrust themselves with complete liberty to his redemptive plan.[39] "Saint Thomas Aquinas offers two penetrating insights on this point: 'our hearts cannot reach out totally to several things at the same time,' and 'the more we cleave to the good things of this earth or to spiritual goods, the more we withdraw from the other' (CG II, 130)."[40]

As religious seek to configure their lives as closely as possible to Christ's way of life through profession of the evangelical counsels, chastity, poverty, and obedience are lived not merely as ideals, but as concrete realities that touch daily life. Even as religious embrace structures that provide a time-tested way to holiness, it is not so much what they renounce or the apostolic service they perform that gives value to their way of life. Of primary importance is who the religious is as one who has been consecrated by God, totally given, and espoused to Christ the Lord. This reality informs the whole of their lives.

THE DISTINCTIVENESS OF CONSECRATION IN THE RELIGIOUS LIFE

It is especially important at the present historical moment in the Church to remember and restate the essential character and identity of religious consecration. Prior to the Second Vatican Council, while exceptions to the rule existed, the significant majority of those in consecrated life were in religious life—

religious sisters and brothers and cloistered contemplative monks and nuns totally dedicated to the Lord. During the decades following the council, a large proportion of religious institutes embraced a misinterpretation of religious consecration. This precipitated a crisis of identity for many individual religious and a confused understanding of the living out of religious consecration. In the same period of time, new gifts of God's Spirit received by the Church gave birth to the flourishing of secular institutes and lay ecclesial movements whose members consist, in part, of consecrated lay women and men living in the world. This confluence of events resulted in confusion regarding the specific character of religious consecration.

The Second Vatican Council proclaimed the universal call to holiness as the vocation of all the baptized. Its concluding work, the *Catechism of the Catholic Church (CCC)*, outlined the distinctiveness of religious consecration from the general pursuit of holiness in this way: "[Religious life] . . . is distinguished from other forms of consecrated life by its liturgical character, public profession of the evangelical counsels, fraternal life led in common, and witness given to the union of Christ with the Church."[41]

> Religious life, as a consecration of the whole person, manifests in the Church a wonderful marriage brought about by God, a sign of the future age, and of the indissoluble union of Christ with his Church. Thus religious bring to perfection their full gift as a sacrifice offered to God by which their whole existence becomes a continuous worship of God in love.[42]

The religious live this reality in "a society in which members, according to proper law, pronounce public vows either perpetual or temporary, which are to be renewed when they have lapsed, and live a life in common as brothers or sisters. . . . The public witness to be rendered by religious to Christ and to the Church entails a separation from the world proper to the character and purpose of each institute."[43]

Essential Elements describes nine elements as being essential to the authentic living of religious life: (1) consecration to God by public vows, (2) stable, visible form of community life, (3) corporate apostolate faithful to charism, (4) personal, communal, and liturgical prayer, (5) asceticism, (6) public witness, (7) specific relation to the Church, (8) life-long formation, and (9) government calling for religious authority based on faith.[44] In the following section, we seek to summarize the essential components that are distinct to the religious way of life as a particular form of consecrated life. They include:

Public vows professed freely in the context of the Church's liturgy by an individual whose call to religious consecration has been ratified by legitimate authority and is received by the Church.[45]

Public witness or visible presence in the Church witnessing to the supreme realities to which religious life is entirely ordered.[46]

Life lived in common with one's sisters manifesting the communion of the Church and reflecting the Trinitarian communion of love.[47]

A certain *separation from the world* proper to the purpose of the institute which signifies the absoluteness of God.[48]

A *corporate apostolate* which is experienced by its recipients as an expression of love of God through the members of a religious family.[49]

Let us now consider each of these essential components of religious consecration in greater detail.

PROFESSION OF PUBLIC VOWS

One of the distinguishing characteristics of religious consecration is the profession of public vows to God accepted in the name of the Church and confirmed by her liturgical consecration.[50] The vows are most fittingly received within the context of the Church's liturgy, in which one unites her total gift of self with the eucharistic sacrifice. The person assumes the title of a "public person," that is, one who represents the Church.[51] Canon 654 defines the consequences of religious vows as threefold: One is bound to observe the evangelical counsels; one is consecrated and incorporated into the institute.

Through the profession of public vows, one enters the way or "state of perfection"[52] not by having arrived at the perfection of charity, but "through his having obligated himself in perpetuity and by means of a certain solemnity to those things that pertain to perfection."[53] Saint Thomas Aquinas defines the meaning of *state of life* and *state of perfection* in the *Summa Theologiae* (ST

II–II, Q183–184). A person's state of life implies permanence. For example, one speaks of the married state or the religious state. Saint Thomas says that bishops and religious occupy the state of perfection within the Church, for they are bound with religious solemnity exclusively to the service of God.

All Christians are called to be holy and to pursue the perfection of charity in their spiritual lives. It is true that a person can be in the state of perfection and yet be deficient in inner perfection. Rev. Gambari explains that religious life is a state of perfection, "not only because it makes consecrated persons belong completely to God in the present time, but also it sets them in pursuit of the common Christian goal through a way of life leading perfectly, in principle, to it."[54] The religious who professes public vows is now obligated by a new bond and enjoys the liberty to strive to love as God loves and to abide in his love. Daily choices should be compatible with this new bond in order to fulfill one's religious vocation.

"More than the words, the facts count: The sacredness of a bond lies in the willingness of giving oneself to God and in the separation of the persons from other aims in order to be reserved for God alone."[55] As *Lumen gentium* states: "The more stable and firm these bonds are, the more perfect will the Christian's religious consecration be."[56] Perpetual profession creates a definitive bond between Christ and the person who is consecrated as a religious, manifesting in the Church a wonderful marriage brought about by God.[57] This bond reaches to the soul of the person; the characteristic of perpetuity implies that there is a lasting effect upon the soul of the religious.

> From the depth of the Redemption there comes Christ's call, and from that depth it reaches the human soul. By virtue of the grace of the Redemption, this saving call assumes, in the soul of the person called, the actual form of the profession of the evangelical counsels. In this form is contained your answer to the call of redeeming love, and it is also an answer of love: a love of self-giving, which is the heart of consecration, of the consecration of the person. The words of Isaiah—"I have redeemed you . . . you are mine"—seem to seal precisely this love, which is the love of a total and exclusive consecration to God. This is how the special covenant of spousal love is made, in which we seem to hear an unceasing echo of the words concerning Israel, whom the Lord

"has chosen as his own possession." For in every consecrated person the Israel of the new and eternal covenant is chosen.[58]

Although, at a later date, someone may be dispensed by the competent ecclesiastical authority from the obligation of the vows, this dispensation does not refer directly to the new bond of religious consecration, arising from perpetual profession, which remains forever.[59] A dispensation is solely a relaxation of ecclesiastical law; for the good of either the person who chooses to leave religious life or of the religious institute, the Church does not enforce the bond. It is not a declaration of nullity. A dispensation does not address the bond itself as received by God. The dispensation does exclude the person from membership in a religious institute and effects a return to the lay state.

The *Code of Canon Law* defines a vow as "a deliberate and free promise made to God concerning a possible and better good which must be fulfilled by reason of the virtue of religion."[60] The binding force of the vows derives from the virtue of religion, defined by Saint Thomas Aquinas as an interior and supernatural habit of the soul that inclines one to render to God the worship due to him. A religious offers the complete sacrifice of herself and thus belongs exclusively to God. As a result, one's entire life becomes an act of worship.

It is often asked why the profession of the evangelical counsels in religious profession is not a sacrament. Saint Thomas Aquinas teaches that the sacramental system was instituted for two reasons: to perfect men in those things that pertain to the worship of God through the rite of the Christian religion, and to act as a remedy against those defects brought about by sin.[61] The sacraments are outward signs instituted by Christ to bestow grace. They use earthly realities as vehicles to communicate God's grace. However, in religious profession, God communicates grace to the soul directly, acting without an earthly, tangible intermediary or channel used in the ceremony.[62]

> By the grace or call of religious vocation, and especially by the grace and act of religious profession, a soul is taken up by God in a most special way, and the state into which the person is assumed is of heaven, heavenly, rather than of earth, earthly. . . . Therefore it is a sign and figure . . . of the eschatological state, one that is not of earth, but rather is a sign in anticipation of the life which the soul

is to lead in the Beatific Vision when it shall be united with God alone.[63]

The vocation to religious consecration and to matrimony both bear witness to the same reality: the union of Christ with the Church (see Ephesians 5); the married, *in via*, and the religious "*in termino*, in heaven, where there is no marrying nor giving in marriage, and where there is no sacramental system."[64] Thus the profession of public vows is not only a supreme act of devotion on the part of the religious. It is also a witness to the people of God of their eschatological destiny.

PUBLIC WITNESS/VISIBLE PRESENCE: A SERVICE OF HOPE

> We are permanent signs, sacraments, of the power of divine grace. . . . The difficulties which torment us, the secret battle between the call of good and of evil, are common to everyone. And we know how fatigue and discouragement lie in wait for the man who depends solely on himself. In this way our life, if it is lived in truth, brings our fellow men a breath of hope. They need to learn how God's power is at work in the world, how this power takes upon itself all human effort directed toward goodness and brings it to transcend itself. The disproportion between our own wretched condition and the fruit which God nevertheless knows how to draw from it by means of our absolute involvement in His service makes it possible for our fellow humans to detect the divine presence. This in turn gives to their own action the foundation of confidence, of peace, without which it could not continue. In this way religious life assumes in the world the service of hope.[65]

Today there is need of lives that silently proclaim the primacy of God. Before all else, religious are to witness to the primacy of God, and to make "Christ present through personal witness."[66] To the degree that the whole of their lives are conformed to Christ, religious stir up the world's thirst for God. Such witness is consistent with the charismatic dimension of religious life, and is the special contribution of consecrated religious to the Church and the world. The human need for signs of the divine presence is heightened in the present historical moment that sees both the deep spiritual poverty of the affluent gripped by a culture of death, and the material poverty of a disproportionate percentage of the world's people. Religious presence is an invitation to an encounter with the ultimate reality, who is God.

The witness of consecrated religious affects the whole of their lives: their separation from the world, their simple community life, their apostolate that has the capacity to make tangible the love of God, and their specifically religious expression of the evangelical counsels. The witness religious give to the world is not the result of self-conscious efforts, but rather is the flowering of willed and desired commitments made to the Lord in a particular institute—the fragrance of a life which has become holocaust. The purpose of the public witness of religious is to proclaim to all men and women the mysteries of the Kingdom of God present here among us and thus give rise to hope. Witness is not only the effect of religious life lived well, but is at the heart of the purpose of this call to consecration: to introduce others to the Person of Jesus Christ. In the encyclical, *Spe salvi*, Pope Benedict states, "God is the foundation of hope: not any god, but the God who has a human face and who has loved us to the end, each one of us and humanity in its entirety. His Kingdom is not an imaginary hereafter, situated in a future that will never arrive; His Kingdom is present wherever He is loved and wherever His love reaches us."[67]

Visible marks of consecration—contemplative prayer especially centered in the liturgy and the sacraments, a visible common life, a corporate apostolate, and an evident religious garb—remain important and cannot be accurately described as the mere nostalgia of the faithful. "The Church must always seek to make her presence visible in everyday life, especially in contemporary culture, which is often very secularized and yet sensitive to the language of signs. In this regard, the Church has a right to expect a significant contribution from consecrated persons, called as they are in every situation to bear clear witness that they belong to Christ."[68]

The great service religious can give is to remind the world of eternal realities. The sign value of religious can only be effective when their vows are given concrete expression. This is possible through living a real and tangible poverty, a vibrantly, self-giving love in chastity, and obedience in maturity and freedom. In this way, religious give testimony to the truth that following God's plan is liberating and fulfilling. In the apostolate, religious are

called to love with delicacy and warmth, so that the persons
entrusted to their care experience the tender providence of God.
It is only the faithful observance of the vows in a life deeply rooted in prayer that makes possible such freedom.

RELIGIOUS COMMUNITY LIFE:
GIFT AND MYSTERY

Religious community life is a privileged way of living the
second great commandment to "love your neighbor as your-
self." It is also a constitutive feature of religious consecration,
even considered by some theologians to be as weighty as a
fourth evangelical counsel.[69] The common life provides stability
and gives concrete expression to the living of the vows. For the
religious, communion in community is received as gift. It is a
sharing in the mystery of the Trinitarian communion and the
communion of the Church, a means to holiness, and an urgent-
ly needed witness of love to modern culture. Therefore, the
vocation to religious life demands not only the human capacities and supernatural grace to live vows of chastity, poverty,
and obedience, but also a commitment to, and aptitude for, participation in a vital and varied common life of an institute
according to its spirit and tradition. A positive assessment of
these capacities is incumbent upon those persons responsible
for inviting new members to a participation in the life of the
religious institute.

The document *Fraternal Life in Community,* interpreting
canon law and the documents of the Second Vatican Council,
states: "Before being a human construction, religious community is a gift of the Spirit. It is the love of God, poured into our
hearts by the Holy Spirit, from which religious community
takes its origin and is built as a true family gathered together in
the Lord's name."[70] It is therefore impossible to understand religious community unless we start from its being a gift from on
high, from its being a mystery, from its being rooted in the very
heart of the Trinity, who wills it as part of the mystery of the
Church for the life of the world.

In creating man and woman in his own image and likeness,
God created them for communion. God the Creator, who
revealed himself as love, as Trinity, as communion, called them

to enter into intimate relationship with himself and into personal communion with one another. "This is our highest vocation: to enter into communion with God and with our brothers and sisters."[71] How far from a flattened, functional purpose of religious community life is this description! Religious do not live a common life primarily as a way of providing an economic, orderly life for its relatively large *family* of followers, nor is it ordered primarily for the sake of the community's apostolate—rather, and of first importance, common life itself has a transcendent, essentially spiritual value for those who live it and for those to whom their witness of genuine, lasting fraternal life brings hope.

The paradigm for all human relations is the Trinity, and the power to live out this ideal comes only through Jesus Christ. This ideal and truth about all human communion can be lived only if we are alert to the fact that supernatural grace never ignores nature. The slow and patient process from selfishness to self-giving is an exodus into freedom. It is often hard-won by religious who willingly take responsibility both for personal growth in self-knowledge and virtue and for active participation in religious community life. "The communion in which consecrated persons live out their belonging to the Lord cannot be reduced to a purely sociological or psychological dynamic: It must ultimately be rediscovered and understood in its theological nature as a gift and mystery."[72]

Through baptism we are offered a participation in God's own life of perfect unity. Religious community life is an incarnational reality allowing for the transformation of love in the human relationships of its members. The Holy Spirit is the soul of such religious community life, which becomes in its prayer, poverty, and apostolic works a channel of grace for the world.

All communion in community is founded in baptism and nourished by the eucharist.[73] In the daily reception of holy communion, Saint Augustine reminds us that we who receive do not so much possess Christ, as are drawn into the life of God—Father, Son, and Holy Spirit. Literally, we are drawn into the life and being of the Triune God; and in the contemplation of God, we recognize his presence in our brothers and sisters. Eucharistic life lends a sacred character to all human relationships, and especially for those called by the Church to be true experts in communion. For a religious, one's social life is a reflection of and at the service of one's contemplative union with God. Human love is a gift and a participation in divine love.

In its form and structure, religious community life is designed to support personal conversion, growth in self-knowledge, and virtue—in essence, to result in the growing holiness of its members. Toward the realization of this goal, common life has an ascetical dimension.[74] To be lived well, religious common life demands those qualities needed for all human relationships: mutual respect, kindness, sincerity, self-control, tactfulness, a sense of humor, a spirit of sharing, joyful simplicity, clarity, mutual trust, capacity for dialogue, and an acceptance of communitarian discipline. If nothing less than union with God is at stake for those who live religious community life, it is incumbent upon communities of religious to be attentive in the years of initial formation, and throughout the lifelong formation of its members, to provide the instruction and experiences needed by members to assure the possibility of fruitful, intelligent living of the common life.

If we were made for love and communion, why then is community life difficult? The answers are as surprising as they are true: because we are blessed by our Creator to be unique and unrepeatable human persons, and because of sin. Sin attacks the communion of persons brought together by love. The word *diabolical* comes from the Greek meaning "to separate or divide." It is for this reason that a rich, warm community life is so significant and prophetic an aspect of religious life.[75] Christ himself said that we would recognize his followers by the love they have for one another. Loving, healthy community life is the most characteristic mark of the Christian people, and it is the longing of so many in a culture that has spawned the breakdown of family life and infidelity in human relationships.[76]

A communion of persons gives evidence of the presence of God and the fruits of the Holy Spirit: love, joy, peace, patience, kindness, goodness, generosity, gentleness, faithfulness, modesty, self-control, and chastity. "The Church . . . has no other purpose than of making possible 'communion' among people, opening the Trinitarian life to all humanity and, since divine life is Trinitarian (communal) life, the Church is the 'sacrament' wherein it becomes possible for people to be saved as members of the one family of God."[77] The joy and freedom found within an authentic communion of persons in religious life is the fundamental Christian witness that love is possible.[78]

Separation from the World

The manner in which each religious institute embodies its fundamental focus on eternal realities, its total belonging to God, and its choice to live radically the call of the gospel gives rise to a distinctive way of life that is recognizably religious. "The public witness to be rendered by religious to Christ and the Church entails a separation from the world proper to the character and purpose of each institute."[79] Certain practices of separation from the world are adopted according to each individual charism in order to provide religious with the most beneficial environment for the living of their vocation.[80] As stated earlier, the religious binds herself to a *state of perfection*, which requires a striving toward holiness that is not temporary or capricious but rather by its very nature stable and life-long. Religious observance fulfills a twofold purpose: first by providing means that have been proven throughout the centuries to assist those seeking the perfection of charity and, secondly, as an external sign to the world of the primacy of God. In fulfilling this supernatural vocation, a religious employs all the spiritual and temporal means that will assist her such as prayer, penance, meditation, spiritual reading, and the common life.

Throughout the history of religious life, the modes of separation have taken various forms, depending on the times, the institute's charism, and apostolate, and whether the institute is contemplative or active. Each institute will adopt concrete ways of living defined by proper law that, when taken together, animate a specific identifiable family spirit. Some of the time-honored means for creating a favorable environment in which the individual and communal living of religious life can flourish include: residence in a religious house in an atmosphere that fosters fellowship among members; silence, recollection, and opportunities for solitude that make room for the mystery of God; some form of cloister; wearing of the religious habit; and a thoughtful and disciplined approach to communication with those outside the community and to the use of the media.[81] Religious institutes' members grapple with media, which, though good in themselves, may be overly intrusive into the life of the community if left unchecked. The changes in technology require attentiveness to the effects upon religious for more rapid communication, often subtly demanding one's immediate attention and possibly distracting from the life of prayer and separation from the world.

Religious serving in the apostolate are in the world but are not of the world. They engage contemporary culture, are attentive and responsive to its needs, but are not absorbed or distracted by it. They are called to be salt and light—a prophetic, countercultural sign—to men and women living in a culture that is often permeated by many forces that degrade the dignity of the human person such as secularism, hedonism, and utilitarianism. These practices of separation do not distance or alienate the religious from the contemporary men and women whom they seek to serve. Rather, they make it clear that a religious' focus is on God who illuminates all things. By purifying their hearts of that which is degrading to the human person, they simultaneously, in the pattern of Mary, open their hearts to those they serve in a more profound way. "While sin divides . . . Mary's purity makes her infinitely close to our hearts, attentive to each of us, and desirous of our true good."[82] Adequate separation from the world enables the religious to have a supernatural perspective in approaching temporal realities and to foster in themselves and others a contemplative outlook that "arises from faith in a God of life, who has created every individual as a 'wonder'" (cf. Ps 139:14).[83]

Exterior practices of separation are efficacious means for those seeking inner freedom and a life of continual conversion, total self-giving, and universal charity within religious life. They should be in keeping with the character and purpose of the institute and the dignity of the human person. Religious observance should not remain an exterior burden but rather be freely accepted and interiorized, so as not to focus on the means to the exclusion of the purpose it serves and the reality it expresses.[84] For the religious, these observances are tangible reminders of the spiritual, theological, and ecclesial realities to which religious life bears witness, and they call the members by way of symbol to a deeper understanding of and living out of their identity in the Church.

Specific norms and customs are not immutable, but taken together, they become a carefully woven fabric that clothes the institute, revealing the unique character of a particular religious family. Individual practices can seem arbitrary, insignificant, or cumbersome at times (for example: permissions from religious superiors, assignment of tasks and responsibilities, or following the *horarium*, which is the schedule, including prayer, common meals, and work of the members) to those unfamiliar with or disdainful of religious life. It is easy to question their importance or be tempted to "pull out a thread" here and there. However, care must be taken lest the *fabric* that protects and upholds the living of that particular expression of religious life become completely unwound. It is similar to the bark that provides a protective outer covering, supporting the inner life of a tree. At times the bark peels off or is carved into, and the life of the tree remains intact. But if the bark is removed in a certain way that exposes the interior of the tree to the elements and cuts off the life-sustaining nourishment received in the roots from reaching the rest of the tree, the tree will die. Observance of religious discipline cannot be done away with without altering the very nature of religious life. Perhaps a faulty interpretation of renewal, or in the words of Pope Benedict XVI, "a hermeneutic of discontinuity and rupture" following the Second Vatican Council led to the rapid, and what now appears to be, in hindsight, indiscriminate discarding of important, practical disciplines and structures. These traditions or practices serve to uphold, protect, sustain, and guide the living of religious life. While respectful of the good intentions of those involved in the decades of experimentation following the council, few hold that the general dismissal of time-tested structures have resulted in a more vibrant expression of lived religious life in America.

The indispensable relationship between separation and discipline is readily acknowledged in such activities as an athlete training for the Olympics or a musician seeking entrance into a conservatory. Their pursuit of perfection in performance affects their manner of living to the minutest detail: what and when they eat and sleep; the demanding schedule of practice that dictates how much personal time they have; submission to the guidance of an experienced trainer, mentor, or teacher (which may require them to move away from family and friends); cultivation of attitudes and ways of thinking and behaving that will motivate them to continue their pursuit even in difficult moments; and a willingness to forgo many things that are desirable and good in order to achieve their noble goal. Pursuing a lofty human goal demands that the proper means be employed with determination, focus, perseverance, and a willingness to sacrifice. If this is true in seeking perfection in the natural order, how much more attention and care must be given to the means that are employed in seeking to aid those who are called to the perfection of charity in responding to a supernatural vocation.

CORPORATE APOSTOLATE

The Church entrusts each religious institute in a particular way with a sharing in the saving mission of Christ according to its founding charism.[85] In imitation of Jesus who was sent by the Father in order to carry out the redemption of the world, men and women religious find in their apostolate the outward expression of their consecration and the sure means to enter into the mystery of salvation.

Throughout the centuries, the Holy Spirit has raised up religious communities to meet the most pressing needs of the times by inspiring founders with an exceptional gift of the Spirit, called *charism*. It is the animating force within the religious institute and is communicated to the world through apostolic service. The manifold spiritualities and apostolates of the various religious communities across the globe bear witness to God's providence present and active in the world and to the Holy Spirit's creative workings within the humanity of those chosen to be his instruments. The Church authenticates a new charism as a gift to build up the Body of Christ upon approval of an institute's constitutions. The constitutions clearly define the particular spirituality and apostolic mission to which the Church entrusts the community. The common apostolate gives concrete expression to the purpose of the institute and is a source of unity and identity among members, affecting all that the religious does and the manner in which it is accomplished.

Major superiors have a responsibility to safeguard the charism when evaluating new works to be undertaken because the common apostolate entrusted to the community cannot be changed without affecting the character of the institute.[86]

The apostolate is always a work of the community within the ecclesial mission of the institute. It is usually undertaken with brothers or sisters of the same religious family in the context of religious obedience. Individual members are "genuinely apostolic, not because they have an 'apostolate,' but because they are living as the apostles lived: following Christ in service and in communion according to the teaching of the Gospel in the Church he founded."[87] The charism is the animating force that impels them forth with a common vision and mission. While the apostolate may be undertaken by an individual member, apostolate always flows from a common mission, bearing witness to the Spirit's gift of unity and communion. The corporate apostolate of a community is an outward expression of an inner reality; it makes the charism tangible in the world and is a privileged place in which the religious encounters Christ.

Traditionally, the apostolates of religious communities have been directed toward caring for the underprivileged, the sick, the needy, and the outcast. Religious have built schools, hospitals, orphanages, and have begun charitable works to meet the needs of the poor. The animating force of these works and institutions is the love of Christ and the charism of the community. Religious communities experience the creative power of the Holy Spirit enlivening and magnifying their efforts with spiritual fruitfulness in unpredictable and marvelous ways as they fulfill the apostolates entrusted to them by the Church. Each religious community has its own collective experience of the Holy Spirit at work as it seeks to communicate, express, and live out its charism.

Consecration and mission are two facets of one reality: a life-giving, creative dynamism that fills one with apostolic zeal and continually calls one back to the wellspring of life. The source of one's apostolic vigor is rooted in the interior life and is strengthened and supported through communion in community. The union of a religious with Christ through prayer and contemplation generates new life within her that overflows into the apostolate bearing fruit in the lives of others. In this way her spiritual maternity is expressed.

The common apostolate entrusted to the community may be expressed in a variety of forms. However the members remain united in their dedication to give their charism expression through their service: to make it real, active, and present in the world today. The apostolate is an expression of their consecration and also a means of sanctification. In the apostolate, the religious is invited to enter into Christ's *yes* to the Father. Her personal preferences and individual likes and dislikes are not the guiding force. The religious who takes the risk of loving in Christ finds her capacities expanded and her love purified. A power greater than her own is at work. It is in this losing of self that she discovers herself.

The annunciation and visitation of Mary provide an apt illustration of the life-giving dynamism operative between consecration and mission. After Mary pronounces her *fiat*, placing her life at the service of God's plan of salvation, she conceives Christ beneath her heart through the power of the Holy Spirit. She then goes forth *in haste* to assist her elderly cousin Elizabeth who is also with child. Upon hearing Mary's greeting, Elizabeth, filled with the Holy Spirit, exclaims: "How does this happen to me, that the mother of my Lord should come to me? For at the moment the sound of your greeting reached my ears, the infant in my womb leaped for joy" (Lk 1:43–44). The Fathers of the Church taught that at the visitation, the power of Christ's presence dwelling within Mary radiated forth, penetrated the womb of Elizabeth, and purified John the Baptist of original sin. This is the life-giving mystery of Marian receptivity that the consecrated religious is invited to enter through the apostolate. In response to God's call, the religious echoes Mary's fiat at her profession and then goes forth with alacrity, generosity, and joy in apostolic service, carrying Christ within, radiating his presence to all within her range of activity, and through her prayer to the ends of the earth. The religious is then privileged to witness the marvels wrought by God in and through her frail humanity.

CONCLUSION

Pope Benedict XVI (then Joseph Cardinal Ratzinger) stated in the book-length interview *Salt of the Earth*, "What we really need are people who are inwardly seized by Christianity, who experience it as joy and hope, who have thus become lovers. And these we call saints."[88] The possibility for this love, this sanctity, is given at baptism, the fundamental consecration and call to holiness of every Christian. For those called into the religious state, baptism is like a seed planted deep within that buds, flowers, and bears fruit in and through their religious consecration.

One cannot long meditate on the gift and mystery of religious consecration without having the words of Saint Thérèse of Lisieux leap to mind: "Everything is grace."[89] Indeed, everything is grace— the call and the ongoing response. In our own day, we witness young women seeking to live vibrantly the essential character of religious consecration and embrace with fervor the demands of public vows, by way of a proper separation from the world and a life lived in common with her sisters. They face the demands of public witness and rejoice in the strength found in a corporate apostolate. God's graces will not be wanting. To the degree that such religious consecration is embraced through the vows and the essential components of religious life, those thus called are "inwardly seized" by Christ, and become "lovers," bearing fruit in the Church and the world in joy and hope.

Chapter 2

THE SPOUSAL BOND

Sister Paula Jean Miller, F.S.E.

I am espoused to him, to him whom the angels
serve, whose beauty the sun and moon admire. My
Lord Jesus Christ has pledged me; my Lord Jesus
Christ has pledged me with his seal. And crowned
me as his spouse, and crowned me as his spouse.

Flor Peeters[1]

I s this twentieth-century liturgical music composer merely utilizing an archaic metaphor, now discarded and disdained? Or is this just a "game of make-believe," an attempt, as many psychologists might claim, to blunt the pain of loneliness and renunciation? Philosophers ask, "What is 'real'?" Can a human know the real, or is the real a "moving target," the product of culture and socially conditioned psyches? Which is more real in human experience—the eternal and spiritual or the temporal and physical—or are they inextricably intertwined, mutually existing only in relationship? Is the mystic's Divine Lover a psychological invention or is the ek-static experience of human love rather a first taste of the Divine Communion? Is the language of love only poetry or is symbol the only adequate language of love? So goes the contemporary debate over the spousal nature of religious consecration through profession of the vows of chastity, poverty, and obedience—a debate often intensified by the emotions tied to rejection of or adherence to fundamental beliefs.

In the thirteenth century, Saint Clare of Assisi responded to Agnes of Prague's similar ponderings in this way:

> When you have loved him, you are chaste; when you have touched him, you become more pure; when you have accepted him you are a virgin; in whose embrace you are already caught up.[2]

To which astonished twenty-first-century teens would probably retort:

> Love lead to chastity? Virginity and the spousal embrace co-exist? No way—not in this life!

The virgin-spouse paradox described by the Lady Clare and again seven centuries later by Flor Peeters—while always a great challenge to human understanding—seems to be particularly incomprehensible to contemporary culture. The inability to hold what seem to be contraries in paradoxical relationship reflects not only a current tendency to define terms univocally, but also an intellectual and spiritual skepticism. Many modern approaches to spirituality, theological traditions, sacred scripture, and God himself manifest a similar reticence to explore the richness of the interpersonal covenant between God and humanity, preferring to restrict the human experience and knowledge of God to the subjective limits of metaphorical attribution, that is, to attribute human qualities and roles to God in a poetic manner. Such theologians do not believe it possible to develop real propositions about God, as has been done historically through analogy, but instead metaphorically attribute human qualities in the superlative degree to God; for them real knowledge is the exclusive domain of the culturally conditioned individual human subject. Any socially shared means of mediating knowledge of God through theological analogy is eliminated.

This metaphorical "non-knowledge" of God-in-himself differs substantially from the knowledge of faith transmitted by the apostles and theologically developed by the Fathers of the Church and their successors throughout the first two millennia of Christianity. In contrast to the metaphorical method that extracts descriptive notions for God from the human condition, the analogical method begins with God as the primary analog. God (by definition) holds particular attributes in their perfection; human participation in any virtuous quality or relation is a real but very imperfect "glimpse" of the full reality as it must exist in its divine perfection. The very fact that the quality or relationship exists at all in the creature totally depends upon its perfect actualization in God in whose Being all beings participate. Hence, the actual existence of these qualities and relationships in creatures, although more unlike than like these same qualities and relationships as they exist in God, still provide us with some real knowledge about God. Analogy asserts objective correspondence based on something shared, albeit in radically different proportions.

Francis Martin differentiates between analogy and metaphor by stating that analogy always includes a judgment concerning an *objective correspondence* between God and humanity; metaphor, on the other hand, *creates* the correspondence rather than asserting the multiple possession of the reality that is imputed to God and humanity.[3] Martin continues:

> In the Christian tradition, knowledge and speech about God are not merely a function of the mind. The mind appreciates the utter mystery of God's being and incomprehensibility, but love seeks to find ways of praising God and declaring his wonders to others. Love seeks for language because the beloved is known in his actions. We may understand Paul's statement that love believes all things (1 Corinthians 13:7) to refer to that interior activity by which the believer yields ever more and more to what is perceived in mystery and presented to faith. This is the rhythm of Christian speech about God. Where there is no living and personal contact with God who has revealed himself in the history of Jesus Christ, there is no desire to speak the mystery of God, and our temptation is to frame our language in terms that express and promote our own experiences.[4]

Hence, real knowledge of God depends on more than intellectual apprehension; the powers of the mind need to be complemented by the affective powers to free us from the limitations of merely human experience. It is Love that opens human knowledge to transcendent dimensions. The diminishment of knowledge to calculating reason beginning in the Age of "Enlightenment" accounts not only for the transition from the analogical understanding of the Divine-human relationship to the metaphorical attribution of human experience to an unknowable God, but also for the contemporary dismissal of the spousal reality of Christ with his Church, and more specifically, of the spousal nature of religious life. The Fathers of the Church surely did not share this view, as for example, in the writings of Origen:

> Do not think that the Church can be called spouse of Christ only once the Savior has come in the flesh; she is his spouse from the creation of the world or even, if we follow Paul on the origin of this great mystery, from before the creation of the world.[5]

The Catholic tradition continues to maintain that the spousal bond at the heart of consecrated life is a living sign of this marital covenant between Christ the Bridegroom and his bride the Church.

As expressed in the Roman Pontifical [*Acta apostolicae sedis* 62] (1970), the consecrated virgin is to be a "spouse of Christ," a

sign of Christ's Virgin Bride, the Church. She is freely and joyfully to bear to Christ the same undivided and perpetual love that
joins Christ and the Church. The Church is the bride of Christ.
Like the Church herself, her vocation is virginal, spousal, and
maternal. She is dedicated to the service of the Church because
she is espoused to Christ, her Bridegroom, forever.

This title of the Church was given by the fathers and doctors
of the church to those like you who speak to us of the world to
come, where there is no marrying or giving in marriage. You are
a sign of the great mystery of salvation, proclaimed at the beginning of human history and fulfilled in the marriage covenant
between Christ and his Church.[6]

Pope John Paul II recognized the broader implications of
this mystery, signed in the consecration of the religious but
intended as a hermeneutical principle for the whole economy
of salvation:

> There is an analogy in God's salvific economy: if we wish to
> understand it fully in relation to the whole of human history,
> we cannot omit, in the perspective of our faith, the mystery of
> "woman": virgin-mother-spouse.[7]

But what does it mean to be a sign of great mystery? The philosophical development of semiotics in the twentieth century by
Charles Peirce can be traced back to Saint Augustine, who first
defined its essential elements.[8] This understanding of the *signum
et res* in the Augustinian tradition culminated in the cosmic semiotics of Bonaventure's theology. Sign does not here mean something dead and inanimate like a signpost, but rather something
alive and participative in the Greater Reality to which it points
because it subsists within it. Saint Bonaventure captures the
dynamics of sign relation in his word *contuition*[9]: "a co-recognition,
a co-knowledge of one object together with another, so that one
cannot recognize one without also recognizing the other."[10]
Hellman finds the basis for this co-recognition in an underlying
structure which is common to both the Uncreated and created
orders. What the human person recognizes in everything created
is the presence of God in a particular *ordo*. Contuition is a simultaneous realization that the same order exists in both the created
and the Uncreated, though one is imperfect and the other perfect.

An example of this for our purposes is that a religious community shares in the *ordo* of the Church: it is a miniature of the

ecclesial community; each member bound to every other member because each is bound to Christ. The body of consecrated religious, like Christ's Body the Church, exists as a sign and instrument[11] "to make visible what is invisible: the spiritual and the Divine," the Divine Communion of the Trinity.[12] Thus the religious, spousally bonded to her community in Christ, makes visible to the world the Church, spousally bonded to Christ. The Church, in turn, is the great sacrament of the Trinity, in which each Person is spousally bonded to the Other. While we don't claim that religious live the spousal bond in perfection as it is in God, it is still really a spousal bond. As such, the Trinity, the Church, and the religious community, spousally bonded to one another in Christ, fulfill what Charles Peirce argues is necessary for a true sign—a three-cornered relation that connects the mind to the object signified.[13] As John Deely argues in his definitive work on semiotics, "the irreducible and unique feature of the sign is triadicity or 'Thirdness': A sign must always involve three terms" and must always include "being toward another" in relation.[14] The religious body is toward, participates in, and makes visible the Church as Body of Christ, which in a less visible manner is toward, participates in, and signs the Trinitarian Communion which is toward all creation, and in a particular way is toward the Church and the religious body, investing them with the mission of spousality. This living, participative *relation* is the sign.

Peirce's philosophical explication (c.1902: CP 2.92) of the sign function specifies genuine mediation as the character of a sign. According to Peirce, a sign is anything which is related to a second thing, its object (e.g., God), in respect to a quality (e.g., spousality), in such a way as to bring a third thing, its interpretant (an observer), into relation to the same object, and that in such a way as to bring a fourth into relation to that object in the same form, ad infinitum. If the series is broken off, the sign, in so far, falls short of the perfect significant character. Deely explains that what signs do specifically is to mediate between the physical and the objective, where the object represents itself in knowledge (both as partially including and as transcending the physical environment) and the sign always represents an object other than itself.[15] The sign depends upon the object in that the object provides the measure or content whereby and according to which the sign signifies. But the object in representing itself also depends upon the sign for being presented (the object determines what is presented, the sign whether it is presented).

The *quality* of the Trinitarian Communion, the Christ-Church covenant, and the consecrated religious community that is shared and mediated to an infinite series of interpretants, is the spousal bond of fruitful love. In the theology of Saint Bonaventure, the Trinity *is* the mystery of Marriage itself that is fully revealed to us in the great sacrament of Christ and his Church (Eph 5:32), which is then made visible for us in two complementary sign-vehicles (using Deely's suggested, improved term).[16] Sacramental marriage makes visible the *kenosis* of the Trinity in temporal reality; religious consecration makes known the same total gift of self as the spiritual marriage of every person to God as an eternal reality. Pope John Paul again states:

> Thus they give themselves to the divine Spouse, and this personal gift tends to union, which is properly spiritual in character. Through the Holy Spirit's action a woman becomes "one spirit" with Christ the Spouse (cf. 1 Cor 6:17).[17]

In the ecclesial sacrament of marriage and family and in the eschatological sign of consecrated religious community, the object (the Trinitarian God), "represents itself in knowledge (both as partially including and as transcending the physical environment)" while, in complementary ways, the ecclesial sacrament and the eschatological sign "represent an Object other than itself."[18] Clearly, in both sacramental marriage and consecrated religious life, "the sign depends upon the object in that the object provides the measure or content whereby and according to which the sign signifies. But the object in representing itself also depends upon the sign for being presented." The degree of intensity in which the spousal bond is faithfully lived, whether in sacramental marriage or in consecrated religious life, measures one aspect of the effectiveness of the mediation of the spousal character of Trinitarian life to the interpretant in any given historical circumstance. However, as Deely explains, the weakness or opacity of the particular human sign-vehicle does not diminish the sign relation itself constituted by the three terms "being toward one another" as such.

The question still remains, then, whether the sign, having mediated the transcendent mystery of the Object to the interpretant, will necessarily be effective within the mind of the interpretant if the interpretant has (as in our contemporary situation) predetermined limits for human knowing. Can the sign of a divine mystery be a sign to a human knower closed to a real relation with the Divine? The insights of Saint Clare into love, virginity, and spousal fidelity with which we began, call these predetermined limits of "human wisdom" into question. Her mystical yet human perception recognizes that human participations in divine relations transcend our fractured cultural experiences of love, virginity, and spousality, and require a deeper look from a different vantage point. For that, it is to the revelations of a "mysterious and hidden wisdom" (1 Cor 2:1–8) regarding the reality of the virginal-spousal bond to which we now turn.

SPOUSAL VIRGINITY WITHIN CHURCH TRADITION — DEFINING LOVE IN PARADOXICAL TERMS

The Church:
Spouse of Christ, born from his side in the sleep of death; Mother of the New Creation, missioned to bring forth, in the water and the blood poured out, a human race purified and redeemed.[19]

The consecrated religious:
The eschatological sign of the Church in its perpetually actualized dynamism as virgin, bride, spouse, and mother.

Spousal Love:

Divine	Human
The redeeming Love of God	A love of choice
Total self-gift for the sake of the world	A special readiness to be "poured out" for the sake of those who come within one's range of activity

Virginity:
A profound yes in the spousal order; the gift of self to Love, totally and undivided. "One cannot correctly understand virginity— a woman's consecration in virginity—without referring to

spousal love. It is through this kind of love that a person becomes a gift for the other."[20]

In the consecration of each religious, the Church conceives a living image of her union with her Divine Spouse and a living image of her prototype, Mary the *Theotokos*—virgin, bride, spouse, and Mother of God.[21] The spousal nature of the Church has always remained veiled in incomprehensible mystery for a secular world that depicts her as a powerful and wealthy institution. Paradoxically, the Church confers her veil on consecrated virgins as a sign of their mission to reawaken and call forth the deepest dignity of every human person—that of being perpetually bonded to Christ the Divine Spouse. Pope Pius XII reflects that "virgins make tangible, as it were, the perfect virginity of their mother, the Church, and the sanctity of her intimate union with Christ."[22] These values and concepts, foreign and counter-cultural to modern society, are simultaneously absolutely necessary to its healing, development, and fulfillment. In a post-Christian culture that denies the possibility of virginity and seeks to vitiate the meaning of marriage, the Church beckons each human person, in and through the sign of the perpetually vowed religious, to the fullness of that virginal marriage with God to which all have been eternally destined.

Virginity, as a consecration of body and soul to God, has been esteemed and reverenced since the earliest days of the Church. The New Testament understanding of virginity went well beyond the ancient honor given to those able to maintain bodily integrity through personal self-discipline. In the gospel of Matthew, Christ recommended virginity "for the love of the kingdom of God" (Mt 19:10–12), but he also made this a special call and gift and not a commandment. By situating the call of virginity in an eschatological setting, Jesus roots what is eternal within time and earthly existence; he anticipates personal and total union with God in the kingdom that is to come by paradoxically initiating it in the *now* of his advent. Just as the eternal kingdom to come is already experienced in the Word made flesh dwelling among us, so is it already experienced in the virgin wedded to that same Word. In his *Theology of the Body*, Pope John Paul II notes that the voluntary virginity proclaimed by Christ was such a departure from tradition that the disciples could only have understood it as a particular trait to be chosen on the basis of the personal example of Jesus.[23] In the same manner, virginity in the twenty-first century is such a departure from current practice that it can only really be understood on the basis of a spousal relationship with Christ.

Saint Paul's comments on virginity in 1 Corinthians 7 are situated within the context of early Christianity's focused desire to be ready to meet Christ the Bridegroom and enter into the wedding feast of the Lamb at whatever moment, but it anticipated that moment would come very soon. Paul's thoughts on virginity convey a certain pragmatism in terms of preparing for the coming of the eschaton, but a pragmatism meant to convey a larger truth, that is, that the fulfillment of the covenant in eternity is begun in the *now* of the Christian's life. Hence, Paul's "bottom line" is that now is the hour to consider the best means to prepare for eternity, whenever it may come; tomorrow may be too late. His counsel regards priorities. Temporal concerns— though very important—should always take second place to eternal concerns. Paul, like John in his *Apocalypse*, wants the Christian to have Christ in the forefront of his/her mind and to be waiting, anticipating him with eagerness like the virgins of the gospel parable. The focused anticipation of the bride in the *Song of Songs*, ready for the return and the knock of the Beloved, is virginity for Saint Paul. Charles Schleck comments:

> Virginity and celibacy are a visible sign or symbol or "sacrament" of an internal attitude that ought to characterize every Christian since our incorporation into Christ demands that we no longer live as pertaining to this world, but with Christ who dwells in the glory of the Father. The virgin and the celibate in this sense are visible signs or symbols to the world that marriage with God is not only possible, but that it is obligatory since in heaven there will be no marriage or giving in marriage, since the Holy City, the New Jerusalem belongs to the Lamb, to Christ, as his bride.[24]

Schleck goes on to propose that virginity can be considered as a special charisma that characterizes the New Covenant, for it is an act of faith in the significance of the Paschal Mystery, an act of hope in the assistance of the Lord to make fidelity to the vow possible, and most importantly, an act of love for the Person or Persons who alone can fulfill the human heart's desire to love.[25] To add to Saint Clare's formula, when you have believed in him, hoped in him, and loved him, you shall be virgin.

The virgin is consecrated by the Church in order that she or he manifest to the world the Consecrated One, Jesus Christ. To be consecrated literally means "to be set aside for God," so the presence of the consecrated virgin necessarily calls to mind the One for whom she is "set aside." The gospel of Saint John (himself a virgin) speaks of a double dynamic in consecration, a mutuality of consent that is essential to a marital covenant. In John 10:36, Jesus is described as the one "whom the Father consecrated and sent into the world"; but in John 17:19 Christ extends and completes that mystery of consecration—"For their sake I consecrate myself." The mystery of consecration, even in Christ himself, is first received and secondly actively affirmed and engaged in as a mission for the world. The virgin—like Christ—is first consecrated by God through the Church and then actively affirms that gift and mission by consecrating her/himself through the vows of chastity, poverty, and obedience for the sake of the world, in order to publicly witness the poor, chaste, and obedient Christ, the Divine Spouse. It is this double consecration—(1) by God through the Church and (2) by personal vow to God through a religious community for the world—that constitutes the spousal bond between the consecrated religious and Jesus Christ.[26] This spousal bond subsumes the whole of salvation history: it incorporates the *covenant in the flesh* made between God the Creator and Israel; it participates in the salvific *covenant in blood* between Christ the Redeemer and his bride the Church; and this day it makes of a particular consecrated virgin "a garden enclosed" within a community of consecrated virgins. As the Church names each *my sister, my bride*, this community is exhorted to corporately witness to the mystery of the free and conscious choice of God and one another, to personal entrustment and to mutual possession, as the sign of and participation in the Church's bridal relationship with Christ.[27]

The scriptural and liturgical tradition described above finds expression today in the writings of Pope John Paul II and Pope Benedict XVI. In his letter to bishops "On the Collaboration of Men and Women in the Church and in the World," Joseph Cardinal Ratzinger speaks of the spousal nature of the human person within the whole context of salvation history as depicted in sacred scripture:

In the course of the Old Testament, a story of salvation takes shape which involves the simultaneous participation of male and female. While having an evident metaphorical dimension, the terms *bridegroom* and *bride*—and *covenant* as well—which characterize the dynamic of salvation, are much more than simple metaphors. This spousal language touches on the very nature of the relationship which God establishes with his people, even though that relationship is more expansive than human spousal experience.[28]

In *Mulieris dignitatem,* John Paul II applies Isaiah's prophetic insight regarding the Divine-human spousal relationship first experienced between Yahweh and Israel to the Church's understanding of the eucharistic mystery[29]:

We find ourselves at the very heart of the Paschal Mystery, which completely reveals the spousal love of God. Christ is the Bridegroom because "he has given himself": his body has been given, his blood has been "poured out" . . . As the Redeemer of the world, Christ is the Bridegroom of the Church. The Eucharist is the Sacrament of our Redemption. It is the Sacrament of the Bridegroom and Bride.[30]

Here Pope John Paul summarizes a theology of spousal love which is not metaphorical but real, as it is actualized in the liturgy of the eucharist. Earlier, in his apostolic exhortation to men and women religious, *Redemptionis donum,* Pope John Paul had developed this spousal theology in relation to the consecrated life. The mystery of consecration, like the mystery of the eucharist—the wedding feast of the Lamb—is the celebration of total self-gift in loving response to the total self-gift of Christ the Bridegroom through which "redeeming love took on a spousal character."[31] In every liturgy the priest (*in persona Christi*) cries out to the Father and to the bride simultaneously, "May my sacrifice and yours be acceptable to God the Father Almighty." And the bridal Church affirms her total bodily self-offering as she prays, "May the Lord accept this sacrifice at your hands, for the praise and glory of his name, for our good and the good of all his Church." Because it is a participation in the salvific love of God made visible in the crucified love of Jesus Christ, who gave himself up for all humanity, all spousal love is now also redeeming love. True spousal love is called to redeem every counterfeit love that masquerades under its name.

Pope Benedict XVI bases his ecclesiology of communion in this same nuptial understanding of the Church, the Body of Christ, a "pneumatic-real act of spousal love."

> [T]his means that Christ and the Church are one body in the sense in which man and woman are one flesh, that is, in such a way that in their indissoluble spiritual-bodily union, they nonetheless remain unconfused and unmingled. The Church does not simply become Christ, she is ever the handmaid whom he lovingly raises to be his Bride and who seeks his face throughout these latter days.[32]

Like the mystery of marriage itself, which finds its prime analog in the Trinity, its prime sacrament in the Church, and its visible sacramental symbol in the married couple, so spousal love finds its prime analog in Christ the Redeemer Bridegroom, its primary sacrament in the Church as bride (and the consecrated religious as its icon), and finally its visible sacramental symbol, in the spousal, faithful love of husband and wife. All Christians are called to participate in the redemptive mission of Christ as priest, prophet, and king through this total self-gift of spousal love in response to the self-gift of the Beloved.[33] Within the total mystery of the Church, consecrated virgins and married couples participate in complementary ways in the spousal bond forged between Christ and his bride the Church on Calvary.

Expressing this same mystery in philosophical terms, Stanislaw Grygiel, a Polish contemporary of John Paul II, sees the vocations of marriage and virginity as complementary responses to the "horizon," that is, the real world defined by that place where the sky meets the earth, where man meets God. The horizon beckons the person who lives the question of his/her own existence in relation to the Truth that transcends him. A person's historical existence is linked to a double meaning that is related to both one's beginning and one's end, and that confronts the person with a fundamental choice. The choice is made in response to the question-call posed by Transcendence to the person who questions the truth of his/her being. The choice is to determine the virginal character of one's spousal being through virginity or the spousal character of one's virginal being through marriage. Either way, the human person is by nature created to be and become both virginal and spousal.

Grygiel explains:

> The person therefore is an eschatologically spousal reality. He
> exists in a spousal manner. All of his being is spousal. . . . To be
> subject therefore means, in the deepest level of one's reality, to
> be betrothed to Transcendence.[34]

The perspective and purpose of marriage is the perspective
and purpose of the Beginning; the perspective and purpose of
virginity is the perspective and purpose of the End, but both
perspectives are essential to all of us as created historical
beings. Looked at within the whole of the divine eschatological
plan, Grygiel concludes that virginity is to marriage as the
resurrection is to the creation. While we are made "toward"
virginity and resurrection, we are made "from" marriage and
creation and utterly dependent upon them. The existence of
virgins does not allow married couples to forget that their
joined bodies must express their virginal, eschatological destiny, while those married remind consecrated virgins that their
virginity must be expressed in relationship with others. "When
the days are finished in eschatological fullness, only the virginal
spousalness of persons to which men have matured through the
two historical states of human existence, marriage and virginity,
will remain."[35] The human being is person in the measure that
he/she lives towards the Transcendence that descends to meet
him/her.

All are called to be virginal; all are called to be spousal; all
are called to maternity/paternity within the body of the bridal
Church. Yet, in the image of the Triune God and in the mystery
of the one Church composed of many members, there is a distinction of charisms and states of life as real and complementary as the distinction between male and female bodies within the
one human race, and with the same purpose of bringing forth
new life in the image of God. Pope John Paul II states:

> In the life of an authentically Christian community the attitudes
> and values proper to the one and the other state—that is, to one
> or the other essential and conscious choice as a vocation for
> one's entire earthly life and in the perspective of the "heavenly
> Church"— complete and in a certain sense interpenetrate each
> other. Perfect conjugal love must be marked by that fidelity and
> that donation to the only Spouse (and also of the fidelity and
> donation of the Spouse to the only Bride), on which

religious profession and priestly celibacy are founded. Finally, the nature of one and the other love is "conjugal," that is, expressed through the total gift of oneself. Both types of love tend to express that conjugal meaning of the body which from the beginning has been inscribed in the personal makeup of man and woman. Conjugal love which finds its expression in continence for the kingdom of heaven must lead in its normal development to paternity or maternity in a spiritual sense (in other words, precisely to that fruitfulness of the Holy Spirit that we have already spoken about), in a way analogous to conjugal love.[36]

The purpose of this chapter, as of this entire work, is to highlight the vocation to consecrated religious life and the unique gift given to those called to witness to the conjugal meaning of the body, that is fulfilled through the total gift of self to the Divine Spouse, through the sequence of virgin, bride, spouse, and mother/father. Only in so far as this vocation is understood can those called to each of the other vocations, in turn, comprehend and live the virginal/spousal dimensions of their own lives within the bridal Church, for all of us exist together within the one mystery as "deep calling unto deep."

THEOLOGICAL DEVELOPMENT OF THE SPOUSAL IDENTITY OF RELIGIOUS LIFE

Patristic Sources Regarding Sponsa Christi

The Fathers of the Church regard virginity as a spiritual marriage, in which the soul is wedded to Christ. This is for them, in fact, the true marriage—marriage in its fullness—since its actual substance is the eternal marriage to which the Christian is destined and for which he/she longs. Pope John Paul II builds upon this patristic insight saying: "A woman is 'married' either through the sacrament of marriage or spiritually through marriage to Christ. In both cases marriage signifies the 'sincere gift of the person' of the bride to the groom."[37] While sacramental marriage is dissolved with death, the marriage of the virgin to Christ transcends death and is eternally indissoluble. The sacrament of marriage, as the temporal and earthly sacramental counterpart of this eternal marriage, makes it visible and desirable, while the spiritual marriage of the consecrated virgin, as an eschatological sign, proclaims the eternal marriage with God for which each and all persons yearn.

The early accounts of Christian virgins were all closely tied to martyrdom, that is, the virgin martyrs who died defending not only the faith, but their own virginity, since they were already "betrothed to Christ." The commentary of Origen on the *Song of Songs* was the first work to separate virginity from martyrdom and place virginity's value in the spiritual marriage of the virgin soul to the Word of God. Methodius of Olympus developed Origen's thought but also saw virginity as a means of restoring to man and woman the state of integrity lost by the Fall, a state in which the union of man and woman had an essentially transcendental orientation, that is, as a natural sacrament of the Divine Communion of Persons. These theological insights into virginity as an immediate and direct participation in the eternal mystery of marriage laid the groundwork for the writings of other early Fathers of the Church.

Saint Ambrose extolled the absolute and perpetual virginity of Mary, the Mother of God and, building upon the images of the *Song of Songs,* spoke of consecrated virgins as "married to God."[38] Saint Augustine, the disciple of Ambrose, added the dimension of spiritual maternity to this developing theology of virginity. Insofar as the virgin is conformed to the model of Christ in the gospels, she is able to be a true bride of the Word. Sanctity—that is, identification with the suffering and redeeming Christ—is at the core of the virgin's relationship with him and is the source of being able to spiritually conceive Christ in and for the world. Augustine exhorts virgins to "Let him who was fastened to the cross be securely fastened to your hearts."[39] Likewise, Saint John Chrysostom says "the root, and the flower too, of virginity is a crucified life."[40]

In this spousal identification with the suffering Christ we can discern the seeds of current papal writings that describe the mission of consecrated religious as a participation in the redemption of the world, and in a particular way, in the redemption of the human body, completing the redemption "in his/[her] own flesh" in likeness to Christ. This redemption of the body through continence anticipates with and in Christ the future resurrection; "it is a sign that the body, whose end is not the grave, is directed to glorification," in absolute and eternal nuptial relationship with God in a union of perfect inter-subjectivity. Pope John Paul interprets Christ's call to continence as a clear message to the apostles that the personal choice for chastity (and it must be a conscious and mature choice that realizes the inherent value in the masculinity and femininity of the human person) is "a decision bound with the will to share in the redeeming work of Christ" and "that decision, viewed in temporal categories, is a renunciation." While renunciation is looked upon by contemporary culture as a negation of one's sexuality and bodily goodness, the Holy Father hastens to clarify that this renunciation is not a negation but "an act of nuptial love, that is, a giving of oneself for the purpose of reciprocating in a particular way the nuptial love of the Redeemer."[41]

In the early Church virginity was principally an interior, personal decision that became publicly manifest only in and through the woman's choice not to marry, or in the case of the virgin-martyrs, to die rather than to betray their betrothal to Jesus Christ. By the time of Saint Ambrose, a ceremony of consecration had been developed in which the veil was conferred upon the virgin as a public symbol of the wedding of Christ to the Church. The fourfold mystery of the virgin Church together with its eschatological mission, as expressed in the consecration ceremony, is interpreted by Saint Fulgentius:

> This is the only-begotten Son of God, the only-begotten Son of a virgin, also the only spouse of all holy virgins, the fruit, the glory, the gift of holy virginity, whom holy virginity brought forth physically, to whom holy virginity is wedded spiritually, by whom holy virginity is made fruitful and kept inviolate, by whom she is adorned, to remain ever beautiful, by whom she is crowned, to reign forever glorious.[42]

The task of the consecrated virgin within the Church is then to witness to the eschatological marriage with Christ in complement to those sacramentally married, whose task is to witness to the spousal relationship of Christ with his Church here on earth. The consecrated virgin is "to be a sign or symbol which will present visibly before men the bride of Christ not *in via* but *in termino*, in heaven, where there is no marrying nor giving in marriage, and where there is no sacramental system."[43] Yet this eschatological mission must be actualized in time, place, and culture; for only that consecrated virginity that is enfleshed in history can proclaim the eternal truth discerned by Saint Augustine: "our hearts are restless until they rest in thee."

Medieval Theology: Saint Francis—
Icon of the Consecrated Life as Spousal

Saint Bonaventure (1221–1274), a contemporary and colleague of Saint Thomas Aquinas at the University of Paris, was designated the Seraphic Doctor because of his mystical theology of love. His theology of marriage and family as an image of the Trinitarian Communion serves as a predecessor to that of Pope John Paul II; Pope Benedict XVI is himself an expert in Bonaventure's thought. Bonaventure's works climaxed the Augustinian symbolic tradition, and the nuptial imagery and marital, spousal terminology of the Fathers of the Church permeate his writings. It is no accident, then, that in Bonaventure's Christology the Bridegroom of the Church is—as two-in-one flesh—the marriage between God and man. In his commentary on the gospel of Luke, Bonaventure expresses his theological definition of the Hypostatic Union in spousal imagery: "the union of the sublimest love and of the mutual embracing of the two natures, whereby God kisses us and we kiss God."[44] That marriage is consummated (*consummatum est*) during the Passion—the time of the nuptials. The whole of earthly and eternal life is a journey into spiritual marriage with God that Bonaventure never tires of contemplating.

The question arises as to how this spiritual marriage between God and the soul occurs—Mary's very question at the Annunciation, "How can this be?" Bonaventure replies that it is sanctifying grace that makes the marriage between God and the soul.[45] Grace is a gift that the human person is free to accept or reject, and with the free and mutual consent (God freely giving, the soul freely receiving) to God's transforming life within the soul, the marital covenant is concluded. Grace by essence is a spousal mystery, a gift "by which the soul is perfected and transformed into the bride of Christ, the daughter of the eternal Father, and the temple of the Holy Spirit."[46] Christ's gift of the Holy Spirit to the Church is the very "ring of espousal for he made the Christian soul his friend, daughter, and bride."[47] The Holy Spirit is called Gift, Bond, *Nexus,* the Life and Love of God who dwells within the Christian, divinizing and transforming, making the beloved deiform through union.

Bonaventure develops in utter mutuality the themes of love and spousal possession initiated by Saint Clare.

> But he who possesses God must be in turn possessed by him in a special way; and he who possesses and is possessed by God must love and be loved by him particularly and uniquely, as one spouse loves and is loved by the other; and he who is loved must be adopted as a child titled to an eternal inheritance. Therefore, sanctifying grace makes the soul the temple of God, the bride of Christ, and the daughter of the eternal Father . . . it could only be brought about through a free gift *divinely* infused; as clearly appears if we consider what it means to be God's temple and his child, and to be joined to him as though in wedlock by the bond of love and grace.[48]

Even the means by which humanity receives grace bespeaks the total intimacy of Bonaventure's theology: there is no instrumental cause of grace; grace is directly and divinely infused with no intermediary body. The words Bonaventure uses to describe the union attained through this divine infusion of grace are *indissolubiliter* and *copulatum,* signifying again the spousal union of the Divine and the human. While the indissolubility of the union is guaranteed by the divine spiritual nature of Christ, it is through his body that Christ is forever conjoined with humanity as his bride. Like a spouse searching the past to discern the first moment of bodily communion, Bonaventure discovers the Christ-Church union, the Hypostatic Union, and eucharistic communion are all present from the very beginning of the revelation of the Divine-human relationship in *Genesis*.

> From the Beginning, according to Genesis, "they were two-in-one flesh," namely God and man. The exchange was contracted by the assuming of flesh; whence we are able to say according to Genesis, "This now is bone of my bone and flesh of my flesh."[49]

From the beginning God's love for humanity is spousal. In Bonaventure's tractatus, *De plantatione paradisi,* the "sleep" of union is experienced already during contemplation as an eschatological anticipation of paradise, for the soul in prayer is taken into spiritual marriage with the Divine Spouse. "After the sixth day the spirit is raised to paradise, in which resting and sleeping in contemplation, it is shown into the secret chamber of spiritual marriage, where the multiform wealth and the ineffable spiritual delights of paradise are truly hidden, like treasures of wisdom and science."[50] As the breath of God enters into the body of humanity in sleep, so the soul is able to return to union with God, through spiritual marriage, in contemplative sleep.

In the journey of the soul to God, there is a progression into ever deeper ranges of nuptial relationship from carnal, to spiritual, to sacramental, to glory. The nuptials of male and female (carnal nuptials) represent the conversion point, since marriage is instituted by God as a state of common life through which man and woman can work to restore all those relationships destroyed by sin: the relationship between man and woman, between humanity and creation, and between humanity and God. Once restored to relationship with God through the free acceptance of the nuptials of grace, the human person exists in the second stage, that of spiritual nuptials. The sacramental nuptials (nuptials of the eucharist) reveal the third stage of relationship, the nuptials between Christ and the Church. And finally, the eternal nuptials, or nuptials of glory, are the nuptials of the Lamb and the spotless bride. It is this final mystical stage of nuptial relationship with Christ that the consecrated life anticipates, both as an eschatological sign of the Christ-Church union in heaven and of the individual soul in its eternal marriage with God. In this mystical union, "The soul quiets and falls asleep, reclining under God's embrace, when the Bridegroom holds the bride with love and the hand of God caresses his beloved."[51]

What human experience opened Saint Bonaventure to this mystical grasp of the spousal relationship between God and humanity? Bonaventure tells us in his *Legenda maior* that it was on the occasion of his being named minister general of the Order of Friars Minor in 1259 that he returned to that sacred place on Mount Alverno where Saint Francis entered into and was marked bodily by his spousal union with Jesus Christ. Anton Pegis comments:[52]

> Surely it is on Alverno, under the wings of the Seraph, that Francis and Bonaventure meet; and it is that meeting which marks, at once, the point of contact of Bonaventure with Francis and the point of departure of Bonaventure as a thinker. For through the labor of study, Bonaventure the learned doctor

is destined to seek the peace that consumed Francis on Alverno.[53]

What was the source of that peace that Bonaventure discovered in this revelatory moment within the life of Saint Francis? The source of spiritual insight for Francis was dual: (1) spousal union with Christ, known and loved intimately in his humanity and in his passion, and (2) the gratuitous love of the Father, manifested in each and every creature given to Francis as brother and sister. The mystical love that marked the life of Francis as a religious totally consecrated to God was both vertical and horizontal—this cross formed his love for God and his community, and was finally *impressed* upon his body by his crucified Spouse, making his body a sacramental sign of spousal love. Through his marriage to Lady Poverty in which he dispossessed himself of all things, Saint Francis was wedded to and possessed Christ his Beloved and the bridal Church, and so regained the gift of the original garden. Saint Bonaventure writes:

> In beautiful things he saw Beauty itself and through his vestiges imprinted on creation he followed his Beloved everywhere, making from all things a ladder by which he could climb up and embrace him who is utterly desirable. With a feeling of unprecedented devotion he savored in each and every creature—as in so many rivulets—that Goodness which is the fountain-source.[54]

It was poverty that released Francis to be chaste and faithful, and freely, consciously, and lovingly obedient like his beloved Spouse. It was poverty that ultimately made the life of Francis abundantly fruitful, as he totally surrendered his own body in total self-gift to Christ by giving unstintingly to all others. Religious consecration meant for Saint Francis the daily conforming of his body, his mind, and his spirit to the Christ of the Gospel in order that he could be "the true bride of the Word." For when the Word was made flesh and dwelt among us, Christ consented not only to reunite with us through the spiritual realities of charity, mercy, and forgiveness, but through conformity to our nature, through an indissoluble oneness of flesh and life with us. In a full return of love, Francis made Christ visible in history by stretching out his arms and, like Christ his Redeemer, "touched God with one hand and humanity with the other."[55] He participated in the redemptive mission of Christ by recognizing that the love of a friar must also be cruciform precisely because it is redemptive: love by its nature must *cross* all egocentric tendencies. Bonaventure's *Vita mystica* expresses why it is "theologically necessary" that religious life as spousal also be a crucified life.

> The day of his marriage is the first day, that day of indignity and blasphemy, of tribulation and misery, of blows and pain, of bonds and death. Such is this wedding day, O faithful soul, and such is the dowry by which your Spouse . . . has betrothed you.[56]

The paradoxical pain/joy of this cruciform spousal life is elucidated through the stark contrast between the first and the last paragraphs of *On the Perfection of Life Addressed to Sisters*. Bonaventure begins:

> First of all, the bride of Christ who wishes to rise to the summit of the perfect life should start at the level of her own self. Forgetting the material world, she must enter the hidden recesses of her conscience, there to explore, examine, weigh with attentive care all her faults, habits, affections, and deeds; all her sins, both past and present. Whatever fault she finds within herself, let her repent with sincere grief. A good way to self-knowledge, dear Mother, is to realize that we commit all our sins and wrong actions through either negligence, or concupiscence or malice. So whenever you think of your past sins, you should bear these three things in mind; otherwise you will never acquire perfect self-knowledge.

Saint Bonaventure proceeds from this rather startling beginning through eight stages of ever more detailed and demanding purification of the human condition, until just as suddenly the bride emerges from under this cross of her natural failings into the beatific vision of the Divine Spouse's very particular love for her! This brief exhortation culminates in images of paradise directly linked to the cruciform life as Bonaventure fairly sings:

> The more we love God here, the more we shall enjoy God there. Therefore, love God much in this life, and you shall enjoy him much in the next; let the love of God increase in you now, so that you may have then the fullness of his joy. This is the truth to be pondered in your mind, proclaimed by your lips; your soul should hunger, your body thirst, your whole substance crave for nothing but this until you enter the joy of your God, until you are clasped in your Lover's arms, until you are led

into the chamber of your beloved Spouse who, with the Father
and the Holy Spirit, lives and reigns, one God, forever and ever.
Amen.[57]

ECCLESIAL STATEMENTS ON THE SPOUSAL MISSION
OF RELIGIOUS LIFE

Redemptionis Donum: Spousal Covenant
(Vertical and Horizontal) in the Cross

The spousal relationship between Jesus Christ and his bride the
Church is lived out in history as a faithful commitment to bring
about the world's redemption. Hence, the spousal fidelity
required is not only to the Divine Community but to the human
community as well. On the feast of the Annunciation in 1984,
Pope John Paul II issued an apostolic exhortation to men and
women religious regarding their participation in Christ's mission of redemption. In it, the Holy Father explains that the
Church was born from the mystery of the redemption and has
continued to live by that mystery throughout history. The
Church shares her identity and mission with consecrated religious in a very special way.

> From the same See of Rome there reach you, with an unceasing
> echo, the words of Saint Paul: "I betrothed you to Christ to pres-
> ent you as a pure bride to her one husband" (2 Cor 11:2). The
> Church, which receives after the Apostles the treasure of mar-
> riage to the divine Spouse, looks with the greatest love towards
> all her sons and daughters who, by the *profession of the evangeli-*
> *cal counsels* and through her own mediation, have made a spe-
> cial covenant with the Redeemer of the world.[58]

Although this mission is mediated through the Church—
since it is above all her mission in union with Christ the Divine
Spouse—still, the invitation to spousal union and participation
in this mission comes directly to the individual person from
Christ, since this is a marriage and marriage *per se* requires the
free and personal consent of the beloved, as well as faithfulness
and fruitfulness. The Holy Father continues:

> The call to the way of the evangelical counsels springs *from the*
> *interior encounter with the love of Christ,* which is a redeeming
> love. . . . When Christ "looked upon you and loved you," calling

> each one of you, dear religious, that redeeming love of his was directed towards a particular person, and at the same time it took on *a spousal character:* it became a *love of choice.* This love embraces the whole person, soul and body, whether man or woman, in that person's unique and unrepeatable "I." The One who, given eternally to the Father, "gives" himself in the mystery of the Redemption, has now called man in order that he in his turn should give himself entirely to the work of the Redemption through membership in a community of brothers or sisters, recognized and approved by the Church. . . . You replied to that look by choosing him who first chose each one of you, calling you with the measurelessness of his redeeming love. Since he calls "by name," his call always appeals to *human freedom.* Christ says: "If you wish" and the response to this call is, therefore, a free choice.[59]

In these few sentences the pope summarizes the nature of the spousal bond between Christ and the religious, a bond that is marital and so includes those qualities essential to marriage—it must be free, faithful, and fruitful. The character of this spousal union must necessarily be personal and faithful—an eternal union with a unique and unrepeatable "I"—not with anonymous humanity. But the spousal bond between Christ and the religious must also be fruitful. Joseph Cardinal Ratzinger observes that the radical gift of virginity breaks through the limitations of cultural definitions of fertility:

> Virginity refutes any attempt to enclose women in mere biological destiny. Just as virginity receives from physical motherhood the insight that there is no Christian vocation except in the concrete gift of oneself to the other, so physical motherhood receives from virginity an insight into its fundamentally spiritual dimension: it is in not being content only to give physical life that the other truly comes into existence. This means that motherhood can find forms of full realization also where there is no physical procreation.[60]

The redeeming love of Christ is simultaneously offered to all eternally, and to each uniquely and specifically in a personal, historical, and intimate encounter. While such a capacity for love and commitment to all and simultaneously to the uniqueness of each is beyond our human powers and even beyond our comprehension, it is the measure of divine Love that also becomes the standard for Christian love, and in a special way, for the committed love of the religious.

Christ offers the opportunity of being "yoked" with him in complete and selfless giving to the work of redemption, the fruit of this spousal union. But John Paul adds here an addendum that specifies the yoking unique to religious life: It is through membership in a community of brothers or sisters, recognized and approved by the Church. Just as love of God is always exercised through love of neighbor, so a vow to God is always fulfilled within a concrete situation in which that love, in all its particularities, can and should be expressed.

> Religious community is a visible manifestation of the communion which is the foundation of the Church and, at the same time, a prophecy of that unity towards which she tends as her final goal. As "experts in communion," religious are, therefore, called to be an ecclesial community in the Church and in the world, witnesses and architects of the plan for unity which is the crowning point of human history in God's design. Above all, by profession of the evangelical counsels, which frees one from what might be an obstacle to the fervor of charity, *religious are communally a prophetic sign of intimate union with God*, who is loved above all things.[61]

Just as the married couple works out their salvation by fulfilling their vows of love to one another and to their family, so too the religious works out his/her salvation by fulfilling the vows made to God through a particular religious community of the Church. With and through a particular community of persons, the vows made to God of chastity, poverty, and obedience are realized. Material goods are shared *with someone,* relationships of chaste love are developed *with someone,* and obedient submission is given *to someone.* What makes the love of this particular community proportional to the divine love of God is that, while it is a personal love of choice, that is, the individual applies to, is accepted by, and makes vows within a specified institute, still the actual community in which the individual religious lives out her vowed existence is *not* personally chosen but given by God to him/her through religious superiors. Each religious is missioned to a particular local community that represents for him/her the universality of the Church and the world. It is the common mission cross they have all agreed to shoulder that binds one to the other in a single body, the Body of Christ the Divine Spouse.

It is not only the particular community to be loved that shapes the life and character of the religious. The evangelical counsels vowed to God specify a unique program of life that becomes the structure for the formation of his/her being, right down to the detailed schedule of the day. The Holy Father recalls that the look of love given to the young man in the gospels is tied to the counsel of poverty, of giving up things in order to focus not on possessing and having, but on being. Submission to daily schedule that provides a structured possibility for lived community also entails a poverty of control over planning (or being able not to plan) one's time. The religious quite literally does not *have time* because even that most intimate history of a person's changing life and development is not his/her own but belongs to God and the community, and as such really shapes and forms his/her being. While the consecration of chastity and the submission of obedience are more interior to the being and call of the religious than the renunciation of private ownership of material goods, there is no question—as was true in the life of Saint Francis—that the vow of poverty constitutes for a materialistic culture the first cross of contradiction as the prophetic charism of the Church. The decision for poverty in its manifold expressions is an essential condition for a way of life focused on personal transcendence.

Pope John Paul discerns why Christ made poverty the precondition for a vocation that answers the fundamental question of the integral importance of having or being to personhood and then poses a deeper question, "Why be a person—and how long?"[62]

> When a person "sells what he possesses" and "gives it to the poor" he discovers that those possessions and the comforts he enjoyed were not the treasure to hold on to. *The treasure is in his heart,* which Christ makes capable of "giving" to others *by the giving of self.* The rich person is not the one who possesses but the one who "gives," the one who is *capable* of giving.[63]

As in so many places in Scripture, Christ reverses values and expectations: The treasure is not to be grasped but to be given away, and what is given away is not what can be stripped away by an outside force but that which can only be given—the intimate self. This is the definitive determination of what constitutes the treasure of personhood. How long does it take and how many layers of externals can and must be stripped away before confronting the real essence of who I am and why I am,

and before facing the gospel paradox of saving one's life by losing it and so, by personal transcendence, following in the foot-
steps of Christ.

The third section of *Redemptionis donum,* on the eschatological nature of consecration in religious life, contains the heart of
John Paul's understanding of the spousal bond, the spiritual
marriage to Christ realized through the practice of the evangelical counsels. Religious are consecrated to God in Jesus Christ as
his exclusive possession and introduce into the universal mission of the people of God *a special source of spiritual and supernatural energy: a particular style of life, witness, and apostolate, in
fidelity to the mission of the institute and to its identity and spiritual
heritage.*[64] What is this source of supernatural energy for the
Church and why is it important or even necessary? How is the
style of life, witness, and apostolate determined by the mission
and spiritual heritage of the particular institute? Why is religious life composed of such a variety of institutes, spiritualities,
and apostolates which seem to bewilder and confuse the aver-
age Catholic?

The Congregation for Institutes of Consecrated Life begins
to distinguish the necessary elements involved in these spousal
communities within the Church:

> In community life, two elements of union and of unity among
> the members can be distinguished:—one, the more spiritual:
> "fraternity" or "fraternal communion," which arises from hearts
> animated by charity. It underlines "communion of life" and
> interpersonal relationships;—the other, more visible: "life in
> common" or "community life," which consists of "living in one's
> own lawfully constituted religious house" and in "leading a
> common life" through fidelity to the same norms, taking part in
> common acts, and collaboration in common services. All of this
> is lived "in their own special manner" in the various communi-
> ties, according to the charism and proper law of the institute.[65]

From this starting point, the document on *Fraternal Life in
Community* hones into the demanding costs of commitment and
dedication as lived in a religious institute, that are, in fact, often
similar to those required of a husband and wife who submit to
the realities of life in common. The vertical spousal bond with
Christ is forged and lived within the horizontal spousal bond of
a local community of a religious institute in fidelity to common

vows, a common liturgy of the eucharist, common prayer, common meals, a common daily schedule, a common habit, founding gift, and apostolate. The document continues:

> Furthermore, *through the daily experience of communion of life, prayer, and apostolate—the essential and distinctive elements of their form of consecrated life*—they are a sign of fraternal fellowship . . . *they give witness to the possibility of a community of goods, of fraternal love, of a programme of life and activity. . . they have the mission of being clearly readable signs* of that intimate communion which animates and constitutes the Church, and of being a support for the fulfillment of God's plan.[66]

As is true of sacramental marriage, the common life requires a daily living witness of fidelity to the choice, a "daily and patient passage from 'me' to 'us,'" that only takes place at and through the cross of Christ. As Nguyen Cardinal Van Thuan said so eloquently from prison in Saigon, "I accept my cross and plant it with my own two hands in my heart." While the mission of the Institute is rooted in the same mission of Christ as prophet, priest, and king as other vocations within the Church, the form of sharing in Christ's redemptive mission is determined by the religious profession of the evangelical counsels. Here the words of Pope John Paul are particularly direct.

> *The religious profession creates a new bond* [emphasis added] between the person and the One and Triune God, in Jesus Christ. This bond develops on the foundation of the *original bond* that is contained in the *Sacrament of Baptism . . .* In this way religious profession, in its constitutive content, becomes *a new consecration: the consecration and giving of the human person to God, loved above all else . . .* religious profession is a new "burial in the death of Christ": new, because it is made with awareness and by choice; new, because of love and vocation; new, by reason of unceasing "conversion." . . . [I]n a much more mature and conscious manner, "the old nature is put off" and likewise, the "new nature is put on."[67]

The Holy Father has here arrived at the heart of his exhortation. The spousal covenant of redemption entered into in this second consecration, in a more mature and conscious manner and as a very program of life, is to unceasing conversion by actualizing chastity, poverty, and obedience within daily life *with* other members of the community. While the religious assumes the baptismal consecration and promise of conversion of the Body of Christ, in an even more profound way the rest of the Body of Christ is also taken up into this second consecration of the religious. Pope John Paul goes on to explain, "The whole messianic people, the entire Church is *chosen in every person* whom the Lord selects from the midst of this people; in every person who is consecrated *for everyone* to God as his exclusive possession."[68] In other words, the religious is an icon of the Church in the deeper sense of participating in the nature of Christ as the Suffering Servant, for as the pope continues, the religious as spouse of Christ seeks to say with him, "For their sake I consecrate myself, in the full force of these words, through self-giving love, through the offering of oneself to God as his exclusive possession. . . . Through the vows of chastity, poverty, and obedience, the Religious responds to the plea of Saint Paul in his letter to the Romans: 'present your bodies as a living sacrifice, holy and acceptable to God, which is your spiritual worship.'"[69]

The challenge proffered to the consecrated religious by the Church, as the spouse of Christ conjoined with him in his mission of redemption, is to immerse her/himself in the Paschal Mystery of the Redeemer

> through the total love of self-giving, to fill your souls and your bodies with the spirit of sacrifice . . . in this way the *likeness of that love which in the heart of Christ* is both redemptive and spousal is imprinted on the religious profession.[70]

As this new life of Christ begins in the consecrated religious, so too does the new creation begin in the whole messianic people of God, for "evangelical consecration has been planted as a particular sign of the presence of God for whom all live." The Holy Father ends this section by assuring that religious consecration is a taking part "in the most complete and radical way possible in the shaping of that new creation which must emerge from the Redemption of the world by means of the power of the Spirit of Truth operating from the abundance of the Paschal Mystery."[71]

This shaping of the new creation is precisely a transformation and renewal of the entire cosmos which has been disfigured through the sins of humanity and can only be reconfigured to Christ through the transformation of the human heart.

> In the economy of the Redemption the evangelical counsels of chastity, poverty, and obedience constitute the most radical means for transforming in the human heart this relationship with "the world": with the external world and with one's personal "I."[72]

While the essential purpose of the evangelical counsels is the renewal of the whole of creation, it begins with the transformation of the disfigured human heart of the one who in trepidation vows to strive for this personal and cosmic transfiguration. If one is to be anxious about "the affairs of the Lord" and "please the Lord" then, John Paul deduces, "one who pleases God cannot be closed in upon himself but is open to the world, to everything that is to be led to Christ."[73] Perhaps the greatest renunciation required is to replace the Christ of subjective imagination with the real beloved Spouse discovered in the world. This law of renunciation that is integral to the Christian vocation through baptism is even more intimately part of the vowed commitment to identify with today's suffering and crucified Christ, as the means of restoring one's own human nature, in order to be the medium through which Christ transfers the power of the Paschal Mystery to the most extensive level of humanity.[74]

The vowed commitment to continuing conversion and transformation of one's own heart in relation to all of creation finds its deepest expression and challenge in the life of obedience. Pope John Paul calls obedience the "unique way between the mystery of sin and the mystery of justification and salvific grace."

> They are in this "place" with all the sinful background of their own human nature, with all the inheritance "of the pride of life," with all the selfish tendencies to dominate rather than to serve, and precisely by means of the vow of obedience they decide *to be transformed* into the likeness of Christ, who "redeemed humanity and made it holy by his obedience." In the counsel of obedience they desire to find their own role in the Redemption of Christ and their own way of sanctification.[75]

The share in the world's redemption to be contributed by the consecrated religious in complement to that of Christ the Divine Spouse is here boldly accented. Christ, the Sinless, Obedient One assumes human nature so that in it and through it he can redeem all of humanity out of pure spousal love. As seen above in Bonaventure's *Address to Sisters*, the consecrated religious recognizes his/her own sinful and disfigured human nature in all of its concrete and willful manifestations and offers that nature to Christ, first begging its own transfiguration into the likeness of Christ through spousal union. Simultaneously he/she asks that the daily process required for conversion and transformation become the medium of grace and transfiguration for the whole of creation. The religious is called to recognize sinful personal choices as the "O Happy Fault" and become a "dispenser of good through one's own human condition"[76]—to allow Christ to use humanness *as it is* as his own instrument of redemption of others. The very process of being personally released from sin while learning obedience to the Father triggers the means of redemption within others.

Mediating the transformation of others through personal conversion and apostolic works is only possible when the obedience promised to Christ is actualized through obedience to the persons in authority within the religious community. While acknowledging the importance of the particular works of religious orders to the life of the Church, the Holy Father cites the community dimension of the apostolate as its principal value. Because they stand together before God as one virginal body with many interrelated gifts, ready and willing to bring forth new life for the Church and for Christ through their common mission, the community is able to assume, in part, the role and responsibility of the Church as bride and mother to the world. The Marian quality of their bridal yes implies faith in God, trust in one another, openness both to the unknown life yet to be conceived and to the demands that it will make upon the real life of the community. Their community apostolate not only opens each religious to society's needs but also profoundly links religious life itself to the Church as spouse of Christ and mother of humanity.

Redemptionis donum, like the magisterial documents for religious that preceded it, was signed on a major feast of the Blessed Virgin Mary, usually the Feast of the Annunciation. What is the significance for consecrated religious of this particular feast, particularly in light of their participation in the mystery of redemption? On the Feast of the Annunciation the Church acknowledges that it was Mary who gave the gift of flesh to the Son of God, making it possible for him to assume human nature and redeem it. The Holy Father recalls that what is essentially and paradigmatically true for Christ the Redeemer, is also true for each member sharing his one Flesh. Because all humanity is one flesh, all flesh continues to be redeemed in and through the redemption of each member. But as Saint Augustine reminds us, although God created everyone without their help he will not save anyone without a willed cooperation. Personal redemption begins with receptivity to God's grace, and conformation to Christ continues through acknowledgement of sin and personal conversion. Mary, Mother of God and Mother of the Church, is, because of her total receptivity to God through Christ, the prototype of and model for the Church and each member who enters into transformation as virgin, bride, spouse, and mother.

Vita Consecrata: Spousal Existence—
"A Road Situated Between Two Lights"

Vita consecrata was written twelve years after *Redemptionis donum* and proclaimed on the Feast of the Annunciation, March 25, 1996. The Holy Father declared once again that "the *consecrated life is at the very heart of the Church* as a decisive element of her mission, since it 'manifests the inner nature of the Christian calling' and the striving of the whole Church as Bride toward union with her one Spouse."[77] While the emphasis of the earlier apostolic exhortation is on spousal participation in Christ's redemptive mission by both Mary and the consecrated religious, the emphasis in this second exhortation is on the incarnation of the mystery of Christ's Transfiguration within their apostolic ministry as an eschatological sign.

The story of the Transfiguration on the mountain "marks a decisive moment in the ministry of Jesus" and the moment when he shares with the apostles his beauty and his glory. It also marks the departure (*exodus*) for Jerusalem: the commitment to the mission of Redemption. John Paul believes it is the theological mystery of Transfiguration that best expresses the full spectrum of the vocation to the consecrated life: the call to contemplation of Christ and intimate relationship with him in a life of holiness; the corresponding need for personal conversion from sin and weakness; the lived tension between the "going up the mountain" to witness the beauty of the Transfiguration and the "coming down to the valley" to serve the disfigured face of Christ in humanity; the personal process of "transfiguration," "conformation," "configuration," "transformation" that marks the life of the consecrated religious as an eschatological sign.

The pope considers the consecrated life as the call to a difficult "exodus journey" that takes place in the toil of daily life on the way to eschatological encounter with the Lord. But there is a "special grace of intimacy" for those "conforming [their] whole existence to Christ in an all-encompassing commitment which foreshadows the eschatological perfection, to the extent that this is possible in time."[78] This "exodus journey" with Christ takes place within the final mysteries of Christ's life. It is made on "a road situated between two lights: the anticipatory light of the Transfiguration and the definitive light of the resurrection."[79] Like the apostles who walked with Christ from the mountain of Transfiguration through the valley of death to the garden of the Resurrection, the journey for those chosen becomes a time for the configuration of their lives to his *way* of relationship as Son to the Father and the Holy Spirit. Through the chastity, poverty, and obedience of filial love, they too become a *confessio Trinitatis,* an image of the Invisible God.

The vocation to the consecrated life begins with a gift, described by Pope John Paul in the images of the Transfiguration: the gift of an intimate encounter with Christ in which the one called is dazzled by his beauty and so is willing, like the chosen apostles, to leave everything behind "in order to live at his side and to follow him wherever he goes."[80] The call to the consecrated life begins, not with a "clenched teeth" determination to deny oneself the happiness that life has to offer, but with being seized by a Love that becomes the inner motivation for a total gift of self to the mission of Christ. Like Mary at the Annunciation, every vocation begins with "spousal receptivity to the Word in order to contribute to the growth of a new humanity by their unconditional dedication and their living witness."[81]

The next movement in this process toward holiness focuses on the activity of the one called: "They strive to become one with him, taking on his mind and his way of life."[82] Like Moses before the Burning Bush, the one called is filled with the fear of the Holy and keenly aware of personal inadequacies and failings. From the human side of the equation, the call is to "complete conversion, in self-renunciation, in order to live fully for the Lord, so that God may be all in all. Called to contemplate and bear witness to the transfigured face of Christ, consecrated men and women are also *called to a 'transfigured' existence.*"[83] John Paul consistently describes this human dynamic within the process toward holiness as *conformation.* The one invited by the Transfigured One to a transfigured existence responds in a whole-hearted effort to form his/her life in likeness to and union with Christ through a process of conversion, renunciation, and asceticism. There is *"an explicit desire to be totally conformed to him,"*[84] . . . and the more consecrated persons allow themselves to be conformed to Christ, the more Christ is made present and active in the world for the salvation of all."[85]

This personal work on the part of the one called opens the religious to the third stage of the process toward holiness, to *configuration* by the power of the Holy Spirit.

> [I]t is he who shapes and molds the hearts of those who are called, configuring them to Christ, the chaste, poor, and obedient one, and prompting them to make his mission their own. By allowing themselves to be guided by the Spirit on an endless journey of purification, they become day after day, *conformed to Christ,* the prolongation in history of a special presence of the Risen Lord.[86]

This is the heart of the spousal dynamic of the consecrated life: the process of becoming two-in-one-flesh with Christ. Each effort of consecrated men and women to actively conform their lives to Christ is assumed and refashioned by the Holy Spirit until they are *"led progressively into full configuration* to Christ to reflect in themselves a ray of the unapproachable light. During their earthly pilgrimage, they press on toward the inexhaustible source of light."[87]

This dynamic process of personal *transformation* is what the Pope considers the first duty of the consecrated life: "to make visible the marvels wrought by God in the frail humanity of those who are called. They bear witness to these marvels not so much in words as by the *eloquent language of a transfigured life.*"[88] The transformation is visible to all, but most especially to the heart of the one called: "I see how I was and what I have become." The Church needs this witness even more than any practical service or apostolic work; the Church needs persons who "allow themselves to be transformed by God's grace and conform themselves fully to the Gospel."[89] Because this personal transformation takes place within a religious community that is formed in a particular charism, a communal asceticism further purifies and transfigures both community and individual existence. In every charism there predominates "a profound desire to be conformed to Christ to give witness to some aspect of his mystery."[90] Only this rich tapestry of charisms begins to make visible the full mystery of Christ that religious life incarnates for the Church and the world. All together "they bear witness, against the temptation to self-centeredness and sensuality, to the true nature of the search for God."[91]

Mulieris Dignitatem: Spousal Love—A Gift for the Other

Mulieris dignitatem was signed on August 15, 1988, the solemnity of the Assumption, the feast that marks the end of Mary's discipleship on earth and places the divine seal upon the holiness of the body that had not only conceived the Son of God but had been absolutely faithful in spousal covenant with the Almighty. The assumption of Mary into heaven provides additional assurance to the Christian called to eternal marriage with God. The bodily resurrection of Jesus the Christ is, after all, the resurrection of the God-Man; the assumption of Mary, body and soul into heaven, is the divinization of one who is totally human. The life of Mary is a particular yet humble manifestation of the perfection of spousal love; a life lived as a gift for the Other and for all others. The Assumption manifests the divine approval of the simplest human life lived in the integrity of love and made fruitful through the power of the Holy Spirit. The Assumption is the divine "yes" in reply to Mary's human "yes" at the Annunciation and forever after. Mary is the evangelical ideal of virginity as described by Pope John Paul:

> The evangelical ideal of virginity. . . cannot be compared to remaining simply unmarried or single, because virginity is not restricted to a mere "no," but contains a profound "yes" in the spousal order: the gift of self for love in a total and undivided manner. Moreover, a man's consecration in priestly celibacy or in the religious state is to be understood analogously.[92]

The "yes" of Mary, the New Eve, reopens for all of humanity the possibility of responding to the covenant with God in a total and undivided manner. Christ the "New Adam" and Mary the "New Eve" give humanity a fresh start in the "New Creation." Mary is the New Israel and the bride of Yahweh just as she is the Church, the bride of Christ. In her humanity and through her "yes," the New Jerusalem begins to be prepared anew as a "collective subject"—the Body and Bride of Christ—for the wedding feast of the Lamb. John Paul explains:

> According to the letter to the Ephesians, the bride *is the Church,* just as for the Prophets the bride was Israel. She is therefore *a collective subject and not an individual person.* This collective subject is the People of God, a community made up of many persons, both men and women. "Christ has loved the Church" precisely as a community, as the People of God. At the same time, in this Church, which in the same passage is also called his "body," he has loved every individual person. For Christ has redeemed all without exception, every man and woman. It is precisely this love of God which is expressed in the Redemption; the spousal character of this love reaches completion in the history of humanity and of the world. . . . In the Church every human being—male and female—is the "Bride," in that he or she accepts the gift of the love of Christ the Redeemer, and seeks to respond to it with the gift of his or her own person.[93]

Christ, who redeemed all without exception, offered his love as Spouse to each and all when he offered his Mother to his beloved disciple John at the foot of the Cross. The gaze of both Mary and John is redirected by Christ in his last moments; he commands each of them to "behold" the other, and in looking at each other to see and love him in each other. The spousal love of each of them for Jesus is expanded to include another, and in that "third" to build the community of the Church that is the image of the Trinity. When Christ founded the Church through the pouring forth of the Holy Spirit on Calvary, he simultaneously established for his Church a visible icon of his own chaste, poor, and obedient life in the virgins, Mary and John. Their transfiguration of life also took place on the mountaintop, and moments later both Mary and John went back down the mountain, into the valley, to expand the community of the Church by finding and loving the disfigured face of Christ in each and every

person they met. The inner transfiguration of the spousal love of
Mary and John that Christ called forth on Calvary is the challenge given to each disciple, but in a particular way to each consecrated virgin called to participate in the community initiated
in Mary and Saint John. The Holy Father explains:

> [A] consecrated woman finds her Spouse, different and the
> same in each and every person... Spousal love always involves a
> special readiness to be poured out for the sake of those who
> come within one's range of activity... In virginity this readiness
> is open *to all people, who are embraced by the love of Christ the
> Spouse.*[94]

This universal love, capacitated by the Holy Spirit, that is
not only ready to meet and recognize Christ the Spouse in each
and every person but ready to be "poured out" like his for the
sake of all those who come into range, demands an incomprehensible and total surrender to God and an absolute dependence upon his grace. It is a radical response to the Christ who
declares that to save one's life is to lose it while to lose it is to
save it. Edith Stein reflects upon this counsel of Christ in regard
to the life and commitment of the consecrated religious:

> Only God can welcome a person's total surrender in such a way
> that one does not lose one's soul in the process but wins it. And
> only God can bestow himself upon a person so that he fulfills
> this being completely and loses nothing of himself in so doing.
> That is why total surrender which is the principle of the reli-
> gious life is simultaneously the only adequate fulfillment possi-
> ble for women's yearning. [95]

Total *surrender*—more "words" rejected by moderns that
require redefinition—not linguistically, but *really* in flesh and
blood existence, in blood and water "poured out," in passion-
filled self-giving love.

Total surrender—"the principle of religious life"—the essence
of the spousal bond forged between Christ and his bride on
Tabor, Calvary, in the eucharist, in the vowed commitment to
chastity, poverty, and obedience in the bonds of community
life.

Total surrender—the principle of spousal love and virginal
receptivity—the only response intense and resilient enough to
transform the world into the New Creation.

Total surrender—when you have loved him, when you have touched him, when you have accepted him in whose embrace you are already caught up.

Chapter 3

THE THREEFOLD RESPONSE

OF THE VOWS

Sister Mary Dominic Pitts, O.P.

The teaching and example of Christ provide the foundation for the evangelical counsels of chaste self-dedication to God, of poverty and of obedience. . . . They therefore constitute a gift of God which the Church has received from her Lord and which by his grace she always safeguards.

Lumen gentium 43

The pursuit of perfect charity by means of the evangelical counsels traces its origins to the teaching and the example of the Divine Master, and . . . it is a very clear symbol of the heavenly kingdom.

Perfectae caritatis 1

Religious life, as a consecration of the whole person, manifests in the Church a wonderful marriage brought about by God, a sign of the future age. Thus religious bring to perfection their full gift as a sacrifice offered to God by which their whole existence becomes a continuous worship of God in love.

Canon 607 §1

The previous chapter on "The Spousal Bond" shows the extent to which the Church specifies the nature of religious life as *marriage*. The present chapter will show the nature of religious life lived as a radical self-giving in the forms of the three evangelical counsels of poverty, celibacy, and obedience. The Lord offers the religious man or woman a marvelous invitation to a life of total self-gift in imitation of his own life—the three evangelical counsels. These make up the radical imitation of the life of the Lord, who "took the form of a slave" (Phil 2:7) in his own poor, chaste, and obedient life both on earth and in the bosom of the Trinity, where he is eternally dependent on and obedient to the Father in self-emptying.

In professing the vows in order to imitate Christ, the religious makes himself or herself over to God "under a new and special title."[1] This is the "evangelical basis of consecrated life"—the "special relationship which Jesus, in his earthly life, established with some of his disciples. He called them to . . . closely [imitate] his own *way of life.*"[2]

> By professing the evangelical counsels, consecrated persons . . . strive to reproduce in themselves . . . that form of life which he, as the Son of God, accepted in entering this world. By embracing *chastity*, they make their own the pure love of Christ and proclaim to the world that He is the Only-Begotten Son who is one with the Father. By imitating Christ's *poverty*, they profess that He is the Son who receives everything from the Father and gives everything back to the Father in love. By accepting Christ's filial *obedience*, they profess that he is infinitely beloved and loving, as the one who delights only in the will of the Father, to whom he is perfectly united and on whom he depends for everything.[3]

Although the evangelical counsels are the defining characteristics of all forms of the consecrated state, the present chapter will consider the religious state, in which the consecrated life of the evangelical counsels is lived in common.

A BRIEF HISTORY OF THE EVANGELICAL COUNSELS AND THEIR BECOMING VOWS

Early Christians strove to live as Jesus had lived—in celibacy and utter poverty, selling all their property (Acts 4:34–5), undertaking these renunciations not only after but in between periods of persecution.[4] To make the renunciation an even greater imitation of Christ, some Christians, both men and women, went out to live in the desert, there to live a life of extreme austerity as solitary hermits. Eventually these early desert fathers, such as Saint Anthony of Egypt, and anchorite women as well, attracted disciples who wished to make the same renunciations. Thus the anchorites are regarded as the beginning of religious life. While they did not make vows, "the seeds of the vows were already there [in their] strict asceticism and [mortification of] their senses," in their celibacy and poverty "out of sheer joy in imitating the Lord."[5]

The gathering of disciples under an eremitic master to live an ascetic life was the occasion for the first religious communities, such as those of Saint Pachomius (d. 346). The advantage of community life was that there could be a shared asceticism which avoided an extreme deprivation on the one extreme or relaxation of the ascetical practices in the other extreme. There were no vows at this time. The only specific promise was that of obedience to the rule, taken by Saint Pachomius "from the holy scriptures" to demonstrate that "the will of God might often be made clear through a human command."[6] The rule composed later by Saint Basil (329–79) also required of the monk a promise of obedience to God in a life in which poverty and chastity were required.

The first rule of life wherein the monk or nun made vows per se was the Rule of Saint Benedict (480–543), under which rule a novice professed the vows of obedience, stability, and reformation of life. Although there was no vow of poverty, Benedict made the father of every candidate "swear that his child should receive nothing whatsoever of the paternal fortune. . . . The parents could only bestow on the monastery itself a donation."[7]

By the High Middle Ages, practices which had been part of the rules of religious orders, such as "works of penance, labour, or prayer," were regarded as part of the religious life along with obedience. Particular among these were poverty and chastity: "Little by little, poverty, chastity, and obedience began to stand out as the three essential and constituent elements. Their presence in various rules caused them, in fact, to be looked upon as belonging of necessity to all religious life."[8] They were, after all, a main component of the life chosen by the Lord and the penances undertaken by the early Christian hermits and cenobites. Saint Thomas Aquinas, writing in the late thirteenth century, clearly states, in medieval scholastic terms, the reason that three vows are necessary: "As regards the practice of perfection, a man is required to remove from himself whatever may hinder his affections from tending wholly to God. . . . First, the attachment to external goods, which is removed by the vow of poverty; secondly, the concupiscence of sensible pleasures . . . and these are removed by the vow of continence; thirdly, the want of order in the human will, and this is removed by the vow of obedience."[9]

Deeper Rooting in Baptismal Consecration

Chapter 1 of this volume describes how every child or adult being baptized is consecrated by the Paschal Mystery of Christ's dying and rising. Particularly since the Second Vatican Council, when the universal call to holiness was made a prominent theme, the Church has been deliberate in reminding the faithful that all the baptized are called to holiness by following the evangelical counsels within their own states of life. All states of life—laity, clergy, and religious—must live chastely, must guard against excessive attachment to material things, and must surrender their wills to legitimate authority. The very holiness of the Church depends upon its members' observance of these counsels.[10]

However, for some Christians, there is this invitation to a radical adoption of the evangelical counsels, a deeper rooting in their baptismal consecration. The persons making vows are "dedicated totally to God" in order to "give themselves to God."[11]

Lumen gentium explains that one called to profess the evangelical counsels by vow desires, in response to the call, to give himself still more fully to God, and to "derive still more abundant fruit from the grace of Baptism." By profession of the evangelical counsels of chastity, poverty, and obedience, one promises to remove obstacles to "fervent charity and perfect worship of God."[12] In this stable, proven way of life, one's desires can be more readily purified from inordinate preoccupation with material things, sense pleasures, and one's own way. The consecrated religious is free to focus on Christ in undivided love. The religious is able to "travel light" in imitation of the Savior, ready for God's will at any time.

Lumen gentium calls the vows of chastity, poverty, and obedience "that manner of virginal and humble life which Christ the Lord elected for Himself, and which His Virgin Mother also chose."[13] *Vita consecrata* refers to them as "that form of life which he, as the Son of God, accepted in entering this world."[14] The Church's tradition has emphasized the role of the counsels of chastity, poverty, and obedience as being particularly Christocentric, having a unique capacity for configuration of the person to Christ. John Paul II explains in *Redemptionis donum* that the transformation of the world will be brought about only from within, through the transformation of the human heart. Thus the evangelical counsels, being the most radical means for effecting this interior transformation, are the most radical means for transforming the world.[15]

As a gift to the Church and to the consecrated persons themselves, the Savior offers this, his chosen form of life, to some of the baptized. Canon 576 enjoins on the Church the "competent authority . . . to interpret the evangelical counsels . . . and by canonical approbation to establish the stable forms of living deriving from them." Thus the life of the evangelical counsels is a juridical reality in the Church here and now, in the present life. At the same time, embraced under vow, the counsels are the spiritual bonds of love that make the consecrated person *already* the Bride of Christ for all eternity. Embracing these bonds, the religious pledges him or herself to the honor and service of God "under a new and special title."[16]

WHY A VOW?

A vow is a deliberate and free promise made to God concerning a possible and better good which must be fulfilled by reason of the virtue of religion.

Canon 1191 §1

A religious institute is a society in which members, according to proper law, pronounce public vows . . . and live a life in common as brothers and sisters.

Canon 607 §2

The life consecrated by the evangelical counsels requires a "stable form of living . . . totally dedicated to God."[17] Although other forms of consecrated life exist, religious consecration requires public vows, ultimately perpetual, as its norm.[18] In order to understand the mind of the Church here, it is fitting to consider the significance of vows, especially in religious life. A later section will consider the meaning and significance of public vows.

A vow, says Saint Thomas Aquinas, is a natural act of *latria*, that is, worship of God.[19] Rooted as they are in Christ's self-emptying sacrifice to the Father and imitating the Lord's life on earth, the evangelical counsels become *latria*, religious acts of the highest kind, when they are professed as vows. In this offering of self under vow, the very being and actions of the religious become a living sacrifice, in conformity with that of Christ.

A vow by its very nature, continues Thomas, fixes the will steadfastly in the good and spurs the will's determination to carry out the intended good without becoming distracted or giving up.[20] By the grace of the vow, the individual receives the supernatural help to fulfill a commitment that lasts an entire lifetime. The vows fix the will of the religious in a stable way on the good of total self-giving to God.[21]

Emphasizing this totality, Saint Thomas quotes Saint Gregory the Great in *Homilies on Ezechiel*, xx: "When man vows to God all his possessions, all his life, all his knowledge, it is a holocaust."[22] The Old Testament holocaust sacrifice, totally immolated as a gift to God, is a fitting image of the vows of the religious life, for a religious who has made vows focuses her whole life exclusively on Christ, offering herself to be "wholly consumed" (*holo-* meaning "total") by his love. The Church has always held in high esteem the holocaust of self made by consecrated persons, regarding the spiritual benefit of their self-gift as equal to that of martyrs. This perhaps explains why *Lumen gentium* places the section on the evangelical counsels immediately after the section on martyrdom, saying:

> The Church, then, considers martyrdom as an exceptional gift and as the fullest proof of love. . . . *Likewise*, the holiness of the Church is fostered in a special way by the observance of the counsels proposed in the Gospel by Our Lord to his disciples.[23]

A vow gives to God not only the good act, but the source of the act, that is, the very will that *wills* the act. Saint Thomas cites in this connection a metaphor used by Saint Anselm, who points out that a gift of fruit is not as great as the gift of the *source* of that fruit, the tree from which the fruit comes.[24]

Vows in and for the Church

Involving as it does a special bond with Christ, the religious state necessarily implies a special bond with the Church. It is only within the life of the Church that the religious life finds its reason for being, and the individual religious, his or her identity.

Throughout the centuries, the vital ecclesial dimension of the religious state has unfolded. This has been preeminently the case during and since the years of the Second Vatican Council. The Church takes very seriously the assertion of the Council, in *Lumen gentium*, that *"the evangelical counsels unite those who practice them to the Church and her mystery in a special way"*[25]:

> [The Church] herself, in virtue of her God-given authority, receives the vows of those who profess this form of life, asks aid and grace for them from God in her public prayer, commends them to God and bestows on them a spiritual blessing, associating their self-offering with the sacrifice of the Eucharist.[26]

When a religious professes the evangelical counsels according to the proper law of the institute, she not only becomes a part of her institute, but by the charity resulting from the vows, she is also joined in an utterly unique way to the Church's life and mystery.

The significance of a *public vow* lies in the reality that, being received by the Church's representative, the vow is not simply the vow of a certain individual. It is a vow of the *Church*.

> In the person taking the vows, the Church offers herself to Jesus . . . In a certain sense, at profession we cease to be ourselves and become the Church. Our personality is not diminished by this fusion with the Church, but our "I" is stamped with the "I" of the Church.[27]

With their very identity thus bound up in that of the Church, the spiritual life and apostolic works of religious "should . . . be devoted to the welfare of the whole Church."[28] The gifts of grace proper to the religious state and to each institute enable religious to "contribute, each in his own way, to the saving mission of the Church."[29]

Both *Lumen gentium* and *Perfectae caritatis* make clear the mutual responsibilities of the Church and religious. These documents from the Second Vatican Council make strong statements of the mutual benefit resulting from the Church's support for religious life and the dedication of religious to the Church. For example, the Church is not merely a passive witness at the Rite of Profession. She has responsibilities touching the very essence of religious life: "to [interpret] these evangelical counsels, [to regulate] their practice and, finally, to build on them stable forms of living."[30] In turn, "the members of these institutes, in fulfilling their obligation to the Church due to their particular form of life, show reverence and obedience to bishops according to the sacred canons . . . because of the need of unity and harmony in the apostolate."[31] They also enrich the Church's life of holiness and lend vitality to her apostolate.

Pope John Paul II, reflecting on the vocation of religious in the light of the mystery of Redemption, offered a profound insight regarding the Church's sense of the ecclesial identity of religious: "The entire Church is chosen in every person whom the Lord selects from the midst of [his] people; in every person who is consecrated *for everyone* to God as his exclusive possession."[32]

The Vow of Chastity

The evangelical counsel of chastity assumed for the sake of the
kingdom of heaven, as a sign of the future world and a source of
more abundant fruitfulness in an undivided heart, entails the
obligation of perfect continence in celibacy.

Canon 599

In one episode in Saint Matthew's gospel, the Pharisees
attempt to trap Jesus in a legal dispute about divorce (19:3–12).
But the Lord counters their interpretation of the Torah on
divorce (Dt 24:14) with his own even more fundamental pas-
sages from the Torah in support of the indissolubility of marriage (Gn 1:27; 2:24). Then, raising the conversation to an
altogether higher level, he gives examples of persons who do
not marry—eunuchs born as such, eunuchs made so—and concludes with a third dimension that had not occurred to them:

Some are eunuchs . . . because they have renounced marriage
for the sake of the kingdom of heaven. Whoever can accept this
ought to accept it. (Mt 19:12)

Here Christ introduces the astonishing suggestion that some
who are capable of marriage and family might actually
renounce these gifts and accept celibacy as an even more desirable state of life because it is offered by God. With the words,
"Not all can accept this saying, but only those to whom it is
given" (Mt 19:11), the Lord clearly shows that he is not making
celibacy the standard state of life for everyone, but rather
inviting certain individuals to consider and to choose chastity
freely, "for the sake of the kingdom of heaven."

According to Genesis 2:24, the universal natural law is that a
man "leaves his father and mother and clings to his wife, and
the two of them become one body." Therefore, when God created man and woman, He willed that they would have a complementarity such that they would naturally be attracted to each
other. This gift of complementarity in men and women "affects
all aspects of the . . . person in the unity of [the] body and soul.
. . . It especially concerns affectivity, the capacity to love and to
procreate, and in a more general way the aptitude for forming
bonds of communion with others."[33] Taken to their natural end,
these bonds of communion fill the emptiness of man's "original

solitude" in the Garden of Eden.[34] John Paul II's catechesis on the book of Genesis declares: "Men and women were created for marriage."[35]

How, then, if every human person is "made for marriage," is anyone able to respond to the Lord's call to perfect chastity? The answer lies in the Lord's election of certain persons, inviting them to allow *Him* to satisfy their innate longing to love and be loved in a total and exclusive way. In response to this invitation, religious choose spousal love with Christ. In *Redemptionis donum*, John Paul II describes this ultimate response by the human heart as a choice of "virginity or celibacy as an expression of spousal love for the Redeemer Himself."[36] What about the person's psychological and physical powers that are "made for marriage"? Does spousal love for God suppress the natural powers of sexuality? On the contrary, those who choose to respond with this spousal love do not lose their masculinity or femininity. They retain the "sexual instinct" natural to their physical and psychological makeup. Furthermore, they are aware that the new and special consecration that they are undertaking "touches intimately the deepest instincts of human nature."[37] In this consecration they allow themselves to be spiritually fruitful and thus fulfilled in the most extreme expression of self-giving possible for a person: the total giving of self, including the sexual powers, to Christ, in response to his prior self-gift. Only this total gift of self can fully justify, fulfill, and motivate a person to undertake voluntary continence for the sake of the Kingdom of Heaven.

Living the call to perfect continence is not easy. Pope John Paul II compares it to the loneliness of original solitude.[38] Pope Paul VI wrote of it to priests and seminarians:

> The Church is not unaware that the choice of consecrated celibacy . . . involves a series of hard renunciations. . . . And yet more careful consideration reveals that this sacrifice of the human love experienced by most men [and women] in family life and given up by the priest [or religious] for the love of Christ, *is really a singular tribute paid to that great love.*[39]

It is a "hard renunciation," and yet we have divine help, says Paul VI: "The response to the divine call is an answer of love to the love which Christ has shown us so sublimely. . . . With a divine force, grace increases the longings of love."[40]

Not only does this choice enable one to be "anxious about the affairs of the Lord," but—being made for the Kingdom of Heaven—it brings this eschatological kingdom close to all people here and now, in the condition of their daily lives, making it already present in the world of time.[41]

AN OUTSTANDING GIFT OF GRACE

The first paragraph of *Perfectae caritatis* 12 reads:

> The chastity "for the sake of the kingdom of heaven" (Matt 19:12) which religious profess should be counted an outstanding gift of grace. It frees the heart of man in a unique fashion (cf. 1 Cor 7:32–35) so that it may be more inflamed with love for God and for all men. Thus it not only symbolizes in a singular way the heavenly goods but also the most suitable means by which religious dedicate themselves with undivided heart to the service of God and the works of the apostolate. In this way they recall to the minds of all the faithful that wondrous marriage decreed by God and which is to be fully revealed in the future age in which the Church takes Christ as its only spouse.

Although each of the evangelical counsels is surely a gift to the Church and to the individual (in the latter case requiring a special grace from God for faithfulness), consecrated chastity is a gift to the Church in an exceptional way. This vow in particular takes the consecration of baptism to its "logical" conclusion here and now. In vowed chastity, virginal and spousal loves are one: the religious wholly possesses himself through perfect continence in celibacy, while at the same time wholly surrendering himself to Christ in self-*giving* love.

A FRAGILE GIFT OF GRACE

Even though chastity is a gift of grace, due to our fallen nature, consecrated chastity must be vigilantly protected both from a supernatural perspective and with natural common sense. The Council Fathers acknowledge this need in Perfectae caritatis:

> Religious must have faith . . . and, trusting in God's help, not overestimate their own strength. . . . Neither should they neglect the natural means which promote health of mind and body. Candidates . . . should have been shown to possess the required

psychological and emotional maturity. They should be . . .
instructed so as to be able to undertake the celibacy which
binds them to God.[42]

With such precautions, religious themselves are protected
from the "false doctrines which scorn perfect continence as
being impossible or harmful to human development."[43] Shortly
thereafter, in *Evangelica testificatio*, Pope Paul VI calls the gift of
evangelical chastity "fragile and vulnerable." Describing dan-
gers from outside the person, the pope makes a statement
which rings even more true in the third millennium than in
1971: "Human love is more than ever threatened by a 'ravaging
eroticism.'"[44] In spite of such external threats, the prudent,
healthy, and faith-filled living of consecrated chastity should
enable the religious to develop a protective "spiritual instinct
against everything that endangers chastity."[45] However, the
pope points out that part of the danger is from within us: "This
gift, fragile and vulnerable because of human weakness,
remains open to the contradictions of mere reason."[46] Rooted in
the lives and example of Christ and his Mother, chastity will be
lived and protected as long as those to whom this gift has been
imparted comprehend its value and make a total gift of themselves to the Lord. Paul VI trusted that the "uprightness and
generosity" of religious would be an antidote for the world's
abuse of human sexuality, for its lack of understanding of religious life, and indeed for its lack of understanding of love
itself.[47]

Perfectae caritatis and *Evangelica testificatio* both offer the
wise advice of reliance on the community as a help for fidelity
to one's vow of chastity. "Chastity is guarded more securely
when true brotherly love flourishes in the . . . community,"
wrote the Council Fathers. Pope Paul VI brings the message full
circle, saying that fraternal love in the community will benefit
from the "uncompromising . . . demand" of God's inexorable
love, which "makes [such] a demand for fraternal charity that
the religious will live more profoundly with his contemporaries
in the heart of Christ."[48]

The Undivided Heart

Perfectae caritatis 12 also emphasizes that consecrated persons give the total gift of themselves to God with an *undivided*

heart. The religious chooses God in a way that excludes any other spouse, as Saint Paul teaches in 1 Corinthians 7: celibacy "frees the heart of man in a unique fashion so that it may be more inflamed with love for God and for all men."[49] The "undivided heart" is free for love and service of God and others. *Evangelica testificatio* quotes *Lumen gentium* 42 on the fruits that derive from such single-heartedness, saying that "[chastity] becomes 'an incentive to charity, and . . . a particular source of spiritual fecundity in the world.'"[50]

In *Vita consecrata*, John Paul II stresses that undivided love for God is the main focus of religious life. In an exegesis of the Transfiguration, he interprets Peter's "Lord, it is good to be with you" (Matt 17:4) as expressing the joy that results from an *exclusive* focus on God: "How good it is to be with you, to devote ourselves to you, to make you the *one focus of our lives!*"[51] One sees the here special aptness of the use of the holocaust as a metaphor for consecrated chastity. The Hebrew word for a holocaust or whole-burnt offering was *olah*—literally, "elevation." The purpose of the holocaust was not primarily the totality of the burning, nor even the burning itself, for these were merely the means for rendering the victim into a form that could be an "elevation" ascending to God. The holocaust sacrifice was meant to rise up in fragrant smoke. It was "a way to place the offering in God by transferring it into the field of the invisible," going up to God.[52] The vow of chastity renders the heart capable of being wholly receptive to and wholly taken up into the love of God.

Eschatological Sign

A third emphasis in *Perfectae caritatis* 12, echoed consistently throughout ensuing documents, is that of consecrated chastity's being a sign of the future age, "[anticipating] in a certain way that *eschatological fulfillment* toward which the whole Church is tending."[53] This fulfillment is none other than the possession of heavenly goods and the eternal heavenly marriage of Christ with his spouse, the Church, realities of which consecrated chastity is a living sign.

The eschatological aspect of religious life is part of the canonical definition of consecrated chastity:

The evangelical counsel of chastity assumed for the sake of the kingdom of heaven, which is a sign of the world to come and a source of more abundant fruitfulness in an undivided heart, entails the obligation of perfect continence in celibacy.[54]

Religious life, as a consecration of the whole person, manifests in the Church a wonderful marriage brought about by God, a sign of the future age.[55]

Here is expressed (1) the motivation for the counsel—"for the sake of the kingdom"—and (2) the obligation it entails— "perfect continence in celibacy." Both the motivation and the obligation are central to a full understanding of the vow. Perfect continence in celibacy looks forward to the end of time, and specifically to that definitive marriage, brought about by God, which religious consecration specifically manifests in the Church.

John Paul II, drawing on the wealth of the Second Vatican Council's teaching as distilled above in the Church's law, helps us to conclude these reflections on the vow of chastity.

The Second Vatican Council . . . states that consecration better "foretells the resurrected state and the glory of the heavenly Kingdom. It does this above all by means of *the vow of virginity*, which tradition has always understood as an *anticipation of the world to come*, already at work for the total transformation of man. Those who have dedicated their lives to Christ cannot fail to live in the hope of meeting him, in order to be with him forever. . . . The one thing necessary is to seek God's "Kingdom and his righteousness" (Mt 6:33), with unceasing prayer for the Lord's coming.[56]

The Vow of Poverty

For you know the gracious act of Our Lord Jesus Christ, that for your sake he became poor although he was rich, so that by his poverty you might become rich.

2 Corinthians 8:9

The evangelical counsel of poverty, in imitation of Christ who, though He was rich became poor for us, entails, besides a life which is poor in fact and in spirit, a life of labor lived in moderation and foreign to earthly riches, a dependence and a limitation

in the use and disposition of goods according to the norm of the
proper law of each institute.

Canon 600

The ultimate message of evangelical poverty is that "God is
man's only real treasure."[57]

Failure to recognize this fact is the great tragedy of the rich
young man who comes to Jesus hoping to find the key to ultimate happiness (Mk 10:17–27): "Good Master, what must I do to
inherit eternal life?" His choice of words is striking: he does not
say "in order that I might gain eternal life" or "receive eternal
life," but *kleronomos* "[in order that] I will inherit," a legal term
in Greek as in English, meaning precisely to "inherit, be an
heir."[58] The rich man seems to approach eternal life the way
that he does all his many possessions, assuming that he has a
right to it. When he finds out that the price of eternal life is to
live in the vulnerability of owning absolutely nothing, however,
he cannot bring himself to be poor like Christ. He goes away
sad.

Reflection on evangelical poverty enables us to see that this
invitation of Christ in the gospel is not an arbitrary one. It, too,
is an aspect of the mystery of redemption and of redeeming
love. It could even be said to be a condition of the spousal love
manifested in religious chastity. "There is no true love without
poverty," writes Dominican theologian Servais Pinckaers, and
the vow of poverty is intended to prepare for and support just
the kind of self-emptying spousal love which enables the consecrated person to receive the self-gift of the Lord.[59]

Defining Characteristics

As a "clear sign of the following of Christ," writes Father Elio
Gambari, "the practice of this evangelical counsel [of poverty]
has always held a special place in religious life," in some cases
beginning dramatically; as in the case of Saint Francis of Assisi,
who abandoned even his clothes; or Saint Anthony Abbot, who
heard the gospel of the Rich Young Man (Mark 10:17–27, quoted
above) and immediately left behind his considerable earthly
goods to become a hermit.[60] *Perfectae caritatis* 13 situates the
motivation for one who embraces gospel poverty in the imitation of Christ who, in the Incarnation, divested himself of the

riches of divinity and lived an earthly life devoid of material wealth, even to the supreme destitution of the Cross.

Canon 600, reflecting *Perfectae caritatis* 13, mandates that consecrated poverty be not only in spirit, but also in fact. The religious may not acquire, control, use, or distribute material goods without the permission of the legitimate superior.

> The religious foregoes the free use and disposal of his or her property, depends through the lawful superior on the institute for the provision of material goods, puts gifts and all salaries in common as belonging to the community, and accepts and contributes to a simple manner of life.[61]

Such limitation and suitable dependence with regard to material goods are the key distinctions between the vow of poverty and the spirit of detachment (which, of course, must necessarily underlie it, and which the vow is meant to foster). The vow entails more than a simple life. There are also specific juridical obligations that follow from the vow of poverty as professed in religious institutes.[62]

Poverty and the Mystery of Redemption

Voluntary poverty "[shares] in the poverty of Christ," (cf. 2 Cor 8:9) as *Perfectae caritatis* reminds us.[63] In *Redemptionis donum*, Pope John Paul II interprets 2 Corinthians 8:9 (quoted at the beginning of this section on poverty) as belonging to the very theology of redemption. The Holy Father describes poverty as part of "the interior structure of the redemptive grace of Jesus Christ." Chapter 12 of *Redemptionis donum* is like a beautiful antiphonal hymn, alternating between the divine richness on the one hand, and, on the other, the human poverty which Christ took to himself. Paradoxically, says Pope John Paul, "a richness . . . such as the Divinity itself could not have been adequately expressed in any created good. It can be expressed only in poverty." Therefore we must have this poverty of spirit in order to understand "the poverty of the one who is infinitely rich."

The Incarnation is the beginning of the Christ's stripping of self which will end with the Cross: "The supreme poverty is that of the Cross . . . the utter dispossession of self which Christ realized on Calvary."[64] This poverty of the Word of God, Son of

the Lord God of Hosts, has been totally—yet sublimely—
incomprehensible to many saints, among them Saint Catherine
of Siena.

> It is overwhelming to see [you], sweet, kind Jesus, who rule
> over and provide for the whole world while [you yourself are] in
> such misery and need that no one can be compared to [you] . . .
> By committing sin [man] had been stripped, had lost the gar-
> ment of grace. [You die] naked upon the Cross so as to clothe
> man once more and cover his nakedness.[65]

The vow of poverty prepares fertile ground for consecrated
obedience. Both poverty and obedience are *kenosis*, self-emptying,
but poverty could be called the forerunner of obedience in this
regard. It is in stooping to the status of a slave that we come to the
even more radical poverty of obedience: "He was known to be of
human estate, and it was thus that he humbled himself, obedient-
ly accepting even death, death on a cross!" (Phil 2:7–8). Thus Hans
Urs von Balthasar concludes, "It would be folly to try to clear a
path to evangelical obedience without passing through this
entrance gate."[66]

Foreign to Earthly Riches:
Poverty in Fact and Spirit

In affirming the necessity of the vow of poverty for the religious state, Saint Thomas uses a comparison employed by Saint
Gregory the Great, which compares religious to athletes training for a mountain climb. They must not only equip themselves
to scale the heights; they must also strip themselves of all
excess weight, overcoming all attachments to creatures.[67] In the
same article, Thomas quotes Saint Augustine in a simple equation of love: "Too little doth he love Thee, who loveth anything
[along] with Thee, which he loveth not for [Thy sake]."[68] One
who loves other things will quickly find love for God weakening
and attachment to things becoming too strong for a total
response to the Bridegroom.

The Code of Canon Law has adopted from *Perfectae caritatis*
the statement that "members [or a religious institute] must be
poor both in fact and in spirit."[69] The symmetry of "fact and spirit" reflects the balance of poverty well-lived. On the one hand,
neither individual religious nor communities should think that
a "poverty of spirit" can take the place of factual poverty:

"[Religious communities] should avoid every appearance of luxury, excessive wealth, and the accumulation of goods."[70] On the other hand, a "letter-of-the-law" approach, observing the legal directives concerning ownership and use of material things, but lacking the true spirit of poverty, errs in the other direction.

With its immersion into Christ's own redemptive poverty, consecrated poverty requires that interior poverty of spirit be expressed and strengthened by the exterior practice of factual poverty. The use and disposition of material goods as one's personal possessions are relinquished, and the consecrated person depends on the community for what is needed for community life and mission.

Thus, consecrated poverty becomes a means of forming the spirit in detachment from material things for the sake of the kingdom, and of forming attachment to God and the things of God. The religious' outward practice of poverty nurtures inward poverty before God, expresses the need for his grace, and fosters humility and hope, virtues that thrive in soil that poverty has cleared of attachment to material things.

The Witness of Poverty

Love that is willing to abandon all things for Christ must naturally be a sign to others. "Poverty [is] . . . recognized and highly esteemed especially today as an *expression* of the following of Christ."[71] The use of the word *expression* is noteworthy. Like chastity, poverty has a powerful sign value: It too is an expression, a sign with meaning. Leaving everything for the Lord's sake *signifies* that the religious has found Christ to be the pearl of great price, for whom the consecrated person "sells all that he has" (Mt 13:45–46). Pope Paul VI seized vigorously on this idea in *Evangelica testificatio*, beginning with its very title: *Gospel Witness*. The document exhorts religious to live their religious poverty as a witness to the involuntarily poor, to the wealthy and powerful, and to Christians of all denominations. "At a time [of] increased danger [of enticement] by . . . possessions, knowledge and power," says the Pope, "the call of God places you at the pinnacle of the Christian conscience."[72] He adds: "The needs of today's world . . . make your poverty more urgent and deep. . . . Its value as a witness will derive from a generous response to the exigencies of the Gospel."[73]

Paul VI suggests a number of ways religious might respond as witnesses of "authentic Gospel poverty," first by [awakening] consciences to the demands of social justice made by the Gospel and the Church."[74] Some religious, indeed, "join the poor in their situation"; all "limit their own use of goods to what is required for their life and apostolate." As to the institutes' use of remunerations and goods, they are urged to "rededicate . . . some of their works" as a response to the cry of the poor."[75]

John Paul II, like his predecessor, points out that evangelical poverty has a witness value in and of itself, even apart from its being a service to the poor. "Its primary meaning," in fact, "is to attest that God is the true wealth of the human heart."[76] Especially in this way does evangelical poverty make its "prophetic appeal" to our materialistic society, whose very sense of the value of money and material possessions is becoming increasingly disordered. The witness set before the world by the practice of the vow of poverty is a "renewed evangelical" commitment to live an example of temperance, self-restraint, and self-denial, motivated by love of God and neighbor.[77]

Foreign to Earthly Riches:
Poverty in the Spirit of Faith

Evangelical poverty is possible only on the basis of faith. With regard for their personal poverty and that of the institute, religious should "banish all undue solicitude and trust themselves to the provident care of their Father in heaven (cf. Mt 6:25)."[78] In religious life, this trust in Providence is realized in a "*dependence* which is inherent in every form of poverty."[79] Religious must internalize a spirit of dependence on the community that includes detachment from the goods themselves: "So do not worry and say, 'What are we to eat?' or 'What are we to drink?' or 'What are we to wear?' All these things the pagans seek. Your heavenly Father knows that you need them all" (Mt 6:31–32). The exact nature of the dependence is determined by "the type of institute [it is] and on the form of obedience practiced in it."[80]

Dependence in religious life is rooted in the serene inner life of the Blessed Trinity, whose Persons eternally give all to each other and receive all in a total gift of each Person to the Other. Religious poverty particularly reflects the total dependence of

Christ upon the Father. Just as "the Son . . . *receives everything from the Father*, and gives everything back to the Father in love" (cf. Jn 17:7; emphasis added), likewise religious receive from their congregations what they need for their life and apostolate.

The Vow of Obedience

> Your attitude must be that of Christ . . . he humbled himself, obediently accepting even death, death on a cross!
>
> Philippians 2:5–8

As with the other vows, the vow of obedience is vital to the life of a religious consecrated to Christ in perfect charity. Vowed obedience is preeminently and mysteriously the seal placed on the totality of response to the Lord who calls.

The vow of chastity is solidly based in conciliar and post-Conciliar teaching, in Church tradition from the early centuries, and in Christ's resolute and unrelenting pursuit of obedience with its climax on the cross. The sections on religious obedience in the documents of and after the Second Vatican Council—*Lumen gentium*, *Perfectae caritatis*, *Evangelica testificatio*, *Redemptionis donum*, and *Vita consecrata*—invariably begin with Christ's obedience *unto death* as the source of religious obedience, and the recent instruction *Faciem tuam*, in section 21, grounds the superior's role in the humility of Jesus: "Whoever wishes to be first among you must be your slave, just as the Son of Man came not to be served but to serve and to give his life as a ransom for many" (Mt 20:27–8). The decree *Perfectae caritatis* identifies and proclaims "the example of Jesus Christ" to be the motive and the power behind humble, self-sacrificial religious obedience:

> By their profession of obedience, religious offer the full dedication of their own wills as a sacrifice of themselves to God, and by this means they are united more permanently and securely with God's saving will. After the example of Jesus Christ, who came to do his Father's will (cf. Jn 4:34; 5:30; Heb 10:7; Ps 39:9) and [who,] "taking the form of a servant" (Phil 2:7) learned obedience through what he suffered (cf. Heb 10:8), religious moved by the Holy Spirit subject themselves in faith to those who hold God's place, their superiors. Through them they are led to serve

all their brothers in Christ. . . . Religious, therefore, in the spirit
of faith and love for the divine will should humbly obey their
superiors according to their rules and constitutions."[81]

The ultimate motive of religious obedience is a loving desire,
after the example of the Son, to do the Father's will. "If you keep
my commandments, you will remain in my love, just as I have
kept my Father's commandments and remain in his love" (Jn
15:10). In faith the religious regards the superior as standing in
the place of God the Father and therefore willingly obeys.

Pope Paul VI's 1971 apostolic exhortation *Evangelica testificatio*, calls religious back to what is noble and holy in religious life,
particularly the imitation of the suffering Christ in religious
obedience:

> What has been said indicates what degree of renunciation is
> demanded by the practice of the religious life. You must feel
> something of the force with which Christ was drawn to His
> Cross—that baptism He had still to receive, by which that fire
> would be lighted which sets you too ablaze . . . Let the Cross be
> for you, as it was for Christ, proof of the greatest love.[82]

Christ is both the exemplar and the mystical wellspring of
"the [dynamic] charity" whereby the religious is able to make a
"total offering of [the] will."[83] *Evangelica testificatio* also makes
clear the cost: "The Lord obliges each one to 'lose his life' if he is
to follow Him."[84] The religious who thus immolates his or her
will enters into the very Paschal Mystery itself with its "fullness
of [the] mystery of death and resurrection . . . [and] the supernatural destiny of man is brought to realization."[85]

In any authentic following of Jesus in religious life, authentic obedience is learned through the cross. Of the three vows,
obedience resembles most closely the self-emptying sacrifice of
Christ described in Philippians 2:8, since "the call [to the evangelical counsel of obedience] derives from this obedience of
Christ 'unto death.'"[86]

Virtues Necessary for Obedience: Humility, Love, and Faith

The Blessed Virgin Mary gives a singular example of perfect
obedience. The epithet "she who has believed" does not simply
express something she has done; it is rather a description of
who she is: the obedient one who gives herself over to God in a
faith that never wavers throughout her life, from her acceptance

of his will at the Annunciation (Lk 1:26–28) to the suffering and death of her Son on the Cross (Jn 19:25–27). The Blessed Virgin had, to a degree surpassing all other creatures, the virtues that support supernatural obedience. She is the exemplar of the humility, charity, and faith that religious cultivate in their striving to live the vow of obedience. Humility, the basis of all virtue, is essential where submission to another is required. Supernatural charity—that is, love of God before all other things—enables the religious, for the love of Christ whom he follows, and in imitation of him, to redirect the fallen will from rebellion to loving surrender instead. The third virtue, faith, requires a fuller exploration.

Obedience and faith

The faith infused at baptism intensifies under the additional consecration of the vows of religion. Faith animates all three of the vows, but most of all obedience, which cannot exist without it. In the theology of religious life, faith allows a religious to see in the commands of superiors the manifestation of the will of God, who has always preferred to work, hidden, through human beings.

The cause-and-effect relationship of faith and obedience is strikingly evident in the life of the patriarch Abraham, whom Saint Paul holds up in the Letter to the Romans as the father of all believers. The patriarch believes in God's promise and acts on it, despite the tremendous odds against its realization (Rom 16:26). Abraham's first act of obedience in faith occurs when God, previously unknown to him, calls him to "go forth from the land of your kinsfolk and from your father's house to a land that I will show you" (Gn 12:1). Abraham sets out, his journey punctuated by God's promises of innumerable descendants. Over the years the wonderful promise of a son seems more and more impossible by natural standards, but Abraham never doubts God.

> He believed, hoping against hope, that he would become "the father of many nations," according to what was said. . . . He did not doubt God's promise in unbelief; rather, he was empowered by faith and gave glory to God and was fully convinced that what he had promised he was also able to do. (Rom 4:18, 20–21)

After the promised son, Isaac, is miraculously born from the hundred-year-old Abraham and "from the dead womb of Sarah" (Rom 4:19), God demands the unthinkable: the sacrifice of Isaac as a holocaust. Though it seems that the promise is to be annihilated, Abraham believes—in faith—in God's supreme command and prepares—in obedience—to carry out God's will. Then God accepts Abraham's *obedient will itself* as the "holocaust" and promises even more abundant blessings because Abraham did not withhold his son (Gn 22:16–18).

The stages of Abraham's journey may be seen to reflect religious life. First, there is the call to the new life by God. Then there is the increasing reliance on faith in religious life when God's promise may seem far away, when both prayer and acts of obedience may seem dry, and when the soul is in darkness. Finally, acts of death to self are required, perhaps over and over, and in ways that seem completely counterintuitive in the person's advance toward God. All of these stages of obedience require a maturing faith in the religious man or woman.

Obedience to God's will mediated by a superior

Ferdinand Valentine makes a comparison between the faith required for religious obedience and that needed to acknowledge the Real Presence of God in the Eucharist: "'To see God in the superior' has therefore a truly Eucharistic significance."[87] Obedience to divine authority hidden in a man or woman thus participates in the very mystery of the Incarnation: "On the Cross thy Godhead made no sign to men; / Here thy very manhood steals from human ken."[88]

Faith is necessary in religious life because the will of God is made known by means of a human person, the superior. This person, however, has received from the Church the legitimate power to govern. Pope Paul VI, in *Evangelica testificatio,* clarifies the point: "apart from an order manifestly contrary to the laws of God or the constitutions of the institute, or one involving a serious and certain evil—in which case there is no obligation to obey"—the religious can be certain that her obedience to the superior is in fact the will of God. The very structure and sacramentality of the religious community is another sign of authenticity of obedience: "Has not Jesus promised to be present where two or three are gathered in his name (cf. Mt 18:20)? Thus, brothers and sisters become sacraments of Jesus and of the encounter with God, a concrete possibility of being able to live the commandment of mutual love. In this way the path of holiness becomes a way that all members of the community follow together."[89]

In recent years, some have questioned whether superiors in fact "hold God's place" and mistakenly equate compliance with obedience.[90] They call for a "theology of discernment" and a "theology of mediation," stating that each religious can best mediate her own situation and determine her own life, for "*a person chooses to shape* his or her Christian discipleship within the framework of a particular state of life."[91] Saint Basil the Great's blunt observation from the fourth century comes to mind: "If [the monk] . . . wishes to do his own will, why has he placed himself under the obedience of a superior?"[92] In reality, the vow of obedience is rooted in the willed choice of an individual, that is, in her intellect and will. Obedience is not conformity. Its exercise is voluntary and responsible. Acting in true obedience, the religious, far from being repressed and dehumanized, is exercising the most mature act that the will can make. It is "a full act of your freedom that is at the origin of your present position. . . . Thus it is that the Council includes among the benefits of the religious state '*liberty strengthened* by obedience,'" and stresses that such obedience "*does not diminish the dignity* of the human person but rather leads it to maturity through that enlarged freedom which belongs to the sons of God."[93]

> All men should take note that the profession of the evangelical counsels, though entailing the renunciation of certain values which are to be undoubtedly esteemed, does not detract from a genuine development of the human persons, but rather by its very nature is *most beneficial to that development.* Indeed the counsels, voluntarily undertaken according to each one's personal vocation, contribute a great deal to the purification of heart and spiritual liberty.[94]

The Council planted religious obedience even more deeply in the Paschal Mystery wherein, "taking the form of a servant," Christ learned obedience through what he suffered. The obedient religious imitates Christ's obedience.

Without legitimate superiors, obedience cannot be lived authentically. "After the example of Jesus Christ, who came to do his Father's will . . . religious moved by the Holy Spirit subject themselves in faith *to their superiors who hold the place of God.*"[95] It should be noted that both the council's teaching on consecrated obedience and the canonical legislation based on it give explicit directives to superiors regarding the way in which they are to perceive and carry out their role. In the past, there was sometimes an overemphasis by certain individuals on authority as control. A superior should rather be animated by a "spirit of service to the brethren," one that is itself docile to the divine will.[96] For the follower of Christ, authority is about serving.

Precisely because they "hold the place of God" when they give legitimate commands, superiors must themselves be concerned for the religious entrusted to them, respecting their dignity and seeking to understand them. They should do all in their genuine spirit of religious obedience. They are to be true spiritual leaders, examples of a genuine spirit of religious obedience in striving for holiness and, at the same time, mindful of their responsibility ultimately to decide what must be done. The recent instruction *Faciem tuam*, whose English title is "The Service of Authority and Obedience," discusses at length the superiors' role in service of the community, particularly in sections 12–4 and 17–0.

Obedience Lived in Community

In 1965, the council issued the decree *Perfectae caritatis*, which not only expressed in a new way the beauty of common life, but also offered deeper insights into the dignity of both subjects and superiors.[97] While promoting the authority of superiors, the decree also pointed out their responsibility to encourage the members of the community to contribute their talents and gifts.

> Subjects should be brought to the point where they will cooperate with an active and responsible obedience in undertaking new tasks and in carrying those already undertaken. And so superiors should gladly listen to their subjects and foster harmony among them for the good of the community and the Church, provided that thereby their own authority to decide and command what has to be done is not harmed.[98]

In 1994, the Congregation for Institutes of Consecrated Life and Societies of Apostolic Life issued a document titled *Fraternal Life in Community* to confirm the necessity of religious life lived in common. *Fraternal Life in Community* emphasized the fact that canonical religious life is, by definition, life lived together in common, so that each member of the institute is not only called to an individual vocation but to a *"con-vocation'*— they are called with others, with whom they share their daily life."[99] Chapter 4 of this book addresses this theme and some aspects of *communio* in religious life.

Three aspects of the interaction of community life and obedience are worth noting. The first is the power of the combined acts of obedience by the members. Each act of obedience is one person's individual act of the will. In community, those acts of the will are bound together with great spiritual power. Additional power comes from the fact that those in the community are obeying by reason of their vow and with the resulting merit in the graced atmosphere that such obedience creates. In the daily life of the community, the decisions and acts of the individuals are united in "a specific mission to be accomplished within the Church."[100] *Vita consecrata* has the same message: "Obedience, enlivened by charity, unites the members of an institute in the same witness and the same mission. . . . In community life which is inspired by the Holy Spirit, each individual engages in a fruitful dialogue with the others in order to discover the Father's will."[101]

The second aspect of the inner workings of community life, alluded to in the previous sentence, is the opportunity, introduced in the Second Vatican Council, for formative "dialogue." *Perfectae caritatis* describes this dialogue: "Subjects should be brought to the point where they will cooperate with an active and responsible obedience in undertaking new tasks and in carrying those already undertaken. And so superiors should gladly listen to their subjects."[102]

The third aspect of obedience is that authority is necessary for good community life. *Vita consecrata* emphasizes the crucial role of the superior's authority in relation to communal dialogue and discernment.

> In an atmosphere strongly affected by individualism, it is not
> an easy thing to foster recognition and acceptance of the role

which authority plays for the benefit of all. Nevertheless, its importance must be reaffirmed as essential for strengthening fraternal communion. While authority must be above all fraternal and spiritual, and while those entrusted with it must know how to involve their brothers and sisters in the decision-making process, it should still be remembered that *the final word belongs to authority.*[103]

Good community life, says *Fraternal Life in Community*, "comes from obedience to the Word of God."[104]

Thus the community aspects of obedience can be seen. Authority, obedience, and life in common are woven together in religious life, but with the authority of the superior always in the ascendant: "In religious communities, authority, to whom attention and respect are due also by reason of the obedience professed, is placed at the service of the fraternity, of its being built up, of the achievement of its spiritual and apostolic goals."[105]

Obedience as Reflection of the Inner Life of the Trinity

Obedience in religious life reflects the inner life of the Trinity. It is an obedience specifically configured to that of the Son, whose total receptive surrender to the Father for all eternity constitutes his very identity as Son; and whose divine filial surrender is "translated" into human terms throughout his earthly life.[106] The profound configuration of religious life to this "mystery of Christ," a theme unfolded in chapter 1 of *Vita consecrata*, "brings about in a special way that *confessio Trinitatis*"—in other words, religious life is a sign of the Trinitarian mystery itself, "the mark of all Christian life."[107] Simple love and mutual deference, eager promptness, and thorough obedience in a religious community all manifest the "loving harmony" within the Trinity, where the obedient Son is infinitely loved by the Father and eternally loves the Father.[108] The Son "delights only in the will of the Father, to whom he is perfectly united and on whom he depends for everything."[109] Religious obedience reflects this divine mutual dependence and delight in doing another's will, the will of one who is seen, in faith, to represent the Father. The religious chooses to obey, subjecting his or her will in perfect freedom. In this particularly significant way, religious obedience imitates Christ.

> Obedience, practiced in imitation of Christ, whose food was to
> do the Father's will (cf. Jn 4:34), shows the liberating beauty of
> a dependence which is not servile but filial, marked by a deep
> sense of responsibility and animated by mutual trust.[110]

This utter obedience by which Jesus trustingly and willingly
lays down his life for love of the Father and for us "is the key to
understanding [the] third evangelical counsel."[111] As Pope John
Paul II says above, obedience is "liberating." Configured to God
the Son, religious obedience entails dependence on the Father
with maturity and intelligence.

THE VOWS:
MEASURE OF THE RESPONSE TO GOD'S CALL

The vows of chastity, poverty, and obedience are a total
spousal response to the Loving God who gives Himself. All
aspects of the vows are total gift—the undivided heart, the leaving all, the obedience unto death. They are the holocaust, the
martyrdom, of oneself, given to God so totally that nothing is
left, nothing is held back. "Go, sell what you have" (Mk 10:21).

Religious profession expresses the person's gift of his life for
the love of God and for the sake of the Church. The Church benefits by the total self-gift of the religious. On a day-to-day basis,
the vows are renewed through the smaller gifts of one's time,
personal talents, and activity. All these expressions take place
in the heart of a religious community, for God intends that the
gift of the religious life be lived in common with others who
share the institute's charism and vows. It is this very *communio*
that will be unfolded in the next chapter.

Chapter 4

COMMUNION

IN

COMMUNITY

Sister Mary Prudence Allen, R.S.M.

RELIGIOUS LIFE FLOWS FROM THE COMMUNION
OF THE THREE DIVINE PERSONS

In 1992, the Congregation for the Doctrine of the Faith, whose prefect was Joseph Cardinal Ratzinger (before he became Pope Benedict XVI), issued a Letter to Bishops of the Catholic Church, titled *Some Aspects of the Church Understood as Communion (communio)*. This paper asked for a deeper reflection on the mystery of the Church as communion, as "a key for the renewal of Catholic ecclesiology."[1]

This Letter to Bishops identifies several principles of ecclesial communion. These include, first, that "the concept of communion lies 'at the heart of the Church's self understanding,' insofar as it is the Mystery of the personal union of each human being with the divine Trinity and with the rest of mankind, initiated with the faith, and having begun as a reality in the Church on earth, is directed towards its eschatological fulfillment in the heavenly Church."[2] The Letter also notes that communion is analogical, and not a univocal concept (3,8); communion is both invisible and visible (4); that in its invisible elements there is a mutual relationship between the pilgrim Church on earth and the heavenly Church (6); and finally, communion occurs among plurality of different forms of life through charity, the bond of perfection (15). While the letter was applied to relationship among different Churches, its principles apply very well to communion in community in religious life. With the new emphasis of the Second Vatican Council on the deep mystery of the Church as *communio*, the particular gift and obligation for renewed authentic living of the community dimension of religious life as a service to other states of life began to manifest itself with increasing clarity.

113

A preliminary survey of the use of the words "common" and "communion" in over fifty documents written by Church authorities from the thirteenth century through the twenty-first century reveals three distinct phases.

In the first phase, from the thirteenth century up to approximately 1964, the word "communion" in relation to religious life simply was not used. Instead, the word "common" was applied in various ways to characterize common property, possessions, rule, mode of living, breviary, life, apostolic endeavor, and obligations.

In the second phase from 1964–1978, the Church introduced the word 'communion' to refer to different kinds of communion brought about in the Church through the action of the Holy Spirit, by participating in the Eucharist, and among the hierarchical offices in communion with the Apostles. In the dogmatic constitution *Lumen gentium* (1964) where "communion" appears thirty-five times to describe a wealth of different kinds of communion in the Church, it never has direct reference to religious communities, even in nos. 43–7, which are on religious life. In no. 15 of *Perfectae caritatis,* the Decree on Religious Life (1965), the word "communion" was introduced once with respect to religious life in common. "Common life, fashioned on the model of the early Church where the body of believers was united in heart and soul (cf. Acts 4:32), and given new force by the teaching of the Gospel, the sacred liturgy and especially the Eucharist, should continue to be lived in prayer and the communion [*communione eiusdem spiritus perseveret*] of the same spirit." Thus, spirituality of communion for religious springs up like a tiny little shoot from this root in *Perfectae caritatis* and the Second Vatican Council.

In the third phase, thirteen years later in 1978, two major documents of the Sacred Congregation for Religious and Secular Institutes (SCRSI), *Mutuae relations (Directives for Mutual Relations between Bishops and Religious in the Church)* and *Religious and Human Promotion* brought religious into the heart of the theme of ecclesial communion. The first document called religious into a unity of communion with the Bishops in the "living organism" of the Church (nos. 1, 5). This call into an organic communion permeates the document and invites religious to full participation in this ecclesial communion.

In no. 24 of the document on *Religious and Human Promotion* (1978–1980), religious are given particular responsibility in the spirituality of communion: "*Experts in communion,* religious are, therefore, called to be an ecclesial community in the Church and in the world, witnesses and architects of the *plan for unity* which is the crowning point of human history in God's design." Religious are mandated not only to witness to ecclesial communion, but also to become architects or designers of such a communion. This is a striking continuity of development in a context of increasing tendencies toward disunion among many among lay, religious, and hierarchal vocations in the Church.

In the same document, nos. 24–5 make the link between common life of religious and spirituality of communion clear:

> Furthermore, through the daily experience of communion of life, prayer, and apostolate—the essential and distinctive elements of their form of consecrated life [ref. to *Perfectae caritatis*,15]—they are *a sign of fraternal fellowship.* In fact, in a world frequently very deeply divided and before their brethren in the faith, they give witness to the possibility of a community of goods, of fraternal love, of a program of life and activity which is theirs because they have accepted the call to follow more closely and more freely Christ the Lord who was sent by the Father so that, firstborn among many brothers and sisters, he might establish a new fraternal fellowship in the gift of his Spirit. From their communitarian way of living flows that form of presence and involvement which should characterize them in the Church's mission and which we now emphasize in view of the options concerning human promotion.

By 1980, after the election of Pope John Paul II, we see a robust theology of religious life in which religious are asked to serve the Church through an authentic spirituality of communion because of their privileged essential characteristic of living in common. This new mission is one of the important ways that religious serve the ecclesial communion of the Church itself.

By 1994, the renamed Congregation for Institutes of Consecrated Life and Societies of Apostolic Life repeated the call to religious to become experts in communion. This time, the sign-value of community for other members of the Church in the here and now is indicated, and religious communion witnesses to the final goal of the eschatological kingdom.

Religious community is a visible manifestation of the communion which is the foundation of the Church and, at the same time, a prophecy of that unity toward which she tends as her final goal. As *"experts in communion,"* religious are, therefore, called to be an ecclesial community in the Church and in the world, witnesses and architects of the plan for unity which is the crowning point of human history in God's design.[3]

Even more, religious no longer just witness to communion, but again are asked to become designers or architects of communion for the world. Two years later, in 1996, John Paul II repeated this same clarion call and pleaded with religious in *Vita consecrata* to willingly and joyfully accept this new mission given to them by the Church:

A great task also belongs to the consecrated life in the light of the teaching about the Church as communion, so strongly proposed by the Second Vatican Council. Consecrated persons are asked to be true experts of communion and to practice the spirituality of communion as "witnesses and architects of the plan for unity which is the crowning point of human history in God's design." The sense of ecclesial communion, developing into a spirituality of communion, promotes a way of thinking, speaking and acting which enables the Church to grow in depth and extension. The life of communion in fact "becomes a sign for all the world and a compelling force that leads people to faith in Christ. . . . In this way communion leads to mission, and itself becomes mission"; indeed, "communion begets communion: in essence it is a communion that is missionary."[4]

In 2002, continuing this same line of thought, the Congregation for Institutes of Consecrated Life and Societies of Apostolic Life elaborated on the meaning of a spirituality of communion in *Starting Afresh from Christ: A Renewed Commitment to Consecrated Life in the Third Millennium.* Repeating the call to become true experts in communion from *Vita consecrata* (46, 51, and 93), and from *Novo millennio ineunte* (43), *Starting Afresh from Christ* mandates religious to develop "a spirituality of communion suitable for the present time."[5] This is the new evangelization of the communion in community of religious life: "The whole Church expects a clear contribution to this undertaking from consecrated life because of its specific vocation to a communion in love."[6]

Awakening deep desires to respond to this expectation with joy and enthusiasm, there is a need to hear the words of caution: "This is a task which requires spiritual persons interiorly shaped by God, by loving and merciful communion, and by mature communities where the spirituality of communion is the rule of life."[7] This book will hopefully lead to further understanding of how contemporary religious can better become these spiritual persons interiorly shaped by God within the specific charism of their own institutes, and how contemporary religious communities can mature so that the spirituality of communion truly is their rule of life.

Longing to become experts in communion, both living and evangelizing the spirituality of communion within the Church and in the world, religious communities may bear witness to the intimate interaction between communion and mission so beautifully captured in *Fraternal Life in Community*:

> [C]ommunion begets communion: essentially it is likened to a mission on behalf of communion. . . . Communion and mission are profoundly connected with each other, they interpenetrate and mutually imply each other, to the point that communion represents both the source and the fruit of mission: communion gives rise to mission and mission is accomplished in communion.[8]

THE STRUCTURES GUIDING COMMUNION IN COMMUNITY

Scientists study nature carefully to discover laws governing hierarchical structures. Each level of reality respects the laws of the lower levels, while at the same time revealing new laws about the structures of the higher level.[9] Thus, laws about water (H_2O), a higher level of organization of the two elements, hydrogen and oxygen, respect the integrity of the laws governing the two lower elements. The Jesuit scholar Bernard Lonergan describes the continuing hierarchical level of reality this way: "Organic, psychic, and intellectual development are not three independent processes. They are interlocked with the intellectual providing a higher integration of the psychic and the psychic providing a higher integration of the organic. Each level involves its own laws. . . ."[10] The laws describe how the forms of real things operate in the real world under particular conditions.

As an example of this natural hierarchical structure of organization, consider a religious woman or man, whose body at the level of physics has a specified number of hydrogen atoms. At the level of chemistry, these hydrogen atoms are organized into blood; at the level of biology, this blood is organized by the cardiovascular system; at the level of psychology, this cardiovascular system both affects and is affected by the individual psyche of the person; at the level of philosophy, the person directs his or her intellect and will with respect to the passions experienced in the psyche, when he or she decides to do a conscious act to build communion within a specified community of persons; and at the level of theology, the blood of Christ unites this community of persons and fills it with a spirituality of communion responding to the words of the priest in Eucharistic Prayer III: "Grant that we, who are nourished by his body and blood, may be filled with his Holy Spirit, and become one body, one spirit in Christ."

In addition to laws of physics, chemistry, biology, and psychology, there are also spiritual laws. For example, Saint Ignatius of Loyola described laws for the discernment of spirits applicable to all men and women; and the Carmelite reformer Saint Teresa of Avila described laws for entering into spiritual marriage. Throughout the recent document of the Congregation for Institutes of Consecrated Life, *The Service of Authority and Obedience*, spiritual laws for good order in religious communities are well articulated. Ignoring or breaking any laws, including spiritual laws, is done at the peril of the religious. Instead, since laws of nature and spirit form a path on which God has set the feet of religious, there is a need to beg God, like the authors of psalms and proverbs, to reveal these laws; and, after they are discovered, freely choose to follow them.

Just as the individual religious man or woman is properly understood to be a hierarchically structured reality, so also is a religious community properly understood as a hierarchically structured reality. The laws which operate within these structures reveal the integrity of identity and process. Laws of natural and spiritual life are different from rules, civil laws, or positive laws, which are man-made and can change at will.

Laws of natural and spiritual life are the paths which God has made for the world, and which the human intellect can discover through the cooperative dynamic of faith and reason, revelation and science.

In this discussion of the spirituality of communion, three *erroneous* claims about religious life often made by contemporary religious need to be addressed. They can be identified by the following three concepts: *pure democracy, evolution,* and *process.* Each one draws those who believe in it off the path of religious life with respect to enduring communion in community.

The Question of Pure Democracy

Some religious argue that their community is "democratic—not hierarchical," implying that these are the two exclusive alternatives.[11] While it is surely true that the renewal of the Second Vatican Council asked for fuller participation in decision-making within a religious institute, and it is also true that it opened possibilities of governing structures to include models other than a strict monarchy, it did not, however, suggest a radical polarization. Often a militant feminism accompanies such a radical polarization.[12]

When this appeal is made to broad-based decision-making and rejection of hierarchical authority, the goal is usually an *absolute* or *pure democracy*, in which each religious has equal say (or vote) about everything, and in which elected leaders function primarily as administrative secretaries for the base religious communities. This is a particular political model of religious community, within more secular Protestant developments. However, as far back as Ancient Greece, Plato and Aristotle had claimed that an absolute or pure democracy tends to deteriorate into anarchy, with small groups vying for power, until a tyrant rises up to impose order.[13]

Contemporary democratic political structures—for example, the parliamentary model of European and Canadian governments and the representative democracy (republican) model of the United States—usually are classified as examples of a "mixed democracy" or "polity." Distinguishing a mixed democracy from a pure democracy is important for this reflection on the kinds of structures that support or detract from communion in community, because a mixed democracy is essentially hierarchical at the same time that it involves the active participation of all members of the society.[14]

A religious community is different from a political government in that its form of government and its particular form of religious authority do not "derive from the members themselves. It is conferred by the Church at the time of establishing each institute and by the approving of its constitutions."[15] However, it may be considered like a mixed democracy or polity in some of the following ways: (1) The members of the community are the electorate, whose votes during a general chapter select the major superiors to lead the community for a specified amount of time, according to their constitutions;[16] (2) once elected, the major superiors exercise their authority by right of office, and for the common good of the community as a whole and of each individual within it; (3) exercising the executive functions of the polity, the supreme moderator, also known as the superior general, is assisted in a consultative dynamic, rather than directed by a general council; (4) ecclesiastical law, canon law, and the constitutions provide a legislative dimension to the governing; and (5) various levels of Church hierarchy and tribunals at the diocesan and pontifical levels provide the juridical dimensions of community life.

Consider the following passage from *Renewal in Religious Life,* which describes the goal of effective renewal of governing structures of a religious community:

> In the first paragraph of n. 4 of *Perfectae Caritatis,* it is stated than an effective renewal and a just, proper adaptation cannot be achieved without the collaboration of all the members of the institute. This principle of government conforms to psychology. . . .
>
> This directive of the Council should awaken in every institute a feeling of responsibility, evidenced in a deepened awareness of the community as an active, conscious unity of mind, heart, resolution and action; it should result in the discovery of the depth of meaning in common life, the head of which is authority but in which everyone else plays an active part (cf. n. 14, 15, of "P.C.").[17]

A mixed democracy with a hierarchical structure of authority is the model proposed by the Second Vatican Council. It should be able to foster a flowering of communion in community.

Those who advocate a "pure democracy" appear to be supporting a system that may tend, on the one hand, toward the destruction of the common good within a community, when a few individuals begin to dominate the whole, from below.[18] It may also tend, on the other hand, toward a new kind of Christian community, which no longer fulfils the essential characteristics of a Roman Catholic religious community.

The Question of Evolution

Sometimes, by applying a Darwinian model of evolution to the structure of religious life, it is falsely argued that the essential structures of religious community simply evolve over time.[19] This evolutionary model of religious life may lead to a situation in which laypersons become members of the community, participate in chapters of election and chapters of affairs, and determine not only the governance but also the apostolic works of particular communities. When this happens, the religious community, considered simply as an "organic lifeform," has mutated into some other kind of Christian community. It no longer fulfils the proper form of a religious community. It may even mutate further into a feminist community, or a socialist community, or some other kind of community involving members from different religions or even with no particular religion, but who share a common aim or goal.

Embedded within this kind of Darwinian evolutionary approach is the underlying premise that change in structures of community is a simple, natural process, much like accommodation to changes in weather or environment, without reference to judgments about better or worse structures for supporting the common good of a religious institute. With this misunderstanding of the meaning of renewal of religious life, this process can actually devolve toward decline and ultimately to extinction.

The evolutionary model is also defended at times by another false polarization between a model based on Platonic essences on the one hand, and on artificially constructed social clubs with contracts on the other.[20] The difficulty with this kind of false polarization is that it does not include the option incorporated in Church documents, based on the analogical application of laws about the real world. What makes for essential elements in the structure of religious communities are neither Platonic Ideas nor mechanistic (materialistic) contracts, but rather elements and laws analogically common to many religious communities, recognized and defined by the Church. In contrast to this Darwinian evolutionary model of religious life, the Second Vatican Council offered good reasons for why the essential structures of religious communities needed to be renewed rather than mutated, and it gave guidelines with reasons for why they should be renewed from within in particular ways.

Consider an example found in chapter 3 on the vows, which includes the element of obedience in community life. If there is no religious authority to ask a sister or a brother to freely undertake an obedience, then this sister or brother is not able to live the vow authentically.[21] In a section on "The Task of Authority" in *Vita consecrata*, John Paul II summarized it this way:

> In the consecrated life the role of Superiors, including local Superiors, has always been of great importance for the spiritual life and for mission. In these years of change and experimentation, the need to revise this office has sometimes been felt. But it should be recognized that those who exercise authority cannot renounce their obligation as those first responsible for the community, as guides of their brothers and sisters in the spiritual and apostolic life.
>
> In an atmosphere strongly affected by individualism, it is not an easy thing to foster recognition and acceptance of the rule which authority plays for the benefit of all. Nevertheless, its importance must be reaffirmed as essential for strengthening fraternal communion and in order not to render vain the obedience professed.[22]

In addition to concluding that an individual religious has a right to be asked to practice the virtue of the vow of obedience, John Paul II emphasizes how the hierarchical exercise of authority is essential for strengthening fraternal communion. A vital service to the common good is given when those in authority are available, attentively listen, encourage sincere dialogue, and welcome with discernment of the Holy Spirit the contributions of each member of an institute.[23]

The Question of Process

The third erroneous description of religious life claims that it is not possible to make vows or life-long commitments because persons and the communities to which they belong are always changing. The problem addressed is: how can someone make a life-long commitment (or religious vow) to a particular person (or religious community) when he or she will change over time?[24] Not only does this kind of argument imply that marriage commitments are practically impossible, but it also implies that religious vows are practically impossible to fulfill.[25]

Sometimes it is suggested that human-made "frameworks" can be used to explain how self-definition might work to create stability over time.[26] In this approach, religious community is viewed as a human-made framework that people choose to help provide stability in commitments grounded in the emotions of love for the God they experience. Thus, they view religious community as beginning with human subjective experience, and then try to build human structures to provide more or less permanent frameworks for ongoing commitments. However, even with a weakened understanding of God's covenant,[27] this kind of process schema cannot account for the way in which the Church understands religious communities as being called forth by God, with a specific charism, for the common good of the Church and its members.[28]

This erroneous description of religious life has been deeply affected by a process philosophy that is rooted in the thought of Alfred N. Whitehead.[29] His metaphysics of process emphasizes the constantly changing dynamic of reality and, more specifically, how a person's identity is always in flux. Process philosophy also presupposes that the experiences of a subject are the foundation for any commitment.[30] The historical linking of process philosophy to pragmatism and feminism has had significant negative effects on the community life in some religious institutes, and can be evident in cynicism or defective qualities which can permeate religious institute members.[31]

Coupled with a rejection of the hierarchical structure of reality, there is also an overemphasis on self-assertion.[32] Since experience is the basis of the person's identity, process thinkers seek stability in exercising the will in autonomous self-definition. This creates a difficulty since the human will, too, is only exercised in the present moment, which is as fleeting as an emotion or experience.

Process is only a temporal reality; but a religious community is brought into being and is sustained by an eternal source.[33] The eternal enters into time and calls it into being and becoming. A religious man or woman makes his or her vows, in time, to the Eternal Lord, outside of time. A religious community is simultaneously living in eternal and temporal dimensions. Process is only an earthly spatial/temporal reality, but a religious community is held together in being by the in-breaking of the kingdom of heaven.

Recall the following passage from *Vita consecrata*:

> The fraternal life seeks to reflect the depth and richness of this mystery [of communion, "a people made one with the unity of the Father, the Son, and the Holy Spirit."], *taking shape as a human community in which the Trinity dwells, in order to extend in history* the gifts of communion proper to the three divine Persons. Many are the settings and the ways in which fraternal communion is expressed in the life of the Church. . . . By constantly promoting fraternal love, also in the form of common life, the consecrated life has shown that sharing in the Trinitarian communion can change human relationships and create a new type of solidarity.[34]

The Holy Trinity creates the paths and the clearings for religious life to take root and flourish; religious men and women, called to live a specified religious life, set their feet on these paths and dwell together in these clearings, where the living God comes to dwell among them. The indwelling Lord spiritually animates the communion in community: "The Risen One, who lives in the community, communicating his own Spirit to it, makes it a witness of the resurrection."[35] While a community of men or women may construct a framework within which to live and love, as a kind of utopian venture, even serving others generously, this process never moves into the range of the life of communion breathed from the Holy Spirit into a religious community of consecrated persons called into being in time by God and called together into a pilgrimage of life toward union with the Holy Trinity and saints in eternal life heaven.

MARY, MOTHER OF GOD,
AS PILGRIM GUIDE TO COMMUNION IN COMMUNITY

Every pilgrimage needs a pilgrim guide. Mary's unique role in guiding religious from communion to mission is usually associated in Church documents with her special place at the Annunciation, the wedding at Cana, the foot of the Cross, and in the upper room at Pentecost. In these situations, Mary was at the center of small communities of persons whom she guided by her prayer and acts. In *Novo millennio ineunte,* John Paul II described how Mary's communion with the Holy Trinity is crucial in mission.

> The missionary mandate accompanies us into the Third Millennium and urges us to share the enthusiasm of the very first Christians: we can count on the power of the same Spirit who was poured out at Pentecost and who impels us still today to start out anew. . . .
>
> On this journey we are accompanied by the Blessed Virgin Mary to whom, a few months ago, in the presence of a great number of Bishops assembled in Rome from all parts of the world, I entrusted the Third Millennium. During this year I have often invoked her as the "Star of the New Evangelization." Now I point to Mary once again as the radiant dawn and *sure guide for our steps.*[36]

This invocation of Mary as a pilgrim guide draws upon John Paul II's encyclical letter, *Redemptoris mater,* which described "The Mother of God at the center of the Pilgrim Church."[37] For a religious community, Mary becomes the pilgrim guide along the paths of communion laid out by God. Usually a person becomes a guide of pilgrims during a particular pilgrimage because he or she has taken the same pilgrimage before. Mary can be a pilgrim guide on the way to the spirituality of communion because she has successfully made the pilgrimage before all other Christians.

> The journey of faith made by Mary, whom we see praying in the Upper Room, is thus longer than that of the others gathered there: Mary "goes before them," "leads the way" for them. The *moment of Pentecost* in Jerusalem had been prepared for by the *moment of the Annunciation* in Nazareth, as well as by the cross. In the Upper Room Mary's journey meets the Church's journey of faith.[38]

Mary is the pilgrim guide in the Church not only of individuals, but also of religious communities. In *Redemptoris mater*, John Paul II described it this way: "Mary's faith . . . in some way continues to become the faith of the pilgrim People of God: the faith of individuals and communities."[39]

The pilgrimage that Mary, Mother of God is leading us on is not just a temporal one, stretched out in time and space, here and now. Her pilgrimage has a vertical dimension, because it is stretching out from the space/time continuum toward the heavenly eternal kingdom. In *Mother of the Redeemer*, John Paul II describes it this way:

> Through her mediation, subordinate to that of the Redeemer, Mary contributes *in a special way to the union of the pilgrim Church on earth* with the eschatological and heavenly *reality* of the Communion of Saints, since she has already been "assumed into heaven."[40]

This pointing to the end time, "the already but not yet" of the kingdom of heaven is captured in the mystery of being an eschatological sign. Recall the introduction of the three-fold dimension of sign in chapter 2, and consider again documents of the Second Vatican Council, such as *Perfectae caritatis,* which stated that a consecrated religious is called to be "a splendid sign of the heavenly kingdom."[41] *The Code of Canon Law* reiterates this eschatological sign-value of a consecrated religious as manifesting "in the Church the marvelous marriage established by God as *a sign of the world to come.*"[42]

In chapter 2, the individual consecrated religious is described as entering into a spiritual marriage, and being thus called to serve as a sign of the eschatological kingdom. How does a religious community itself also serve as an eschatological sign of the kingdom of heaven? In developing an answer to this question, a profound depth and richness of the religious mission to live a spirituality of communion that is so vibrant that it becomes a living sign of the communion of saints in union with the Holy Trinity in heaven will be discovered.

Léon [Leo] Joseph Cardinal Suenens, whose 1963 book *The Nun in the World: Religious and the Apostolate* contributed so greatly to changes in the post–Vatican II self-understanding of apostolic work of religious communities, defended the necessity of religious living in community. He considered it as an essential sign of a religious community for the whole Church.

> The religious community as such constitutes a "sign" by which the Master ought to be able to make Himself known; a convincing sign of brotherly love lived according to Jesus' words, "So they may perfectly be made one. So let the world know that it is thou who hast sent me." It is a fraternal community trying to continue in the world the prototype of the primitive Church described in the Acts of the Apostles.[43]

Cardinal Suenens offered two reasons for his definitive affirmation of the importance of a spirituality of communion in a particular religious community living communally. The first was that it "constitutes a public affirmation of the transcendency of God and the reality of the supernatural."[44] The second was its important place as a sign of the heavenly kingdom in the context of a secular world:

> Communism is trying to impose by force a new social order . . . ; it is more important that the Church should be able to offer the world the picture of living communities, where a voluntary communism reigns, based on divine worship and brotherly love, as a foretaste of what in many aspects a society open to social Christianity and faithful to the Gospel would be.[45]

It did not occur to Cardinal Suenens, even with all of his suggestions for changes in other areas, to ask religious to forgo living together in community, because it was such an important vibrant sign of the reality of Christian life for the Church and for the world.

THE CALL INTO A RELIGIOUS COMMUNITY

All Christian life flows from the trinitarian life of communion in charity. At baptism—which is conferred on a person within the communion of the Church—the person is brought into the supernatural communion of the Holy Trinity, being adopted by God, the Father, though Jesus Christ, the Son, and in the Holy Spirit. "In the mystery of the Church, unity in Christ involves a mutual communion of life among her members."[46] As we noted in chapter 1, the vocation to religious life, as a new and special bond, "is considered to be *a special and fruitful deepening of the consecration received in Baptism*."[47]

> This is the meaning of the call to the consecrated life: it is an
> initiative coming wholly from the Father (cf. Jn 15:16), who
> asks those whom he has chosen to respond with complete and
> exclusive devotion. The experience of this gracious love of God
> is so deep and so powerful that the person called senses the
> need to respond by unconditionally dedicating his or her life to
> God, consecrating to him all things present and future, and
> placing them in his hands. This is why, with Saint Thomas, we
> come to understand the identity of the consecrated person,
> beginning with his or her complete self-offering, as being com-
> parable to a genuine holocaust.[48]

In other words, God the Father calls, and the person
responds.

It has sometimes been erroneously suggested that the religious vocation springs from "an integrated and integrating
enterprise or spiritual project [of a particular human being],
organized around in function of the God-quest."[49] This falsely
places the initiative for religious life in the passions or power of
a human person, who is so involved in the search for a relationship with God that he or she subsequently gives the whole self
in celibacy to this quest, much like an artist or scientist who is
completely dedicated to his or her work. In this mentality, religious persons together simply "constructed a 'world' . . . or a
'space' . . . to foster the God-quest."[50]

Rather, the call comes from God to enter into a specified religious institute, or in some situations to found a new religious
institute. This is an essential element of the vocation. "Religious
consecration establishes communion between religious and
God and, in him, between members of the same institute. This
is the basic element in the unity of an institute."[51]

Therefore, even though human beings work together on a
common quest, it does not follow that any group, even if their
members share a common spiritual quest, is a religious community *per se.* "A shared tradition, common works, well-considered
structures, pooled resources, common constitutions, and a single spirit can all help to build up and strengthen unity. The
foundation of unity, however, is the communion in Christ established by the one founding gift. This communion is rooted in
religious consecration itself."[52] *Fraternal Life in Community* sums
it up this way:

> Religious community is not simply a collection of Christians in
> search of personal perfection. Much more deeply, it is a partici-
> pation in and qualified witness of the Church-Mystery, since it
> is a living expression and fulfillment of its own particular "com-
> munion," of the great Trinitarian "*koinonia*," in which the Father
> has willed that men and women have part in the Son and in the
> Spirit.[53]

As early as 1987, some religious mistakenly defined actions
of the Persons in the Holy Trinity by suggesting that there are
two distinct and conflicting sources of religious life, one based
in a "christomonistic ecclesiology" and the other in a "pneumatological ecclesiology."[54] However, the call of the Father is not
isolated, but Trinitarian; it comes from a Communion of Divine
Persons. John Paul II elaborates in *Vita consecrata*: "This special
way of 'following Christ,' at the origin of which is always the initiative of the Father, has an essential Christological and pneu-
maticological [Holy Spirit] meaning: it expresses in a
particularly vivid way the Trinitarian nature of the Christian life
and it anticipates in a certain way that eschatological fulfillment
towards which the whole Church is tending."[55] Religious life is
located at the "heart of the Church" and not at its outmost
extremities. Religious life "manifests the inner nature of the
Christian calling."[56]

FORMATION OF A RELIGIOUS IN A SPECIFIED COMMUNITY

Once a person accepts his or her religious call, then formation begins within the specified community with its founding
charism.[57] The formation of the religious aims at conforming
him or her to Jesus Christ in the common life of the religious
community held within the community of the Church.[58]
"Formation is a sharing in the work of the Father who, through
the Spirit, fashions the inner attitudes of the Son in the hearts of
young men and women."[59] One writer adds that the formation
of the individual religious is analogous to the way Jesus Christ
was formed by the Father, with the help of Mary and Joseph, in
the Holy Spirit.[60] The formation of the individual religious is
also analogous to the ways that Jesus Christ formed his own disciples in community.[61] Pope John Paul II, in *Vita consecrata*,
describes:

During his earthly life, the Lord Jesus called those whom he
wished in order to have them at his side and to train them to
live, according to his example, for the Father and for the mission which he had received from the Father. . . . By constantly
promoting fraternal love, also in the form of common life, the
consecrated life has shown that sharing in the Trinitarian communion can change human relationships and create a new type
of solidarity.[62]

Formation or conforming the religious to Jesus Christ is a
permanent, essential element of a religious community. "If, in
fact, consecrated life is in itself 'a progressive taking on of the
attitude of Christ,' it seems evident that such a path must
endure for a lifetime and involve the *whole* person, heart, mind,
and strength (cf. Mt 22:37) reshaping the person in the likeness
of the Son who gives himself to the Father for the good of
humanity."[63] Not only is the individual religious formed, but
also the community itself is formed. *Fraternal Life in Community*
describes "[b]eing a community in permanent formation":

One of the goals of such initiative is to form communities that
are mature, evangelical, fraternal, and capable of continuing
permanent formation in daily life. Religious life is the place
where broad guidelines are implemented concretely, through
patient and persevering daily efforts. Religious community is,
for everyone, the place and the natural setting of the process of
growth, where all become co-responsible for the growth of others. Religious community is also the place where, day by day,
members help one another to respond as consecrated persons,
bearing a common charism, to the needs of the least and to the
challenges of the new society.[64]

While all Christians are called to be conformed to the pattern of the life of Jesus Christ and educated analogously to the
way Jesus formed his own apostles, Christians called to a religious community have a further specified charism or character
which penetrates their lives and service. *Vita consecrata*
describes how formation of a religious always should occur
within the boundaries and with the unique impetus of a specific charism which flows from God and back to God.

In the first place, there is a need for *fidelity to the founding
charism* and subsequent spiritual heritage of each Institute. It is
precisely in this fidelity to the inspiration of the founders and
foundresses, an inspiration which is itself a gift of the Holy

Spirit, that the essential elements of the consecrated life can be more readily discerned and more fervently put into practice. Fundamental to every charism is a threefold orientation. First, charisms lead *to the Father*, in the filial desire to seek his will through a process of unceasing conversion. . . . Secondly, the charisms of the consecrated life also lead *to the Son*, fostering an intimate and joyful communion of life with him, in the school of his generous service of God and neighbour. . . . Finally, every charism leads *to the Holy Spirit*, insofar as it prepares individuals to let themselves be guided and sustained by him, both in their personal spiritual journeys and in their lives of communion and apostolic work. . . . This is so because in every charism there predominates "a profound desire to be conformed to Christ to give witness to some aspect of his mystery."[65]

RATIO INSTITUTIONIS SPIRITUALIS AS COMMUNITY PLAN OF FORMATION

The Church calls the particular plan of spiritual formation of a religious community a *"ratio institutionis."* After the Second Vatican Council, each religious community was asked to renew itself by developing such a *ratio. Vita consecrata* succinctly states this aspect of the call for renewal, which is "to draw up as soon as possible a *ratio institutionis*, that is, a formation programme inspired by their particular charism, presenting clearly and in all its stages the course to be followed in order to assimilate fully the spirituality of the respective Institute."[66]

The *ratio* concerns "the *spirituality* of the respective Institute," which is supposed to enable a religious community to "pass on the Institute's spirit so that it will be lived in its integrity by future generations, in different cultures and geographical regions; presenting clearly and in all its stages the course to be followed in order to assimilate fully the spirituality of the respective Institute."[67] Rev. Elio Gambari states that the *ratio* "aims at covering what constitutes the life plan or the divine design relating to the spiritual life as it is lived in actual practice in that institute . . . a manner of living conceived by God and shown by Him to a soul so that this soul may accept it and embody it in his [or her] own life."[68]

Because the *ratio* is spiritual, it pertains to an interior, invisible, formative dimension of religious life. As Fr. Gambari describes it further, "the 'Ratio' represents the guideline holding together all the elements of the spiritual life, both general and specific, and helping to achieve a unified life."[69] In *Renewal in Religious Life*, a diagram for writing a *ratio* depicts how "life in common" and "life of the community in charity and as an eschatological community" grow as branches from the roots and trunk of the Church, which draws its life-force from the Holy Trinity.[70]

Life in common could be characterized as a more visible aspect of community life. The invisible aspect of community life is "the more spiritual 'fraternity' or 'fraternal communion,' which arises from hearts animated by charity. It underlines 'communion of life' and interpersonal relationships."[71] Although all religious institutes have had some changes in their visible structures, one commentator has mistakenly suggested that in communities in which visible structures of common life have remained more or less stable, no renewal has occurred in the spiritual dimensions of community.[72] Some commentators have even radically polarized religious communities which no longer live a common life and religious communities which keep the external structures of common life, failing to inquire whether the latter are religious communities that have spiritually renewed and are presently renewing their communion in community through a *ratio institutionis* based on updating their founding charism.[73] *Vita consecrata* describes the Trinitarian participation of this renewal:

> . . . the Church is essentially a mystery of communion, a "people made one with the unity of the Father, the Son, and the Holy Spirit." The fraternal life seeks to reflect the depth and richness of this mystery, taking shape as a human community in which the Trinity dwells, in order to extend in history the gifts of communion proper to the three divine Persons. . . . The consecrated life can certainly be credited with having effectively helped to keep alive in the Church the obligation of fraternity as a form of witness to the Trinity.[74]

THE EUCHARIST AS KEY TO RELIGIOUS' PARTICIPATION IN CHURCH *COMMUNIO*

The sacrament of charity, or the Eucharist, binds the religious together intensely. In *Essential Elements* we read that "the

local community, as the place where religious life is primarily
lived, has to be organized in a way [in] which its center is the
Eucharist in which the members of the community participate
daily as far as possible and which is honored by having an orato-
ry where the celebration can take place and where the Blessed
Sacrament is reserved (cf. ET 48)."[75] The privilege accorded by
the Church to religious men and women of Jesus Christ's
Eucharistic presence in the convent or monastery demonstrates
how this sacrament of charity provides a perpetual source for
their communion in community.[76] John Paul II, in *Starting
Afresh from Christ*, also emphasizes that the place of the
Eucharist in the life of the consecrated religious allows for:

> the fullness of intimacy with Christ [to be] realized, becoming
> one with him, total conformity to him to whom the consecrated
> persons are called by vocation. . . . The Eucharist, the
> Sacrament of unity with Christ, is at the same time the
> Sacrament of Church unity and community unity for the conse-
> crated person. Clearly it is "The source of spirituality both for
> individuals and for communities."[77]

The Second Vatican Council emphasized that the Church is a
communio. Karol Wojtyla, in *Sources of Renewal*, writes that "the
Church . . . is oriented towards the resemblance there ought to
be between [its members] united in truth and charity . . . and
the essentially divine unity of the divine persons in *communione Sanctissimae Trinitatis*."[78]

In *Vita consecrata*, John Paul II developed the *communio*
dynamic of different vocations in the Church. "The vocations to
the lay life, to the ordained ministry and to the consecrated life
can be considered paradigmatic, inasmuch as all particular
vocations, considered separately or as a whole, are in one way
or another derived from them or lead back to them, in accordance with the richness of God's gift. These vocations are also *at
the service of one another*, for the growth of the Body of Christ in
history and for its mission in the world."[79]

Religious life, at the heart of the Church, serves the priestly
and lay vocations by its witness to the union and charity of the
eschatological life, while the vocation to the priesthood serves
religious life by nourishing it through the sacrament of charity,
the Eucharist. Some contemporary women religious seem to
reject this *communio*-dynamic of vocations being at service of one

another, especially with respect to the clergy.[80] Rather, precisely the gift of willing service by the priest, *in persona Christi capitus*, in offering the sacrament of the Eucharist in a religious community or parish, reveals complementary relations of self-gift in love. In Pope Benedict's words: "[T]he priest is 'the servant of the Church as communion . . .'; [and the] consecrated life, too, of its very nature, is at the service of this communion . . . by constantly promoting fraternal love, also in the form of common life." He states further: "It is indispensable that, within the Christian people, every ministry and charism be directed to full communion"; and that "whoever . . . lives the Eucharist, makes progress in love of God and neighbor and thus contributes to building the Church as communion. We confirm that the 'Eucharistic love' motivates and founds the vocational activity of the whole Church."[81]

Since the religious vocation flows from the Holy Trinity in such a way that religious are called to become experts in communion for the Church, to the extent that they do enter into and embrace the descending love of agape-charity and integrate this love into their common life and into the missions, to that extent will religious be able to serve as living signs of the eschatological communion in loving union with God. The renewal initiated by the Second Vatican Council propels religious to a deeper community love for and participation in the Eucharist, and thus to a more perfect living of the call of the religious vocation. *Starting Afresh from Christ* says it this way:

> Meeting these conditions the community of consecrated persons which lives the Paschal Mystery renewed daily in the Eucharist, becomes a witness of communion and a prophetic sign of solidarity for a divided and wounded society. In fact, the spirituality of communion, so necessary to establish the dialogue of charity needed in today's world, is born in the Eucharist.[82]

THE CHURCH AFFIRMS THE *ANALOGICAL REALITY* OF RELIGIOUS COMMON LIFE

Communion within a particular religious community occurs within the community of the Church. The Church confirms the distinct charisms of each religious institute. By using the notion of analogy, the Church is following a long tradition since

Thomas Aquinas, which distinguishes between words with *equivocal* meaning (where the same word has two entirely different meanings); *univocal* meaning (where the same word means exactly the same thing in two separate applications); and *analogical* meaning (where the word has simultaneously some meaning that is the same and some meaning that is different). This distinction of analogy is extremely important when describing the essential elements of religious life. Some argue wrongly that there are no consistent similarities among religious communities; while others argue wrongly that religious communities are exactly the same. Religious communities *are* analogous to one another, that is, they are simultaneously similar in some respects and different in other respects.

Just consider the way in which each of the over one hundred religious institutes belonging to the CMSWR analogously live their common life today. If we looked closely at the specific ways they lived their common life, we would discover that there are simultaneously both similarities and differences. Turning from the contemporary example to an historical analysis of magisterial statements, we also discover the similar principle that all religious ought to live a common life, but it is lived differently in some respects in different circumstances of time and place. For example, in the thirteenth century, the Church asked religious to "mutually show themselves to be members of the same household."[83] In the sixteenth century, the Council of Trent asked religious to "faithfully observe . . . special precepts particular to any rule or order which belong to their essential nature and to the preservation of common life. . . ."[84] In the early twentieth century, Pope Leo XIII defended the common life of a religious community when secular governments "forcefully removed [them] from their domiciles."[85] The centrality of common life to religious community was reaffirmed again in the later twentieth century, for example, in Norm 12 of *Essential Elements*: "Religious should live in their own religious house, observing a common life."[86]

Some religious have argued that common life is not an essential element in religious life, and they have acted on this faulty premise to disband their common houses, or to send individual religious away to live alone or to return to their families. Acting on this faulty premise has caused agonizing suffering and perhaps even a hidden martyrdom for many religious. The rejection of common life for religious is based on erroneous understandings of the relation between religious community and the Church.

A faulty epistemological/metaphysical argument against common life goes generally like this: There must be one essential way that common life has been lived to make it a universal and necessary characteristic of religious life. A socio-historical review of different "life-styles" of common life among religious communities reveals that there are many different ways that religious communities organize themselves. There is no one essential way that common life has been lived. Therefore, (they erroneously conclude) common life is not an essential characteristic of religious life.[87]

The Church also applies the notion of the analogical lived reality to the way that a religious institute lives out its charism and its mission. Consider the following statement in *Fraternal Life in Community*: "It is impossible to speak of religious community *univocally*. The history of consecrated life witnesses to a variety of ways of living out the one communion according to the nature of various institutes."[88] This Church document elaborates the fundamentally analogical way that religious communities live their charism and mission:

> From participation in the various aspects of Christ's mission, the Spirit makes different religious families arise, characterized by different missions, and therefore by different kinds of community. . . .
>
> There are thus various kinds of religious community that have been handed down over the centuries such as monastic, conventual, and active or "diaconal."
>
> It follows that "common life lived in community" does not have the same meaning for all religious. Monastics, conventuals, and religious of active life have maintained legitimate differences in their ways of understanding and living religious community.[89]

COMMON LIFE A *NECESSARY CONDITION* FOR COMMUNION
IN RELIGIOUS COMMUNITY

Common life is a necessary condition for communion in community. Sr. Elizabeth McDonough, O.P., wrote:

> Two basic legal requirements for the category of religious institutes are public perpetual vows and common life (c. 607, #2). Related to these requirements are a public witness in the Church and a certain separateness of lifestyle (cc. 607, #3; 662; 673). Religious Institutes are supposed to be generally and somewhat identifiable through such characteristics as observance of community life (cc. 674–75), governance structures with superior and councils and general chapters (cc. 617–33), or recognizable exterior indications of membership (c. 669). And these specifications apply whether the religious institute is pontifical or diocesan (c. 589), clerical or lay (c. 588), apostolic (c. 675) or monastic (c. 574).[90]

A religious community has particular juridical realities established not only by the charism of his or her community, but also by its constitutions.[91] Elio Gambari, S.M.M., considers the framework for renewal after Vatican II: "While using moderation, especially at this point, it is nevertheless necessary that the constitutions depict the religious life as a life in common, expressing even in a tangible way the reality of the Mystical Body."[92] These juridical structures are meant to recognize essential elements for the flourishing of a religious vocation. Father Gambari describes further how this dynamism unfolds:

> Love, the most genuine expression of freedom, will lead the religious to cling to the constitutions in mind and in heart. . . .
>
> Thus will be actualized the encounter and fusion between the internal law of charity and the external juridical law. The law of charity becomes the soul and the motivating principle of the juridical law; the latter becomes the true and genuine expression of the interior law of love. The fusion is effected by the Lord, who is the ultimate source of both.[93]

In contrast to this positive and synergetic description of the integration of juridical and spiritual realities in the life of a religious, recently some religious have articulated an erroneous historical/experiential argument against common life which goes something like this: Common life is primarily a monastic way of living religious community. While it was forced on all religious communities by the Church in Tridentine (pre-conciliar) times, it is especially unsuited for contemporary active religious communities with apostolates (ministries) in the world.[94] In addition, it was an unhealthy form of community life, which kept religious in an immature and unreal state of existence.[95] Arguers reach the faulty conclusion that religious should personally reject common life as essential to community life, and that they should seek alternate forms of self-selected congregational group living.[96]

These objections to common life radically polarize two options. This polarization contains what we philosophers call a fallacy of false alternatives: either pre–Vatican II common life or no common life at all. No one would deny that the way many communities lived their common life before the Second Vatican Council needed to be renewed, integrating updated principles from psychology, sociology, philosophical anthropology, and theology. However, to conclude from historical experience that common life itself should be rejected in favor of radically different experimental structures is not supported by the evidence.

In a kind of "divorce mentality," many religious concluded that they had no other option than to leave common life.[97] Let us summarize the fallacy of false alternatives contained in this kind of argument: The beginning premises set up two alternatives: (1) either updated common life is *impossible per se* [in itself], or (2) updated common life is personally and ministerally *counterproductive*. Then each premise is contradicted: since a religious first cannot choose something that is impossible *per se*, and second, *should not* choose something that is counterproductive to her own vocation, the conclusion (by ignoring any other than the two alternative premises) erroneously claims a religious must reject common life.

This fallacious argument does not grasp the meaning of renewal asked for by the Second Vatican Council.[98] For example, *Starting Afresh from Christ* does not suggest a superficial updating of the status quo, but rather a renewal which dynamically integrates contemporary advances of understanding the human person and community life into essential structures of religious life.

> Thus, the constant search for unity in charity will become a
> school of communion for Christian communities and an exam-
> ple of people living in communion.
>
> Particular attention must be given to cultural formation in
> line with the times and in dialogue with the research of the
> meaning of human life today. This calls for a greater prepara-
> tion in the philosophical, theological and psychological fields
> and a more profound orientation to the spiritual life, models
> more adapted to the cultures in which new vocations are being
> born and well-planned programs for ongoing formation.[99]

Thus, common life must be renewed from within, so that it
can flourish with real communion in community.

Fraternal Life in Community describes the impact of these
false alternatives: "The tendency, in some institutes, to *empha-
size mission over community*, and to *favour diversity over unity*, has
had a profound impact on fraternal life in common, to the point
that this has become, at times, almost an option rather than an
integral part of religious life."[100] The document reaffirms that
common life is an essential element of religious life: "Religious
should live in their own religious house, observing a common
life."[101] It concludes with the following prescription: "Should
there be institutes in which, unfortunately, the majority of
members no longer live in community, such institutes would no
longer be able to be considered true religious institutes."[102]

RELIGIOUS LIFE *FLOWS OUT FROM* COMMUNION IN COMMUNITY

While common life is a necessary condition for religious life
and for its dynamism of communion in community, it is not a
sufficient condition. Something more is needed for a true spirituality of communion to occur than simply living together in a
common house as a local community. In other words, even if
religious are living a common life, the fullness of communion
in unity and charity may not have permeated their lives together. The Holy Trinity must vivify a religious house with a Divine
spiritual source of communion at the same time as the religious
members work to build their community. For a religious community to be living a true spirituality of communion involves
above all a continuous Divine-human cooperation. *Fraternal
Life in Community* describes it this way:

> Before being a human construction, religious community is a
> gift of the Spirit. It is the love of God, poured into our hearts by
> the Holy Spirit, from which religious community takes its origin
> and is built as a true family gathered in the Lord's name.
>
> It is therefore impossible to understand religious communi-
> ty unless we start from its being a gift from on high, from its
> being a mystery, from its being rooted in the very heart of the
> blessed and sanctifying Trinity, who wills it as part of the mys-
> tery of the Church, for the life of the world.[103]

Communion involves living a continuous Divine-human
cooperation "in accordance with the orientation of the charismatic gift received by the founder from God and transmitted to
his or her disciples and followers."[104] The unity in the religious
community has as its foundation "the communion in Christ
established by the one founding gift."[105]

A religious who has pronounced his or her vows is united in
"a new and special bond" with Jesus Christ. As was well
described in chapter 2, this spiritual bond, likened to a spiritual
marriage and to a perfect friendship, is the prime relation of
love in the life of the consecrated religious. It is strengthened by
individual and common prayer, especially the Eucharist and the
divine office, and by being in one another's presence in
various ways. "Prayer needs to be seen also as time for being
with the Lord so that He might act in us and, not withstanding
distractions and weariness, might enter our lives, console them
and guide them. So that, in the end, our entire existence can
belong to him."[106] This new and special bond with Jesus Christ
is interpersonal between a human person and a Divine Person.
Interpersonal relations among religious in a local community
are the subsequent primary interpersonal set of relations
dependent upon the foundational bond with Jesus Christ.
Fraternal Life in Community continues:

> From the gift of communion arises the duty to build fraternity,
> in other words, to become brothers and sisters in a given com-
> munity where they are called to live together. . . .
>
> In our days, and for our days, it is necessary to take up again
> this "divine-human" work of building up the community of
> brothers and sisters, keeping in mind the specific circum-
> stances of present times in which the theological, canonical,
> social, and structural developments have profoundly affected
> the profile and life of religious community.[107]

The obligation for spreading a spirituality of communion in the Church and the world had recently been mandated of religious communities. In *Vita consecrata* (1996) this task is actually entrusted to us: "The Church entrusts to communities of consecrated life the particular task of spreading the spirituality of communion, first of all in their internal life and then in the ecclesial community, and even beyond its boundaries, by opening or continuing a dialogue in charity. . . ."[108] Then *Starting Afresh from Christ: A Renewed Commitment to Consecrated Life in the Third Millennium* (2002) repeats that "one of the tasks of consecrated life today is that of *spreading the spirituality of communion*, first of all in their internal life and then in the Church community. . . ."[109] For further emphasis, in *The Service of Authority and Obedience* (2008), the essential nature of this mandate is vividly described.

> The building of fraternal community constitutes one of the fundamental tasks of consecrated life, to which the members of the community are called to dedicate themselves, moved by that same love that the Lord has poured out into their hearts. In fact, fraternal life in community is a constitutive element of religious life, an eloquent sign of the humanizing effects of the presence of the Reign of God.[110]

The practical question now arises: how can members of religious communities learn to live an authentic spirituality of communion in their own religious community; and how can they share their knowledge and experience with others in a new evangelization of the spirituality of communion?

CONCRETE WAYS TO BUILD SPIRITUALITY OF COMMUNION IN RELIGIOUS COMMUNITIES

Some ways that primary interpersonal relations of religious can be strengthened have recently been articulated by philosophers and theologians. Let us consider four such examples: (1) identifying authentic ways of participating in interpersonal relations, (2) learning how to engage in dialogue as a new way of charity, (3) developing virtue-friendships and friendships of charity, and (4) welcoming the hierarchy of truth and authority which guides communion in community.

AUTHENTIC WAYS OF PARTICIPATION
IN INTERPERSONAL RELATIONS

Within the framework of a personalist philosophy, Karol Wojtyla describes in part 4 of *The Acting Person* how persons can participate together with others to improve interpersonal relations in different kinds of communities. His general principles are extremely helpful for contemporary religious because they are rooted in a realistic understanding of human dignity and human love. Wojtyla states that "everyone ought to strive for that kind of participation which would allow him [or her] in acting together with others to realize the personalistic value of his own action; [and] any community of acting . . . should be conducted so as to allow the person remaining within its orbit to realize himself [or herself] through participation."[111] In other words, a religious community should be so structured that each person in it can flourish as a person at the same time as the person in the community supports the flourishing of each other person and the community as a whole. Cardinal Wojtyla argued that this goal of serving the common good needs to avoid the two extremes, first, of *individualism*, in which a person concentrates only on his or her own good, and second, of *reverse individualism*, in which the community sees the individual as an enemy of the common good.[112]

In *The Acting Person*, Karol Wojtyla describes practical methods for developing genuine participation in building the common good in a community. The first method is called an *attitude of solidarity* which means "a constant readiness to accept and to realize one's share in the community because of one's membership within that community."[113] In the Second Vatican Council Pastoral Constitution *On the Church and the Modern World*, *Gaudium et spes,* there is a beautiful elaboration of the Christian foundation and goal for this attitude of solidarity.

> As the firstborn of many brethren, and by the gift of his spirit, he established, after his death and resurrection, a new brotherly communion among all who received him in faith and love: this is the communion of his own body, the Church, in which everyone as members one of the other would render mutual service in the measure of the different gifts bestowed on each.

> This solidarity must be constantly increased until that day
> when it will be brought to fulfillment: on that day mankind,
> saved by grace, will offer perfect glory to God as the family
> beloved of God and of Christ their brother.[114]

This constant increase in solidarity until the end of time is in the heart of the mission of religious communities to serve as a living sign of the eschatological kingdom.[115]

In addition, according to Wojtyla the attitude of solidarity also encourages "the mutual complementariness between members of a solidaristic community; every member of a community has to be ready to 'complement' by his [or her] action what is done by other members of the community."[116] In a discussion of Saint Edith Stein's (Saint Benedicta) analysis of "Individual and Community," Sister M. Regina van den Berg, F.S.G.M., describes how mature members of her religious community act as "carriers of communal life": "They carry the community by placing their energy at its disposal, and by making the community's ideals their own. A carrier identifies his [or her] good with the communal good. . . ."[117] Anyone who has observed sisters in early formation may have experienced recognizing the moment when a young sister moves from imitating what she sees in other sisters of her institute to generously initiating some new aspect of the institute's charism. In this later state of her formation, she has begun to become a carrier of the common good of her own institute.

Sisters or brothers of a religious community should be alert to temptations to *not* engage actively in building the common good, when he or she may fall into what Wojtyla describes as an *inauthentic attitude of servile conformism*. When this temptation is yielded to, the religious simply goes along with others, complies, or remains resigned to an attitude that his or her participation in discussions about an important community value is useless. Wojtyla summarizes the negative effects of this inauthentic attitude on communion in community: "Conformism brings *uniformity* rather than *unity*."[118] When this occurs, both the religious person and the community lose the personalistic value of authentic participation, a dynamic acting together with others, and community life becomes deadened, rather than enlivened.

Another difficulty occurs if a religious decides that his or her participation is altogether impossible. Wojtyla describes this as an *inauthentic attitude of noninvolvement in community*, in which a person isolates the self from the community, and ultimately becomes unfulfilled in his or her religious vocation. In the first case, the religious remained in the community, but simply conforms; in the second case, the religious withdraws emotionally and even physically from the community. *Fraternal Life in Community* offers an example of how this attitude negatively affects religious community.

> [I]f we know little or nothing about the lives of our brothers or sisters, they will be strangers to us, and the relationship will become anonymous, as well as create true and very real problems of isolation and solitude. Some communities complain about the poor quality of the fundamental sharing of spiritual goods. Communication takes place, they say, around problems and issues of marginal importance but rarely is there any sharing of what is vital and central to the journey of consecration.
>
> This can have painful consequences, because then spiritual experience imperceptibly takes on individualistic overtones. A mentality of self-sufficiency becomes more important; a lack of sensitivity to others develops; and, gradually, significant relationships are sought outside the community.[119]

Thinking of how much communication and love is exchanged among the Divine Persons—Father, Son, and Holy Spirit—and of how religious are called to live in likeness to this Trinitarian love within their religious communities, a religious can be encouraged to recognize those times when he or she slides from authentic to inauthentic ways of relating to religious brothers or sisters. *Starting Afresh from Christ* offers an important incentive for trying to live authentic interpersonal relations in religious communities:

> The spirituality of communion which appears to reflect the spiritual climate of the Church at the beginning of the third millennium is an active and exemplary task for consecrated life on all levels. It is the principle highway for the future of life and witness. Holiness and mission come through the community because in and through it Christ makes himself present. Brother and sister become Sacraments of Christ and of the encounter with God, the concrete possibility, and even more,

the unsurpassable necessity in carrying out the commandment
to love one another and bring about Trinitarian communion.[120]

Some religious may long to be actively engaged in the task of
building interpersonal communion in their communities, but
do not know how to begin again. This brings us to the second
practical area for consideration.

DIALOGUE AS A NEW WAY OF CHARITY

Karol Wojtyla sets out some philosophical structures of dialogue
in *The Acting Person*:

> The principle of dialogue allows us to select and bring to light
> what in controversial situations is right and true, and helps to
> eliminate any partial, preconceived, or subjective views and
> trends. . . . Consequently, it seems that in a constructive com-
> munal life the principle of dialogue has to be adopted regardless
> of the obstacles and difficulties that it may bring with it along
> the way.[121]

At times religious have to overcome the temptation to evade
the difficult work that dialogue calls for, by either conforming or
being uninvolved. This is especially important when the goal is
to build the common good of a religious community in love.

With this backbone of the philosophical value of dialogue in
relation to truth, it is not surprising that in *Vita consecrata*, John
Paul II encourages this authentic attitude of interpersonal
engagement.

> The experience of recent years widely confirms that "*dialogue is
> the new name of charity,*" especially within the Church. Dialogue
> helps us to see the true implications of problems and allows
> them to be addressed with greater hope of success. *The conse-
> crated life*, by the very fact that it promotes the value of fraternal
> life, *provides a privileged experience of dialogue.*[122]

In 1964, Pope Paul VI, in Chapter III of *Ecclesiam suam,* had
previously declared that "to this internal drive of charity which
seeks expression in the external gift of charity, We will apply
the word 'dialogue.'"[123] Rooted in the dialogue that persons have
with God, and aiming for an authentic dialogue of *The Church
and the Modern World*, which he called "the dialogue of salvation," Pope Paul VI outlined the proper characteristics of dialogue. These are also essential for engagement within religious

communities: Dialogue should be intelligible; accompanied by
Christian meekness; stated with confidence and good will of
both persons; and oriented by a prudent attention to the receptivity of the hearer. He concluded that "in a dialogue conducted
with this kind of foresight, truth is wedded to charity and understanding to love."[124]

In *Ut unum sint*, especially paragraphs 28–36, Pope John Paul
II elaborated further essential characteristics of dialogue in the
context of ecumenical relations among Christians. This elaboration contains an excellent summary of fundamental guidelines
for the place of dialogue in a spirituality of communion.

> If prayer is the "soul" . . . of the yearning for unity, it is the
> basis and support for *everything the council defines as "dialogue."*
> This definition is certainly not unrelated to today's *personalist
> way of thinking.* The capacity for "dialogue" is rooted in the
> nature of the person and his dignity. As seen by philosophy,
> this approach is linked to the Christian truth concerning man as
> expressed by the Council: man is in fact "the only creature on
> earth which God willed for itself"; thus he cannot "fully find
> himself except through a sincere gift of himself." Dialogue is an
> indispensable step along the path *towards human self-realization,*
> the self-realization both of *each individual* and of *every human
> community.* Although the concept of "dialogue" might appear to
> give priority to the cognitive dimension. It involves the human
> subject in his or her entirety; dialogue between communities
> involves in a particular way the subjectivity of each.
>
> This truth about dialogue, so profoundly expressed by Pope
> Paul VI in his Encyclical *Ecclesiam Suam,* was also taken up by
> the Council in its teaching and ecumenical activity. Dialogue is
> not simply an exchange of ideas. In some ways it is always an
> "exchange of gifts."[125]

More particular characteristics of an authentic way to participate in dialogue include a presupposition in the other person of
a "desire for reconciliation, for unity in truth"; undertaken in "a
manner proper to the dignity of the human person and his
social nature"; "in a common quest for truth" and with a heart
"submissive to Christ's prayer for unity."[126] Dialogue among
persons undertaken in the spirit of humility toward the truth
and charity toward one another serves as "an examination of
conscience" leading to a possible "dialogue of consciences"; and
when continuing, it may become "a dialogue of conversion" and

an "authentic dialogue of salvation" taking place both on the horizontal level among the human participants, and on the vertical level invoking the presence of Jesus Christ through the Holy Spirit.[127]

Walter Cardinal Kasper applied these principles of dialogue from *Ut unum sint* directly to communion in religious community, when he addressed the Council of Major Superiors of Women Religious on "Communion through Dialogue." Emphasizing the importance of dialogue for a religious vocation, he said: "We do not only have dialogue, we are dialogue, we are encounter."[128] A human person can only be fulfilled through gift of self to others, and in receiving the gift of another. Dialogue, according to this view, "is the way through which we come to know about truth and through which we find the truth of our own existence."[129] The importance of dialogue in religious community has been confirmed in the document *The Service of Authority and Obedience* (June 2008): "In addition to listening, persons in authority will value sincere and free dialogue— sharing feelings, perspectives and plans: in this atmosphere each one will be able to have his or her true identity recognized and to improve his or her own relational abilities."[130]

It must be noted that at times dialogue can be, and has been, misused to avoid acts of self-gift. In these cases, one or both persons engaging in dialogue may be operating out of one or more of the following inauthentic attitudes: (1) assuming a relativist stance that predisposes him or her to view dialogue as simply the sharing of various opinions, without being motivated by a deeper desire to discover what is true; (2) trying to manipulate a superior or sister into a particular position by sharing only selective amounts of information while withholding significant things that are essential to the dialogue; (3) using emotionally charged words or tones of voice conveying a hostility which annuls the purpose of the dialogue; and (4) some other similar inauthentic way of relating through speech to the very persons in one's community with whom one should be the most forthcoming. This may involve deception or using the religious institute to promote one's own end, which may counteract the end of the religious community. As the Document on *The Service of Authority and Obedience* points out, integral dialogue demands "keeping in mind that bonding must come about 'in a

spirit of faith and love in the following of the obedient Christ'
and not for other motivations."[131]

Cardinal Kasper points out that even though human persons
do the hard work of building a relationship, dialogue "is ultimately a spiritual event. Establishing a consensus is a spiritual
process. It can be achieved only when we open our hearts, puri-
fy our thoughts, overcome our prejudices and grow in love for
Jesus Christ and one another in Christ. Dialogue is possible
only together with profound conversion and growth in holiness,
i.e., in life in the Holy Spirit."[132] Finally, the spiritual dimension
of dialogue makes regular conversation "an eschatological
process; . . . [and if] dialogue is accompanied by trust, human
friendship and Christian communion in prayer, it can make real
progress."[133]

VIRTUE-FRIENDSHIPS AND FRIENDSHIPS OF CHARITY

Beginning with Aristotle, philosophers classified friendships
into three categories according to whether they were based on
pleasure, utility, or virtue: "Perfect friendship is the friendship
of men who are good, and alike in virtue; for these wish well
alike to each other qua good, and they are good in themselves."[134] Jesus Christ elevated his friends from servitude: "No
longer do I call you servants . . . but I have called you friends,
for all that I have heard from my Father I have made known to
you" (Jn 15:15). Jesus also taught about what friends can actively do for one another: "Greater love has no man than this, that a
man lay down his life for his friends" (Jn 15:13).

Christian authors viewed virtue-friendships as an important
part of the Christian life. In the twelfth century, Aelred of
Rievaulx, a Cistercian monk, wrote extensively about friendships among those in monastic life. In his classic text titled
Spiritual Friendship, Aelred followed Augustine's lead in viewing
Christian friendship on earth as preparation for friendship in
heaven.[135] In the thirteenth century, Thomas Aquinas added to
Aristotle's understanding of a virtue-based friendship as the
spiritual dimension of the infusion of the charity of God. The
Dominican friar, in his *Summa Theologica*, elaborated in detail
the four essential characteristics of Christian friendship:

> *[1] [W]e love someone so as to wish good to him. . . . [2] [A] certain mutual love is requisite . . . ; [3] founded on some kind of communication.* Accordingly, since there is a communication between man and God, inasmuch as He communicates His happiness to us, some kind of friendship must needs be based on this same communication. . . . The love which is based on this communication, is charity: wherefore it is evident that *[4] charity is the friendship of man for God.*[136]

Friendship-charity is the foundation for religious friendship in the spirituality of communion.

In *Vita consecrata*, Pope John Paul II elaborated further on the value of Christian friendship in religious life: "To the degree that they deepen their friendship with God, consecrated persons become better prepared to help their brothers and sisters through valuable spiritual activities. . . ."[137] Friendship becomes the way that an initial relation with Christ is transformed. "After the enthusiasm of the first meeting with Christ, there comes the constant struggle of everyday life, a struggle which *turns a vocation into a tale of friendship with the Lord.*"[138] Friendship with God becomes the fruitful source of religious life. "True prophecy is born of God, from *friendship* with him, from attentive listening to his word in the different circumstances of history."[139] Meditation on the Scriptures in common calls religious "to prayerful reading of the Scriptures, in which God speaks to people as friends (cf. Ex 33:11; Jn 15:14–15) and lives among them (cf. Bar 3:38), so that he may invite and draw them into fellowship with himself."[140]

Pope Paul VI, in *Evangelica testificatio*, also identifies friendship as an important aspect of religious community life. "There is no doubt that community spirit, relationships of friendship, and fraternal cooperation in the same apostolate, as well as mutual support in a shared life chosen for a better service of Christ, are so many valuable factors in this daily progress."[141] The affirmation of the importance of friendship in contemporary religious vocations is repeated by the Sacred Congregation in *Essential Elements*:

> Sharing of prayer, work, meals, leisure, common spirit, "relations of friendship, cooperation in the same apostolate, and mutual support in community of life chosen for a better following of Christ, are so many valuable factors in daily progress" (ET

> 39). . . . Its unity is a symbol of the coming of Christ and is a
> source of apostolic energy and power. . . . The capacity to live
> community life with its joys and restraints is a quality which
> distinguishes a religious vocation to a given institute and it is a
> key criterion of suitability in a candidate.[142]

In religious life, local communities should not usually be self-selected on the basis of friendships already established, but their members chosen by religious authority, as directed by the Holy Spirit. Christian friendships can then flourish anew within the subsequent framework of a vibrant common life, when they fulfill the four-fold criteria identified by Thomas Aquinas. Being sent into a local community by properly constituted authority offers the opportunity to discover charity/friendships through learning how to live a spirituality of communion.[143]

In addition, religious life also demands differentiating friendships of pleasure and utility from friendships of virtue. To have a proper orientation towards pleasure, the Congregation for Institutes of Consecrated Life and Societies of Apostolic Life identifies in *Fraternal Life in Community* (1994) the need for consecrated religious to integrate their "affectivity correctly, both inside and outside the community."[144] Second, to overcome tendencies to use others, a religious also needs to be open to the true value of self and of others:

> To love one's vocation, to hear the call as something that gives
> true meaning to life, and to cherish consecration as a true, beau-
> tiful, and good reality which gives truth, beauty, and goodness
> to one's own existence—all of this makes a person strong and
> autonomous, secure in one's own identity, free of the need for
> various forms of support and compensation, especially in the
> area of affectivity. All this reinforces the bond that links the
> consecrated person to those who share his or her calling. It is
> with them, first and foremost, that he or she feels called to live
> relationships of fraternity and friendship.[145]

Starting Afresh from Christ further reaffirms the relation between genuine friendships, religious life, and the spirituality of communion:

> But what is the spirituality of communion? With incisive words,
> capable of giving new life to relationships and programs, John
> Paul II teaches: ". . . The spirituality of communion also implies
> the ability to see what is positive in others, to welcome it and to

prize it as a gift from God, and to know how to make room for others, sharing each other's burdens. Unless we follow this spiritual path, the external structures of communion serve very little purpose. . . ."

The divine and human value of being together freely in friendship and sharing even moments of relaxation and recreation together as disciples gathered around Christ the Teacher is being *rediscovered*.[146]

This is one of the great gifts of religious life, namely to be able to share charity-friendships with persons whom one would not have ordinarily chosen on the basis of natural preference. The Holy Spirit brings about a new union of virtue-love for unexpected neighbors. This real feature of charity friendships in religious life is why religious communities can be a living sign of the eschatological kingdom.

The Church Commissions Religious to Become "Experts in Communion"

How can a religious community of persons today be a living sign for the Church? Pope John Paul II, in *Vita consecrata*, explicitly links the communal dimension of religious consecration to the mission of being a sign as a common call, within a specified charism of religious walking along the same path within the Church.

This testimony of consecration takes on special meaning in religious life because of the community dimension which marks it. The fraternal life is the privileged place in which to discern and accept God's will, and to walk together with one mind and heart. Obedience, enlivened by charity, unites the members of an Institute in the same witness and the same mission, while respecting the diversity of gifts and individual personalities. In community life which is inspired by the Holy Sprit, each individual engages in a fruitful dialogue with the others in order to discover the Father's will. At the same time, together they recognize in the one who presides as an expression of the fatherhood of God and the exercise of authority received from God, at the service of discernment and communion. Life in community is thus the particular sign, before the Church and society, of the bond which comes from the same call and the common desire—notwithstanding differences of race and origin, language and culture—to be obedient to that call.[147]

In recent documents, the Church has addressed different objections to this understanding of mission. A *first danger* it identifies is self-selecting communities which act as a counter-sign to spirituality of communion. The Church's response to this danger is well described in *Fraternal Life in Community*:

> [T]here are some motives which are questionable, such as same-ness of tastes or of mentality. In this situation it is easy for a com-munity to close in on itself and come to the point of choosing its own members, and brothers or sisters sent by the superiors may or may not be accepted. This is contrary to the very nature of religious community and to its function as sign. Optional homo-geneity, besides weakening apostolic mobility, weakens the Pneumatic strength of a community and robs the spiritual reality which rules the community of its power as witness.
>
> The effort involved in mutual acceptance and commitment to overcoming difficulties, characteristics of heterogeneous communities, show forth the transcendence of the reason which brought the community into existence, that is, the power of God which "is made perfect in weakness" (2 Cor 12:9–10).
>
> We stay together in community not because we have chosen one another, but because we have been chosen by the Lord.[148]

A *second danger* occurs when considering community as an obstacle to the mission. This, by analogy, is similar to a couple who do not want to take time with each other because their marriage is so demanding: ultimately their relationship suffers as they become more estranged. In a section of *Fraternal Life in Community* titled "Fraternity as Sign," the Church invites reli-gious institutes to ponder the deep roots of their communion in community and to welcome it as part of their common mission.

> For some, "building communion" is felt as an obstacle to mis-sion, almost a waste of time in matters of secondary impor-tance. All must be reminded that fraternal communion, as such, is already an apostolate; in other words, it contributes directly to the work of evangelization. The sign par excellence left us by Our Lord, is that of lived fraternity: "By this all will know that you are my disciples, if you have love for one anoth-er" (cf. Jn 13:35).
>
> Along with sending them to preach the Gospel to every creature (Mt 28:19–20), the Lord sent his disciples to live togeth-er "so that the world may believe" that Jesus is the one sent by the Father and that we owe him the full assent of faith (Jn 17:21). The sign of fraternity is then of the greatest importance

because it is the sign that points to the divine origin of the Christian message and has the power to open hearts to faith. For this reason, "the effectiveness of religious life depends on the quality of the fraternal life in common."[149]

Communion in community is thus supremely encouraged by the Church as an essential part of the mission of a religious institute in the contemporary world.

> Religious community, in its structure, motivations, distinguishing values, makes publicly visible and continually perceptible the gift of fraternity given by Christ to the whole Church. For this very reason, it has as its commitment and mission, which cannot be renounced, both to be and to be seen to be a living organism of intense fraternal communion, a sign and stimulus for all the baptized.[150]

A recent example of this radiating effect can be seen in the 2007 publication of the Congregation for Catholic Education titled *Educating Together in Catholic Schools: A Shared Mission Between Consecrated Persons and the Lay Faithful*. In two sections subtitled "Educating in Communion and for Communion" and "Consecrated Persons and the Lay Faithful in Schools," the Church demonstrates how communion among the consecrated and lay teachers and administrators provides the environment in which those being educated can discover true Catholic communion: "It is precisely the presence and life of an educational community, in which all the members participate in a fraternal communion, nourished by a living relationship with Christ and with the Church, that makes the Catholic school the environment for an authentically ecclesial experience."[151]

To conclude this chapter, let us return once more to the 1978 seminal document on *Religious and Human Promotion* and repeat its articulated mission for religious institutes to live in community as an effective sign of charity for complement vocations in the Church:

> *Experts in communion*, religious are, therefore, to be called to be an ecclesial community in the Church and in the world, witnesses and architects of the *plan for unity* which is the crowning point of human history in God's design.
>
> Above all, by the profession of the evangelical counsels, which frees one from what might be an obstacle to the fervor of charity, religious are communally a prophetic sign of intimate union with God, who is loved above all things.

Furthermore, through the daily experience of communion of life, prayer, and apostolate—the essential and distinctive elements of their form of consecrated life—they are a *sign of fraternal fellowship*.[152]

For those individual religious who either live alone, or live in small self-selected communities, this essential mission given to them by the Church becomes very difficult to live out. In contrast, those religious communities which have accepted this mission, and whose members give it a high priority, serve the other vocations in the Church in a particularly efficacious way: "In this way, a religious community becomes a centre radiating outwardly, a spiritual force, a centre of animation, of fraternity creating fraternity, and of communion and ecclesial collaboration, where the different contributions of each help build up the Body of Christ, which is the Church."[153]

Chapter 5

EVANGELICAL
MISSION

Sister M. Maximilia Um, F.S.G.M.

The Second Vatican Council's Decree on the Adaptation and Renewal of Religious Life, *Perfectae caritatis*, describes apostolic religious communities as those for whom "apostolic and charitable activity belongs to the very nature of the religious life."[1] For these religious institutes, engagement in the apostolate is not simply an option or an afterthought, but, rather, defines them as such. Concerning the apostolate, the decree also states:

> [I]t is a holy service and a work characteristic of love, entrusted to [these religious] by the Church to be carried out in its name. Therefore, the whole religious life of their members should be inspired by an apostolic spirit and all their apostolic activity formed by the spirit of religion. Therefore, in order that their members may first correspond to their vocation to follow Christ and serve Him in His members, their apostolic activity must spring from intimate union with Him.[2]

Thus, the decree indicates why certain religious institutes are founded with the express intention of fulfilling an apostolic task, while also describing the spirit in which such service ought to be carried out. These religious participate in particular works (according to the charism of founders, spiritual patrimony, signs of the times, etc.) precisely as a sharing in the one mission of the Church. Hence, they engage in such works in *nomine Ecclesiae*, in the Church's own name. Furthermore, in reaffirming the close relationship between the spirit of religion and apostolic work, the decree indicates a path for developing an understanding of the dynamism of mission which takes account of the primacy of prayer in the life of *every* religious without rendering the apostolate extraneous.

The exploration of these two strands of thought will be the main purpose of this chapter. The first point—that the Church herself is the subject of mission—is critical since this must be understood adequately before addressing the reality of its many expressions according to various historical and personal inflections (charisms, vision of founders, the needs of the times, etc.). Furthermore, central to developing this reflection adequately is a correct understanding of the relationship between contemplation and action, the second point. Together, these two points will constitute the central pillar of this chapter.

Preceding this central pillar will be a section whose object is to clarify the theological foundation for the Church's mission, namely her Trinitarian and Christological roots. A third and final section will examine the exercise of specific apostolates of institutes of religious life, attempting to identify the manner in which they articulate the mission of the Church. This will be done within the context of discussing the prevailing attitudes of contemporary Western culture.

MISSION IN GOD?

Any attempt at placing mission at the heart of the Church's identity must begin by asking how this diffusive movement is related to God. This inquiry, in turn, cannot be made apart from considering the mission of the Person of Jesus Christ. According to the *Catechism of the Catholic Church*, Christ was sent by the Father to redeem a world that had fallen into sin, a state of "disgrace."[3] However, this claim must be understood concretely if it is to retain its relevance, not only as a theological affirmation, but as the deepest reality embracing every human person. The first thing to notice in this regard is that the gospels do not narrow Christ's mission to a well-defined agenda. Rather, it is a pervasive reality—that measure by which he identifies his very Person ("my food is to do the will of the one who sent me"). Although there are numerous ways of attempting to understand this relationship of Person and mission in Christ, it is particularly useful to broach the issue by way of considering Christ's proclamation of the kingdom of God.

In both St. Matthew's and St. Mark's gospels, directly after his temptation by Satan in the desert, Jesus begins to preach that the kingdom of God is at hand (see Matthew 4:17, Mark 1:15). The preaching of the kingdom is omnipresent in the gospels (see Matthew 13, Mark 4:26–34, Luke 13:20–20).

Enigmatically, Christ indicates that the kingdom has both a future dimension and, at the same time, is already present (see Matthew 12:28). And although he does not give a description of the kingdom, Christ puts himself at the center of this new reign—it somehow has to do with him.

In fact, this proclamation of the kingdom is the hinge on which the entire public ministry of Jesus turns. Through parables, Jesus sets about the task of communicating the ineffable dimensions of this new reign. The kingdom comes about through the intervention of God, such that it grows in unexpected ways. In likening the proclamation of the kingdom of God to sowing seed, leaven in dough, or to the mustard bush, he points to the fact that the kingdom begins and grows very humbly—out of the immediate range of man's sight. Hence, it is possible for a merely earthly gaze to miss its presence. Neither does it emerge as a pristine reality, rigidly distinguishable from the world (the wheat and tares grow together). On the other hand, Christ exhorts his listeners to accept the kingdom. While it is God's own initiative, it requires a response from man. Without appropriation, the kingdom does not exist in its fulfilled form.

Jesus' proclamation of the kingdom finds a particularly concrete form in his miracles. More than offering merely empirical proof of his divinity, the Scriptures show us that these prodigies consist of both an exterior and interior dimension. Jesus restores the sight of the blind, cleanses lepers, and mends lame limbs. He meets a physical need. The greater miracle, however, is that he also restores the healed person to the community and stirs within him an unexplainable gladness. This interior dimension is aptly described by Luigi Giussani:

> The greatest miracle, which left a deep imprint on the disciples every day, was not the healing of crippled legs, the cleansing of diseased skin, or the restoration of sight to the blind. The greatest miracle of all was that truly human gaze which revealed man to himself and was impossible to evade. Nothing is more convincing to man than a gaze which takes hold of him and recognizes what he is, which reveals man to himself. Jesus saw inside man. No one could hide in front of him, and before him the depths of conscience had no secrets.[4]

Thus, the physical event is accompanied by the wonderment (miracle—*mirari*) of being understood and loved infinitely. The kingdom is no abstract program or ideology. It is *Christ himself* who walks among men, both eliciting their deepest desires and revealing himself as the object of their fulfillment.[5] The miracles of Christ cannot be understood at a merely biological level, but concern the whole of man.

Christ's mission of proclaiming the kingdom of God has everything to do with the problem of man's happiness. It is true that Christ's mission centers on the Person of the Father: He is sent by the Father and his life is defined by fulfillment of the Father's will. However, it is no less true that the Father wills that man should be saved. The anthropological dimension of Christ's mission is no incidental or instrumental orientation. He himself says that "God so loved the world that he gave his only Son, that whoever believes in him should not perish but have eternal life" (Jn 3:16) and that he "came that [man] may have life, and have it abundantly" (Jn 10:10). That this mission is oriented to the Father and is undertaken for his glory does not cancel out its other term—man.

Having considered the matter of Christ's mission from the point of the economy, the pertinent question becomes "What does it have to do with God himself?" The International Theological Commission reports:

> The consciousness Jesus has of his unique filial relationship is the foundation and presupposition of his mission. . . . This "Coming" of his can have no other origin than God. . . . The mission he received from the Father is not something imposed by an outside source. It belongs to him so intimately as to coincide with his whole being. It is his whole life, his food, he seeks nothing else, his will is consumed entirely by God's will, his words are the words of his Father, his works are the Father's, so much so that he can say of himself, "He who sees me sees the Father." . . . *His mission (in time), in fact, is not essentially separable from his (eternal) procession: it is a "prolongation" of it. His human consciousness of his mission "translates," so to speak, the eternal relationship with the Father into the idiom of a human life.*[6]

The Commission affirms, in the Thomistic tradition, that the only difference between the eternal procession of the Son and his earthly mission is the factor of temporality.[7] Thus, without exhausting the mystery of eternal generation, the Person of Jesus Christ in the flesh is altogether the same Person who eternally proceeds from the Father. Moreover, the implications of this statement reach both "back" into Trinitarian theology and "forward" into soteriology.

The Trinity is not simply a dogma alongside all other dogmas.[8] Rather, the claim that God is triune has decisive implications for all of created reality. In other words, creation itself is not only *from* a triune God, but, as such, *structurally* images his triunity. Its likeness to God is neither incidental nor static, but living and dynamic, precisely while being different from him.[9]

"Otherness" originates within God himself before being posited externally. That God exists does not merely mean that he is "there." Rather, his existence is coincident with his manner of being. Thus, that God the Son is generated eternally by the Father does not simply mean that he was born before time began and has been the Son of the Father "ever since." Rather, the Son is being generated "now," such that he is always receiving his being from the Father. In a manner of speaking, he is wholly dependent on the Father for his being. By the same token, the very existence of the Father depends on having a Son. The terms of the Trinity are essentially relational. This is confirmed by the peculiar "anonymity" of the Holy Spirit in the Godhead. As St. Augustine notes, the Third Person of the Trinity is both Holy and Spirit. In other words, he simply sums up what can already be said of the Father and the Son, such that there is nothing uniquely distinguishing about him.[10] St. Augustine, however, also concludes from this that he is totally referential to both the Father and the Son, participating into their communion not as a "third term" alongside the other two, but precisely as communion (both the bond between them and fruit of their exchange).[11] God's essence is identical to the relations of origin within the Godhead.[12]

The implications of this claim are entirely revolutionary. The reality of the Godhead is no moral union, but, rather, the mystery of love itself, which is none other than a giving and receiving which *constitutes the very Persons*. To say it again, that God exists is coincident with how he exists. Communion is not simply a divine attribute, but the mode of God's very being. This manner of being precedes any phenomenon that can be understood as "choice." To frame it in analogously human terms, if God's being is identical to the relations of origin, the content of his power is not sheer independence to do or be this or that, but precisely its inverse.

Therefore, what exists in the Godhead is the utter positivity of otherness—the fullness of life as the ever-new exchange of love with another. Although our human relationships are constantly fraught with the danger of frustration due to non-reciprocation, this is not so with God. His freedom does not imply the possibility of rejection or refusal. *To say that creation is made in this image, then, means first of all that it is entrusted to itself in order to be given away (to God and to others).* In this way, although we often experience the radical openness of our lives as the occasion for being wounded, for exactly the same reason, it is also the privileged place of communion.[13] To be like God, then, entails the radical entrusting of the self to another, assuming the inherent risks, and guaranteeing the initial gift with the further gift of forgiveness.[14]

This fundamental truth of human life is what Christ comes to reveal. And he reveals it by proclaiming the kingdom of God in the flesh. His body is not simply an instrument he uses to communicate a message, but is already the content of the message itself. What it bespeaks is the love of a God ready to hand over his only beloved Son to whatever fate man will decide for him, a giving so complete and irrevocable that it looks remarkably like weakness and folly. In doing so, God also reveals himself as the one rich in mercy—the one who comes to meet man, conquering sin with forgiveness.[15] The unfathomable love of the Father is what Christ discloses in forgiving sins and eating with sinners. And so Christ builds the kingdom not only *for* persons but *in* them—by making possible an entirely new existence through an encounter which reveals both God and man.

The foregoing reflection may be summarized in three points.

(1) The theological category of "mission" cannot be reduced to a simple action that is subsequent to the person's being. Although the terms of person and mission are uniquely united in Christ, as we will soon see, it is also analogously true for the Church.

(2) Christ's mission is a temporal translation of his eternal generation from the Father (i.e., sonship). This point cannot be over-emphasized because it discloses the inner heart of what it means to be "sent." *Before accomplishing a particular task, to be*

sent means that one belongs to another and brings into every con-crete action the consciousness of this belonging. An essential dimension of this belonging is to understand one's entire self and every aspect of one's life as coming from and being directed to another. Therefore, the actions of Christ are nothing other than concrete expressions of coming from and returning to the Father. It is this total dispossession of self which is reflected in Christ's desire to do the Father's will at every moment.

(3) Through his unique relationship with the Father lived in time (mission), Christ reveals the meaning of human existence. Since man is created "in Christ," he is called to share in communion with the triune God, not simply individually, but *qua filius in Filio* (as son in the Son). In a word, the reality of man's nature is such that its fulfillment lies in receiving one's being entirely from another and making a total gift of oneself. This gift character, because of its outward orientation (i.e., man's source and destiny lie outside of himself), is often felt by man as sheer poverty and weakness. What Christ reveals and makes effective is the positivity of this condition because of its participation in his own sonship.

MISSION OF THE CHURCH

Just as the mission of Christ is a communication of his being as Son, the mission of the Church is a communication of herself. In this regard, it is essential to see that the communion Christ generates among his followers is both with himself (and, through him, with the Father) and with each other. It is both vertical and horizontal, not as separate events, but as two dimensions of the same event. Fellowship with God is precisely that which guarantees fellowship with each other. Without Christ's disclosure of the Father, it is inconceivable that man should be capable of seeing and loving one another as God sees and loves him. Thus, these two dimensions of communion are not simply extrinsically connected. And although there is a hierarchy, it is dangerous to dismiss the human dimension of communion as merely instrumental to its divine dimension. Rather, as Alexander Schmemann contends, creation itself is the very "stuff" of our communion with God.[16] In a word, these two dimensions somehow imply each other, such that it is existentially impossible to separate them. This is more easily grasped when one understands that communion is not a physical, tangible thing, but a relation.[17] And it is precisely in relation to God, and only in relation to him, that man is in relation to other men. Indeed, "[w]hile the various currents of human thought both in the past and at the present have tended and still tend to separate theocentrism and anthropocentrism, and even to set them in opposition to each other, the Church, following Christ, seeks to link them up in human history in a deep and organic way."[18]

Furthermore, this two-fold relationship of communion which makes the Church be who she is must be understood in concrete terms. The span of time which constitutes the life of a person is given not as a lump sum, but at each instant. Paradoxically, it is precisely the fleeting moment which mediates the fullness of eternity to man, such that the meaning of Christianity may be said to consist in the revelation of "the infinite value of the instant"—the true worth of all flesh (i.e., the creation world, everything *human*).[19] Only the merciful gaze of Christ penetrates through appearances to the dignity of man, helping him to see the true possibility for his frail humanity. What man experiences for the first time in Christ's presence is a love totally devoid of the taint of calculation.

Man's salvation is neither an achievement nor a possession, but simply communion with God and other men. Perhaps it is for these reasons that *Lumen gentium* speaks of salvation in terms of unity.[20] The Dogmatic Constitution describes salvation in the context of the Church's predestination, that is, the Father's "utterly gratuitous and mysterious design . . . to [create] the whole universe, and . . . to raise up men to share in his own divine life."[21] Salvation, then, is the restoration of this plan in Christ. However, in describing the characteristics and dimensions of salvation, the document simply *describes the Church*: the sacraments, the various members of the Christian faithful, and the universal call to holiness.[22] We conclude, therefore, that man participates in divine life beginning here and now, and this life consists of none other than belonging to the people God has redeemed. Salvation is a radically communitarian reality.[23]

Thus is the manner in which the Church participates in the mission of Christ—by being the "place" of communion in the world as "both the means and the goal of God's plan."[24] In other words, the Church is the sacrament of salvation. The notion of the Church's sacramentality is already implied in the way Christ generates communion among men. God's communion with man in Christ—in which salvation consists—occurs in and through his Church. In this regard, the Church's role is more than merely instrumental. Rather, when one claims that man is created for communion with the Triune God, one affirms the mystery of the Church as already the immediate term of *communio*'s realization. Henri de Lubac insists that "the Church is not only the first of the works of the sanctifying Spirit, but also that which includes, conditions, and absorbs the rest. The entire process of salvation is worked out in her; indeed, it is identified with her."[25]

These comments illustrate the manner in which the Church's mission is more than something she takes on subsequent to being constituted. This *defunctionalization* of mission is what Paul VI intends to convey in his encyclical on the Church, *Ecclesiam suam*. The document describes the Church's mission to the world in terms of the dialogue of charity (by nature *ad extra*) whose source is a profound self-awareness leading to renewal (by nature *ad intra*).[26] This dialogue of charity is organically related to the Church's understanding of her own identity precisely because her self-examination is none other than the discovery that Christ himself is her deepest center. The energy of the Church for mission is the spontaneous movement of gratitude for and wonder at God's gift. This is the energy which pulses through every concrete Christian apostolate.

What has been said in this section is summarized by the simple claim that communion begets mission, not as an instrument, but because communion itself extends outward by nature.[27] Moreover, this point cannot be understood in its proper depth without also affirming that this communion-mission bipolarity exists at the level of each member of the Christian faithful in the form of contemplation-action. Contemplation is never simply a self-enclosed activity, but rather that adoration of God which serves as the opening for action. Action, then, is the way of preserving what one has received in contemplation—precisely because true prayer is "ecstatic" in the original sense of the term—that is, oriented to a source outside of the self.

Thus far, the attempt has been made to transcend a consideration of particular apostolates by looking at mission's interior dimension—the soul of every concrete apostolate. Having laid out the basic theological structure of mission, it is now possible to proceed to a discussion of how the consecrated religious engages the "field" of mission in a postmodern society marked by cynicism and a weakened sense of the sacred.

THE APOSTOLATE OF RELIGIOUS TO CONTEMPORARY MAN

The collective attitude of postmodern culture is embodied in the pervasive conviction that the fulfillment of the human person lies in the exaltation of self. According to the Catechism of the Catholic Church, this mistaken position is marked by "a false conception of human autonomy, exaggerated to the point of refusing any dependence on God."[28] It is this rejection of dependence that lies at the heart of the cynicism and disbelief of this present age—not only an intellectual refusal arrived at after calculated deliberation, but an existential one. As it were, man finds the thought of being fundamentally related to another entirely abhorrent, and thus rejects it as a violation of his innate dignity-freedom.

It is precisely at this point that it becomes crucial to understand properly the motivation for this rejection. Although not entirely erroneous, to identify pride alone as the impulse for this rejection amounts to a facile position. If the refusal to depend is indeed rooted in pride, then the question needing to be addressed has to do with pride's source. While pride is the unfortunate patrimony of man's fallen nature, it is not simply an unintelligible given. Rather, pride itself has a structure which the *Catechism of the Catholic Church* intimates in its description of original sin: "Man, tempted by the devil, let his trust in his Creator die in his heart and, abusing his freedom, disobeyed God's command. This is what man's first sin consisted of. All subsequent sin would be disobedience toward God and lack of trust in his goodness."[29]

Thus, pride does not exist in and of itself as the simply inevitable fate of man, but as the bitter fruit of fear. Fear of what? Fear that he will no longer receive what he needs from the hand of a Provident Father. In describing the anthropological dimensions of original sin, Jean-Pierre Batut states:

> This sin is the rejection of sonship. We might offer the following definition of this rejection: to be no longer a son means to stop desiring that what one possesses exists only in being given and received. And, if this definition seems a bit complex, we could simplify it by saying: the original sin begins the moment man *distrusts* God. The image of the Father who loves and who gives is substituted with that of the avaricious, self-serving Master. His promise of life places me in uncertainty; it renders me entirely dependent on him. And if he were to change his mind, if he were to stop giving? Would it not be better if I took into my own hands that which, for the time being, I possess only by receiving it?[30]

Thus, the great mystery of original sin is rooted in the mystery of man himself. Although it cannot be adequately elaborated here, Batut speaks truly when he states that man possesses everything as given and received (i.e., he is generated by Another). In fact, he possesses his very being and all of creation as a gift, returning it to the Father through the worship of gratitude.[31]

This being the case, original sin cannot be understood as an isolated transgression man simply commits, but rather as an action by which he loses the very truth of himself. Man does not, cannot, exist outside of God's gift of Himself. Philosopher Kenneth L. Schmitz explains that God's gift of Himself outside of Himself, positing "someone" other than Himself (i.e., man) results in a relationship wherein man is absolutely dependent such that "the creatureliness of the creature—its being-a-creature—is not a received condition which it has; nor, strictly speaking, is being-a-creature even a received condition that it is; rather, the received condition itself is *it*."[32] In other words, the donation of the gift of being and the positing of its receiver are coincident. Prior to creation, it is not simply the case that man does not "yet" exist. Rather, he has no claim to existence. The notion of "rights" can only be appealed to from the perspective of established subjects in the world. However, the act that founded the life of every individual person was and remains a gift of the All-Good God.

Hence, the decision "to eradicate belief in God is based upon his understanding of the situation in which an allegedly all-powerful God stands over, against, and above man and his world . . . [such that creaturehood cannot but be] a radical humiliation."[33] From a Christian perspective, we discern that this position is not without its problems—on a metaphysical level first of all. It operates out of an erroneous and distorted conception of God as tyrant.

Does this radical viewpoint aptly represent the stance of contemporary Western society? Although it is rarely explicitly articulated, an underlying suspicion of God's otherness and the fear of being overcome by him inform many of our social attitudes. In contemporary Western culture, the patrimony of this way of living and thinking is held not under the guise of the "unknown God" or even the "unwanted God," but simply the *"irrelevant God"*; the fact that God exists has become inconsequential to daily life.

At the foundation of this fragmented view of the person lies the erroneous conviction that man can be happy without God. According to *Gaudium et spes*, man finds himself in a sincere gift of himself.[34] Postmodernity, however, has been built upon an anthropology which exalts as truly human only the man who controls his own destiny. Given the fact that this is both an existential and ontological impossibility, man cannot but lose hope faced with such a negation of himself. Even when man achieves a measure of domination, the thirst to do more and have more deprives him of any lasting satisfaction.

In short, man's crisis of faith results in a thwarted search for meaning. Centuries of forgetfulness have eroded man's capacity to see himself essentially as a creature, that is, as someone whose ultimate happiness depends on relatedness to Another. And this in turn has perpetuated and deepened mankind's common oblivion before the mystery of life. The truth is that the man of today, who has every luxury and convenience at hand, finds life bland and without meaning. This very fundamental crisis has been aptly described in the curial document, *New Vocations for a New Europe*, which, in reference to young people and the problem of promoting vocations, states:

> It is a great sadness to meet young people, even intelligent and talented, who have no will to live, to believe in something, to

work towards great ends, to hope in a world which can become better even thanks to their own efforts. They feel themselves *superfluous* to the game or drama of life, as if they have resigned in the face of it, been wounded along the broken paths which have been reduced to the minimum level of tension in life. Without vocation, but also without a future, or with a future which, at the most, will be a photocopy of the present.[35]

The document also claims that contemporary mass culture tends to produce "young people possessing an incomplete and weak identity" who "do not possess the 'elementary grammar' of existence."[36] This last statement is absolutely critical, because it identifies the vocation crisis as a deeper crisis of apprehending the meaning of all reality. It underscores Giussani's claim that what has been stunted in man is precisely what he refers to in other places as the "religious sense."[37] By this term is meant man's capacity (and so his restlessness) for the infinite. A religion that does not promote man's religiosity will, in the end, find itself unable to lead him to the source of life.

The field of mission is not a place; it is man himself in every place where he dwells. Furthermore, it is the concrete man of today to whom the Church is sent. Contemporary man no longer believes he needs redemption precisely because he fails to grasp its depth and scope. The Christian proposal, then, must concern itself with more than spreading orthodox doctrine or performing token good deeds. Precisely in doing these things faithfully, she is called to evangelize (or re-evangelize) the very roots of the culture in such a way that man is unafraid to stand before the mystery of life and commit himself to living it as a risk and promise. Because it extends Christ's own mission down through the centuries, the Church is called ever anew to engage man in the ultimate question of his own happiness. The gospel has not changed—the truth about man is that his path to fulfillment lies not in doing and having more, but by giving himself away in response to the God who gives all.

Thus far, the attempt has been made to sketch a profile of the gospel's anthropological significance—namely, the positivity of man's life as gift, both as received and in its aptness to be given away in turn. It has likewise been illustrated that the angst of modern man lies precisely in his inability to decode and understand the secret of his own nature. Indeed, this secret is unknowable apart from the revelation of Christ. In what remains of this reflection, the unique vocation of religious and the distinctive manner in which they engage in the mission of the Church will be discussed.

The *Catechism of the Catholic Church* affirms that "the entire Christian life bears the mark of the spousal love of Christ and the Church. Already Baptism, the entry into the People of God, is a nuptial mystery; it is so to speak the nuptial bath which precedes the wedding feast, the Eucharist."[38] Thus, "Christian perfection has but one limit, that of having none."[39] It is thus that the Christian vocation as such admits to a certain totality. The grace of baptism itself imparts an objective holiness by which the Christian is bound to strive subjectively for the perfection of charity.[40] It also seminally implies the call to mission (this is seen with greater clarity in the Eastern tradition of chrismating immediately after baptism). Thus, the Christian state of life, conferred at baptism, exists already as the state of perfection. However, it is likewise true that the Church has consistently taught the objective superiority of the state of the evangelical counsels.[41] The paradox, therefore, is the existence of an objectively superior state of perfection (religious life) *within an already unsurpassable state of perfection* (Christian life). The conundrum needing to be resolved concerns the content of and reason for the difference.

In intimating a response to this query, John Paul II seems only to raise more paradoxes beyond resolution. He affirms that "[r]eligious profession creates a new bond between the person and the One and Triune God, in Jesus Christ. This bond develops on the foundation of the *original bond* that is contained *in the Sacrament of Baptism*."[42] The bond of religious consecration, then, is radically new and does not simply grow out of the consecration of baptism as a "necessary consequence."[43] However, it cannot exist without a baptismal foundation. Nor is the cryptic nature of this observation resolved by his claim that religious life "manifests the inner nature of the Christian calling."[44] While maintaining the existence of a difference between the two forms of consecration, it is only ever framed in terms of baptism. Paradoxically, it appears that what makes religious life different from the other states is that it is *preeminently Christian*.[45]

In the end, the difference between the various Christian vocations can only be understood properly when considered in relation to one another. Therefore, while the foregoing remarks seem to be merely self-referential, they point to the radical truth that religious consecration serves the flourishing of baptismal consecration. This can be seen more clearly in John Paul II's comment that "in every consecrated person the Israel of the new and eternal covenant is chosen. The whole messianic people, the entire Church, is chosen in every person whom the Lord selects from the midst of this people; in every person who is consecrated *for everyone* to God as His exclusive possession."[46] He also adds that "the evangelical counsels in their essential purpose aim at 'the renewal of creation': 'the world,' thanks to them, is to be subjected to man and given to him in such a way that man himself may be perfectly given to God."[47] Thus, for John Paul II, the profession of vows exceeds the boundaries of a merely individualistic act. Rather, it already implies a relation to the entire Church, such that God chooses every member of the Church in his choice of the individual religious, and the professing religious somehow gives all of creation to God.

Again, understanding this point requires thinking of consecration in concrete terms. John Paul II identifies the heart of consecration as the "love of *self-giving.*"[48] Hence, the religious understands profoundly that "religious profession touches upon *the very roots of humanity,* the roots of man's destiny in the temporal world."[49] *The anthropological truth to which the profession of the evangelical counsels points is simply that man finds himself "in a sincere gift of himself."*[50] The superiority of the religious state, then, is not to be thought of in quantitative terms, but insofar as it *gathers up the truth about man and fulfills it in a way that is both exemplary and open to some manner of participation by others.* Religious consecration sets some members of the Church apart by making them permanent signs by which all are called to live the Christian vocation of love. In this way, the preeminently Christian character of religious life, as the content of its difference from the baptismal state, constitutes not simply a boundary, but a place of communion between all the members of Christ's faithful.

Religious life's preeminence within the dignity of the Christian vocation already constitutes the reason for engagement in mission. Various apostolates exercised by the myriad of religious families have the purpose of communicating the beauty of a life totally given to God as the truth of man. Religious life communicates this truth as a visibly lived reality, such that its mission is inseparable from the reality of religious consecration and common life.

To illustrate the claim made above, this reflection now briefly turns to a consideration of two areas of apostolic service and how consecrated persons transform this work into a genuine apostolate by virtue of who and what they are. The first area is that of healthcare. In his apostolic letter on the Christian Meaning of Suffering, *Salvifici doloris,* John Paul II states that "suffering is something which is still wider than sickness"[51] and that "joy comes from the discovery of the meaning of suffering."[52] The experience of being ill and weak, then, presents man with an opportunity of embracing the truth about God and himself. However, the one who suffers needs to be taught the meaning of his plight. For various reasons, the chief of which is that man remains a mystery to himself (this is heightened by suffering's all-consuming and subjugating character, and because technology claims to be the master over sickness and death), the grace of suffering as an expression of "the truth of love" is not apprehended.[53]

The gospel of suffering as a participation in the redemptive suffering of Christ needs to be proclaimed to the infirm. John Paul II insists that "in suffering there is concealed a particular power that draws a person interiorly close to Christ" and that it constitutes a vocation in and of itself.[54] In other words, the deepest truth about man's nature and destiny—that he fulfills himself in giving himself away—is never thwarted. This reality, however, remains inaccessible until one overcomes "the sense of the uselessness of suffering."[55] Those who have made a total gift of themselves through the profession of the evangelical counsels are in a unique position to proclaim this gospel of suffering. Doing this effectively will depend primarily not on technical skill, but on a "heart [which] sees where love is needed and acts accordingly."[56] Only a heart which sees the dignity of another's distress is capable of communicating Christ's merciful gaze. And this merciful gaze is the only way by which the one who suffers understands his condition as a gift and a task for the Church.

The second apostolate to be mentioned in this consideration is education. Benedict XVI has said that "first and foremost every Catholic educational institution is a place of encounter the living God who in Jesus Christ reveals his transforming love and truth."⁵⁷ To this end, the educator is called to practice "intellectual charity" by leading those entrusted to his care to the truth about life.⁵⁸ In the curial document, *Reflection and Guidelines on Consecrated Persons and Their Mission in Schools*, the specific contribution of religious in this apostolate is highlighted as "in its being a sign, a memory and prophecy of the values of the Gospel"⁵⁹ such that:

> Whatever their specific task, the presence of consecrated persons in schools *infects* the contemplative glance by educating into a silence that leads to listening to God, to paying attention to others, to the situation that surrounds us, to creation. Furthermore, by aiming at the essential, consecrated persons provoke the need for authentic encounters, they renew the capacity to be amazed and to take care of the other, rediscovered like a brother.⁶⁰

It is interesting to note that the document identifies the mission of religious in schools to imbue the environment of the school with a contemplative gaze capable of generating communion because it sees Christ in all things. This is why "there is no need for consecrated persons to reserve exclusive tasks for themselves in educational communities."⁶¹ Through the profession of vows and a life educated into spiritual maturity, the religious is already a powerful witness to the primacy of God and man's vocation to order all things accordingly. The interior movement of recognizing Christ in all things, which gives the religious the capacity of living every circumstance as the gift of the Father, constitutes the basic "charism" of every religious institute. In this way the universality of the Church's mission is present in the defined of particular religious institutes.

However, this depth can only be attained when religious themselves are profoundly converted to the reality of their ecclesial vocation through what Paul VI calls in *Evangelica testificatio*, "a certain experience of God,"⁶² that is, a profound knowing and being known by him which gives the capacity of introducing "into the universal mission of [the People of God] a special source of spiritual and supernatural energy."[63] John Paul II, in *Vita consecrata*, refers to this source experience in the language of the Transfiguration:

> [F]or an overall picture of [the] essential characteristics [of the consecrated life], it is singularly helpful to fix our gaze on Christ's radiant face in the mystery of the Transfiguration. . . . The disciples who have enjoyed this intimacy with the Master, surrounded for a moment by the splendor of the Trinitarian life and of the communion of saints, and as it were caught up in the horizon of eternity, are immediately brought back to daily reality, where they see "Jesus only," in the lowliness of his human nature, and are invited to return to the valley, to share with him the toil of God's plan and to set off courageously on the way of the Cross.[64]

The continuity between the splendor of Tabor and the shadow of the valley lies in the person of Jesus Christ himself. Moreover, the beauty shining forth from the face of Christ necessitates the movement back down the mountain. Although Peter would stay, "he is invited to return to the byways of the world in order to continue serving the Kingdom of God. . . . in order that, through the brightness and beauty of good works, [he might] possess in charity what is symbolized in the Lord's white garments."[65] Peter is not allowed to keep and enjoy the splendor of Tabor for himself. To put it another way, the only way for Peter to preserve this gift is to return to the toil of his everyday life. However, precisely because the beauty of the transfigured Christ has taken root in him, his everyday life is now suffused with this light.

What is the significance of this light? The *"special experience of the light which shines forth from the Incarnate Word"*[66] reveals him as "the infinite beauty which alone *can fully satisfy the human heart."*[67] Although it will mature through the scandal of the Cross, the utter surprise of the Resurrection, and through the gift of the Holy Spirit, Peter encounters already on the mountain that peerless love which alone has the power to make sense of his whole life. As a good teacher, it is this embryonic experience which Christ nurtures in the challenge laid on Peter to respond with his entire person: *configured* to Christ in the *disfigurement* of suffering and *transfiguration* in glory. In the end, an experience lacking such depth is unable to be communicated unto the Cross. Therefore, in recalling the event of the Transfiguration, John Paul II indicates both the source of the mission of consecrated persons and its manner of communication. Only a life wholly given over to God, which has as its genesis and consistency a fascination with Christ, has the innate power of "inviting the men and women of our time to lift their eyes, not to let themselves be overwhelmed by everyday things, to let themselves [in turn] be captivated by the fascination of God and of his Son's Gospel."[68]

CONCLUSION

Sister Mary Judith O'Brien, R.S.M.

Sister Mary Nika Schaumber, R.S.M.

The preceding chapters have expressed the understanding of religious life as lived by different religious institutes, each with its own unique charism. The various perspectives offered by each author from different theological and philosophical disciplines are rooted in a strong love for religious life and for the Magisterium, and reflect in a small way the rich diversity of the many charisms in the Church. The chapters began with an understanding of baptismal consecration as the foundation for the call to consecrated life and of the uniqueness of religious consecration, which witnesses to the spousal bond of Christ and his Church. In response to that divine invitation to spousal relationship, the individual religious vows chastity, poverty, and obedience within a specific institute. This religious consecration builds upon and strengthens communion with God and, in him, communion among members of the same institute, in order to foster the spirituality of communion within the entire Church. In this way, communion leads to mission.

The authors bear witness to the importance with which the Church has held religious life from its beginnings. The introduction explains that active non-ordained congregations were first approved as religious by *Conditae a Christo,* and traces an evolution of the understanding of the bond that united those institutes to the Church until the Second Vatican Council. In the early decades of the twentieth century, non-ordained religious institutes were considered private societies, although the vows professed were public. Individuals strove for perfection in a religious congregation or society that was somewhat parallel to the Church, rather than *for* and *in* the Church. In a private allocution, Pius XII foresaw a more direct ecclesial relationship which was further clarified in the documents of the Second Vatican Council.

The Second Vatican Council returned to the teaching of Saint Thomas Aquinas that says that each of the three states of life—the laity, ordained priesthood, and religious life—are essential for the perfection of the Church.[1] The Council recognized religious life as an integral part of its ecclesiology.[2] At the same time, the documents were unable to resolve certain questions regarding the origin of religious life and the nature of religious consecration. As the preceding chapters have drawn heavily upon the ecclesial documents from the Second Vatican Council forward, this conclusion will place those documents in an historical context, especially tracing the evolution of the Church teaching regarding the nature of religious life. This historical study is by no means complete. Rather, the summary is intended solely to reveal a growing awareness of the close relationship between religious life and the Church.

THE UNDERSTANDING OF RELIGIOUS LIFE
IN THE SECOND VATICAN COUNCIL

On January 24, 1959, Pope John XXIII uttered those words that shocked the Church and the world, words that came "like a flash of heavenly light": Ecumenical Council.[3] There had only been twenty such councils in the history of the Church, the last having been interrupted by the Italian invasion of the Papal States in 1870. The primary purpose of the twenty-first Ecumenical Council was to safeguard the sacred deposit of Christian doctrine and "to expound Church teaching in a manner demanded by the times."[4] The Second Vatican Council could well be called the council that explained the organic structure of the Church. This is most clearly seen in the Constitution on the Church, *Lumen gentium,* which has been frequently quoted in the preceding chapters.

Lumen Gentium

Lumen gentium is considered "the great achievement of the council," the center to which all the other decrees must be referred, both because of its important contents and because of its central place among the Council documents.[5] Perhaps none of the other documents underwent such drastic revisions before the text was finally approved. The Council Fathers desired their reflections on the nature of the Church to be more biblical and more historical than the theological manuals published between the two world wars. Even a brief look at the evolution of the chapter headings of *Lumen gentium* reveal the Council Fathers' willingness to struggle to understand the constitution of the Church and the place of religious within this structure.

In preparation for the Council, Pope John XXIII had requested input from all the bishops of the world. Their responses filled fifteen volumes that covered 9,420 pages. A sub-commission worked out a comprehensive draft that was presented soon after the opening of the Council on October 11, 1962. The twelve chapters of this first draft followed the basic structure of the Church as outlined in the Code of 1917: the nature of the Church militant, the members of the Church and the necessity of the Church for salvation, two chapters on the episcopacy and the priesthood, the state of evangelical perfection, the laity, the teaching office of the Church, the relationship with the State, missionary activity, ecumenism, and a chapter on the Virgin Mother. The second draft in 1963 consisted of only four chapters. After a beginning chapter on the "Mystery of the Church," there followed chapters on the episcopacy, the laity, and the *call to holiness*, which was to refer to religious life. The final version reflected one of the most pivotal doctrines developed by the Council Fathers: the article of faith that all are called to holiness, that all the faithful are called to live the counsels in imitation of Christ. Clearly this doctrine was based in the very words of Christ and was the constant teaching of the Church, but the major focus in the writings and canonical doctrine of the preceding decades was the hierarchical structure of the Church. This was evidenced in the structure of the *Code of Canon Law, 1917.* To reflect the universal call to holiness, *Lumen gentium* begins with the "Mystery of the Church" and "The People of God." Then it speaks of the episcopacy, the laity, the call of the whole Church to holiness, and only then of religious. It must be said that some religious objected to this order, for they felt "banished to a sort of appendix." They feared that one of the surest signs of vitality in the Church, the life consecrated to God, would "lose some of its value in the eyes of the Christian people."[6]

The *iter* or development of chapters 4 and 5 of *Lumen gentium* might indicate some of the factors involved in the

decision of the Council Fathers. The first draft presented in
1962 under the title "Of those who bind themselves before the
Church to the Evangelical Counsels" was presented and rejected
by the Theological Commission in May of 1963. The draft was
judged insufficiently related to the mystery of the Church
because it treated the religious state as a privileged state for
chosen souls, a spiritual aristocracy and obscuring the basic
doctrine that all Christians are called to holiness.[7] A revised text
titled "The Call of the Church to Holiness" was intended to be
submitted to a joint meeting of the Theological Commission
and the Commission for Religious. This never happened, however, due to the suspension of the council following the death of
Pope John XXIII. When Pope Paul VI resumed the Council, the
coordinating commission decided to print the revised chapter
without the formal approbation by the two commissions. The
text provoked bitter arguments even after the debate on
the Council floor. Why did the description of religious life in the
constitution on the Church cause such difficulty? It will be
impossible in this chapter to delve into all the questions raised
by the Council Fathers. They were many and varied including:
(1) debate on the appropriateness of calling religious life the
state of perfection if all are called to be holy; (2) question of
whether to describe the religious state as an intermediate state
between the clergy and the laity or whether to say that religious
may be called from both the lay and clerical states (thus reject-
ing the term *religious state*); and (3) disagreement regarding the
order in the listing of the evangelical counsels, since some considered chastity to be the vow that defines religious consecration most particularly. An area of concern raised by the Council
Fathers which was not able to be fully resolved and that still
needs further clarification is the difference between religious
and secular institutes. This question became predominant in
the debates regarding the very title of chapter 6: Religious.

The Title of Chapter 6: Religious

Historical background is necessary in order to understand
the concern regarding the title of chapter 6 of *Lumen gentium*.
In the beginning of the fifteenth century, Saint Francis of Rome
organized a group of oblates of Saint Benedict who, while living

in their own homes, went out to exercise the spiritual and corporal works of mercy. Many similar groups arose in the subsequent centuries, including the Ursulines, founded by Saint Angela Merci, and the Priests of the Sacred Heart, founded by Pierre de Cloriviere. In 1947 Pius XII recognized these groups as having a distinct vocation within the Church. In *Provida mater ecclesia*, he granted approval to *secular institutes*, which are marked by a distinct secularity and whose followers seek a "state of perfection in the world." Following the Second Vatican Council, Paul VI responded to the question of the theological-canonical nature of secular institutes by stating that theirs is "a form of new and original consecration, springing forth from the Holy Spirit to be lived amidst temporal reality."[8]

During the Council the place of secular institutes within the structure of the Church was understandably unclear. Having only been approved in 1947, this was a new reality, inspired by the Holy Spirit but awaiting further canonical development. Chapter 6 of *Lumen gentium*, which was titled "Religious," addresses those who bind themselves by vow or other sacred bonds similar to a vow.[9] What did this mean? Religious, according to the canonical doctrine of the time and reaffirmed in the *Code of Canon Law, 1983*, profess vows and not any other form of *sacred bond*. Members of secular institutes take a *sacred bond*. Was this reference implying that members of secular institutes were religious? Or, perhaps, was the *sacred bond* referring to the innovation of *Renovationis causam*, an interim instruction on religious life, that permitted religious institutes "to replace temporary vows with bonds of some other kind."[10] (This permission was revoked by the *Code of Canon Law, 1983.*) It is not clear exactly what the reference to *sacred bond* in this chapter referred to, but it is known that a last minute revision of *Perfectae caritatis* (*PC* 11) clarified that members of secular institutes are not religious.[11] Nonetheless, the title of chapter 6 which addresses those who profess vows or sacred bonds remained "Religious."

The Ecclesial Dimension of Religious Life

In reflecting on the nature of the Church, *Lumen gentium* firmly affirmed the ecclesial nature of religious life, making it an essential part of its ecclesiology. In paragraph 13c, the Council Fathers refer to different ranks (*ordines*) within the Church:

> This diversity among its members arises either by reason of their duties (*officia*), as some exercise the sacred ministry for the good of their brethren, or by reason of their condition or way of life, as many enter the religious state and, pursuing sanctity by the narrower path, stimulate their brethren by their example.

By this statement both the ordained priesthood and the religious state are seen as necessary if the catholicity of the Church is to be realized.[12] Moreover, it is not that individuals decide to seek holiness by this narrow way, but rather that God raises some from among the people for the sake of the Church.[13] "The evangelical counsels unite those who practice them to the Church and her mystery in a special way." They are "committed to the honor and service of God under a new and special title . . . [they are] more intimately consecrated to divine service." For this reason "although the religious state constituted by the profession of the evangelical counsels does not belong to the hierarchical structure of the Church, nevertheless it belongs inseparably to her life and holiness."[14] This profound statement by the Council Fathers cemented the ecclesial dimension of religious life.

By religious profession, a person is united not just to the particular institute but to the Church, as Augustine Cardinal Bea insisted: "It is necessary . . . that religious, living in fidelity to their Rule and to the spirit of their proper Order, Congregation, or Institute, know themselves at the same time and in a greater measure, members of the Church."[15] Moreover, the religious is dedicated to the welfare of the entire Church, taking on the duty of strengthening the kingdom of Christ. Each religious becomes "a sign that can and ought to attract all the members of the Church."[16] This was the first time that an ecclesial document definitively recognized religious life not as a way of personal asceticism, but as integral to the holiness of the Church.

Lumen gentium is a crucial document for religious life. While it did not resolve the distinction between religious and secular consecration, it affirmed religious life as a constitutive aspect of ecclesiology.

Perfectae Caritatis

The *iter* of *Perfectae caritatis*, the decree on the Appropriate Renewal of the Religious Life, was no less challenging than chapter 6 of *Lumen gentium*. The first draft presented to the preparatory central commission of the Council contained about two hundred articles. A synthesized text was requested. This work commenced under the chairmanship of Archbishop Paolo Phillippe, O.P., and was presented to the coordinating commission on March 27, 1963. The draft met with many criticisms including: (1) the title "Of Religious" did not apply to secular institutes; (2) the term "state of perfection" could be misunderstood; (3) there was a lack of theological and biblical explanations; (4) there were not sufficient guidelines for renewal; and (5) provision was not made for a more appropriate involvement of religious in the world. The secretary general of the Council received a rigorously abbreviated draft of fifty-two articles in nine chapters on May 8, 1963. This, however, was met with strong opposition. The responses of the Council Fathers ran to over two hundred pages with widely differing opinions. The criticisms posed regarded: (1) the inappropriateness of the title, "On the states that aim at perfection"; (2) the juridical tone; (3) the lack of differentiation between contemplative and active religious; (4) the omission of guidelines for closer collaboration between bishops and religious institutes; and (5) the Latinized uniformity of religious life in the Church. A letter from the coordinating commission on January 23, 1964, stated that the schema could only contain essential points of appropriate renewal in the form of short guiding principles. The final text was scarcely four pages long and consisted of nineteen articles. The schema was again revised and the fourth redaction was circulated to the Council Fathers under the title "On the Appropriate Renewal of Religious Life." A record number of fourteen hundred *modi*, or modifications of the text, were considered before the final edition. The *modi* were often so contradictory that it was extremely difficult for the commission to come to a consensus.[17] The many concerns that were raised reflect both the interest of the Church in religious life and the fact that this form of life was probably not well understood by many of the experts and the Council Fathers.

The decree in Latin begins with the phrase *Perfectae caritatis,* the perfect charity reflected in the teaching and example of Christ and lived through the exercise of the evangelical counsels. While it is considered the *Decree on the Appropriate Renewal of the Religious Life,* this decree is also addressed to members of secular institutes and societies living a community life without the exercise of vow (now referred to as "societies of apostolic life"). Although the decree indicates that "the special character of both groups is to be maintained," *Perfectae caritatis* did not define that special character.[18] The only difference noted in the decree appears to be that members of secular institutes "reside in the world."[19] Articles 10 and 11 treat respectively lay religious life and secular institutes, but they are incredibly similar. Article 10 describes religious life as "one of total dedication to the profession of the evangelical counsels," and article 11 states that secular institutes make a "profession of the evangelical counsels which is genuine and complete."

The final decree issued general guidelines to be entrusted to the general chapters of three forms of institutes: religious, societies living a community life without vows, and secular institutes. The guidelines could be distilled to two principles: (1) return to the source of all Christian life and to the original inspiration of a particular community, and (2) adjust to the changed conditions of the times.[20] For many years the Vatican had been asking major superiors of women's communities to revise their customs. In 1952 Pius XII urged superiors to update those customs that had lost their significance, to adopt habits that were suitable and met the requirements of safety and hygiene, and to be educated to the same degree as their lay counterparts.

For example, in the United States, there was concern regarding sisters being ill-prepared to enter the classroom as teachers or the hospital room as nurses. In 1955 there were three million students in parochial schools. Against the advice of the Vatican, some religious institutes cut short their time of spiritual formation in order to staff these schools, resulting in poorly formed religious unable to handle the crisis that was about to erupt.[21] Within the institutes, some superiors misused their power and were overly restrictive about normal human activities. Some institutes were too preoccupied with themselves and not with the needs of the Church.[22] Renewal of institutes was needed, and *Perfectae caritatis* sought to inspire both a renewal of spirit within each institute and an adaptation to the external circumstances of society.[23]

The Council Fathers anticipated the revision of the *Code of Canon Law* to take place shortly after the conclusion of the Council. For that reason, they deliberately did not try to legislate but rather offered the underlying guidelines that could inspire both a renewal of spirit in religious institutes and a revision of the *Code*.

Ecclesiae Sanctae

Shortly after the close of the Second Vatican Council, Pope Paul VI published an apostolic letter, *motu proprio Ecclesiae sanctae,* which did provide some norms for certain of the Vatican II documents, including *Perfectae caritatis*. Clearly the intent of these norms was to give to each institute the opportunity and responsibility for its own renewal and adaptation, especially through the work of the general chapter. However, serious *lacunae* or gaps in the documents caused an unexpected and undesired result.

Through *Ecclesiae sanctae II,* the general chapter of each religious institute was given autonomous authority—exercised previously only by the Holy See—for a significant period of time. During the experimental period, the general chapters were permitted to alter norms of the constitutions, even if contrary to the common law, "as long as the purpose, nature and character of the institute [were] preserved."[24] *Ecclesiae sanctae* contained the provision that experiments contrary to the common law should be embarked on only "with prudence." However, the apostolic letter concluded by saying these experiments "will be willingly permitted by the Holy See as the occasions call for them."[25]

Such permission to change constitutions was a derogation of the existing common law, which had meticulous directions for any alteration of norms in religious institutes. Membership in general chapters had been specifically determined. Rules pertaining to adequate representation required for a vote and the number of votes necessary to introduce changes to the particular law of each religious institute had been strictly enforced. Suddenly all these safeguards ensuring proper representation of

all the members of an institute were gone, together with the
necessity of submitting proposals for the approval of the Sacred
Congregation. For example, in some instances, chapter dele-
gates were allowed to self-select, to choose to participate or not
in the chapter, rather than being selected by the members
themselves. This allowed groups who may not have represent-
ed the viewpoints of the majority to have an inordinate voice in
promoting radical change. *Ecclesiae sanctae II* permitted alteration of constitutions for an experimental period that in certain
circumstances could be as long as sixteen years, while it did not
mandate the method to be followed to assure fair representation
or accountability.[26]

In promulgating *Ecclesiae sanctae II*, Pope Paul VI recognized
that the cooperation of all superiors and members was necessary for true renewal.[27] Surely the Holy Father anticipated that
any constitutional change would be entrusted to the discernment of every member of the institute, as *Perfectae caritatis* had
stated: "In decisions which involve the future of an institute as a
whole, superiors should in appropriate manner consult the
members and give them a hearing."[28] Perhaps he presumed that
the method already established in constitutions would be followed, but, according to the *motu proprio*, those very procedural
norms could also be subject to experimentation. Specific guidelines for the procedures, such as the number of votes required
for a change to be approved or the means to assure adequate
representation in the chapter, were not given. *Ecclesiae sanctae
II* left to the discretion of the superior the choice of the best
means to renew, without the need to follow their own constitutions or the guiding documents of the Church; this was a significant gap in the norms, which resulted in significant changes in
some institutes.[29] The responsibility thus placed in the hands of
superiors was astounding.

The intention of *Ecclesiae sanctae II* was the promotion of a
"renewal of spirit" within religious institutes based on the guidelines of *Perfectae caritatis* and *Lumen gentium*.[30] The period of
experimentation it initiated was to be "undertaken prudently"
by special general chapters until the definitive approval of their
revised constitutions.[31] However, because the period of experimentation could last so long, in many institutes what was a trial
became a normal condition of life. An experiment can never be

"so long as to make a doubtful condition of mind a permanent rule of conduct."[32]

THE POST-CONCILIAR CHURCH

The period of Church history that followed the Second Vatican Council can be aptly characterized as one of light and shadow. The Second Vatican Council was received, on the whole, with tremendous zeal, and the fruits of the *aggiornamento* cherished. At the same time, however, there was a "partial and selective reading of the Council, as well as a superficial interpretation of its doctrine . . . a lack of discernment of spirits."[33] This misinterpretation often led to an acceptance of the secularized mentality prevalent in society, and a certain estrangement from the Church.

In the aftermath of the Council, religious were described as "stupendously enthusiastic, and more than ever in love with their ecclesial mission."[34] There was a "virginal primeval evangelical vitality," a vision of wide horizons.[35] The Holy Spirit had spoken through the supreme pontiff in union with the college of bishops: it was the time for renewal. The norms of *Ecclesiae sanctae* gave religious institutes a magnificent challenge for renewal of life and discipline and a surprising autonomy for experimentation. A selective reading of *Lumen gentium*, *Perfectae caritatis*, and *Ecclesiae sanctae*, however, as well as an interpretation of these texts from the perspective of secular values, caused a shadow to be cast over the ecclesial dimension of religious life as described in Vatican II. In this diminished light, the true nature of religious life as inseparable from the "life and holiness" of the Church was overshadowed by a pronounced desire for self-fulfillment and by purely organizational questions related to power. A strange dichotomy arose in many religious institutes, as evidenced in the United States: there was a concerted effort both to distance the religious institute from the institutional Church, and, at the same time, to demand jurisdictional powers proper only to the hierarchy. Examples of the former will follow, while the question of jurisdiction will be addressed in the section on the *Code of Canon Law.*

Desire for Separation from the Institutional Church

Caught in the societal cry for liberation from all authority that was so prevalent in the 1960s in the United States, some religious claimed that such a charismatic life repels the rigidities of human law. They refused to recognize the appropriateness of a common law to regulate religious life. The "Sisters' Survey" of 1967 put out by the Conference of Major Religious Superiors of Women's Institutes in the United States included this statement: "All authentic law is by its very nature flexible and can be changed by the community in which it is operative."[36] R. Coursey even proposed that statistical law may be appropriate for religious life:

> In stating a law, the modern scientist is satisfied if "most of the elements of a certain group act in such a way most of the time." . . . Thus, "religious must attend daily Mass" can be understood to mean, without evoking casuistic rationalizations, that most religious will be at daily Mass most of the time.[37]

For many, religious law was meaningless. In that light, religious superiors were seen as not only superfluous, but even detrimental to the ecclesiology of communion. Pope Paul VI described the extent of this phenomenon in 1968:

> There exists today a widespread attitude whereby, after the manner of the skeptic, it is distrustful of or rejects canon law and everything which, as it were, represents or in any way derives authority from it; and so this attitude bypasses or even despises all such things.[38]

Although contrary to the vow of obedience, and thus to very essence of religious life, this anti-authority attitude permeated religious institutes, especially in the United States.

REVISION OF THE CODE OF CANON LAW

In the midst of this widespread confusion regarding the role of law and of authority in the Church, the Pontifical Commission for the Revision of the *Code of Canon Law* sought to integrate the vision of Vatican II within the stability of canonical prescriptions. Although the commission was set up by Pope John XXIII on March 28, 1963, the completed *Code of Canon Law* was not promulgated until 1983. The following section will consider the structure of the *Code of Canon Law* with regard to religious life, some of the concerns raised by the norms, and particularly the question of authority and obedience which would ultimately determine the response of individual institutes to the directives of the Church.

Institutes of Consecrated Life and Societies of Apostolic Life

The various names given to the sub-commission responsible for the norms on religious life is revealing. At first, the sub-commission bore the title, "On Religious." In 1968 that was changed to "On Institutes of Perfection," and in 1975 to "On Institutes of Consecrated Life" in order to embrace all who profess the evangelical counsels.[39] There were many debates among the commissioners if this was the correct course, but faced with three forms of life—religious, secular, and societies of common life (now referred to as institutes of apostolic life)—they decided to consider all three together.

Many authors questioned this decision, particularly in regard to placing religious and secular institutes under the same heading. A. Bandera wrote:

> Not all of this seems very clear to me. By placing the religious institutes under the generic concept of *institutes of consecrated life,* an ambiguity is introduced that, if I am not mistaken, diminishes the ecclesial assessment of religious life. I think, further, that the category consecrated life, without intending to and without wanting to, leads to inconsistencies between the Code of Canon Law and Vatican Council II, and although the latter is the source of the former, it is not always followed. While I express this opinion, I can only wish that I am mistaken.[40]

Jean Beyer notes that a project to clarify the typology of consecrated life was proposed for the commissioners, but it was rejected. He continues, "Such a typology will one day be of major importance for an ecclesial life that is concerned over truth and renewal."[41]

Religious and Secular Consecration

The norms of the *Code* specify differences between religious and secular institutes. They do not, however, clarify the distinction between religious and secular consecration and, on the contrary, actually introduce more confusion. C. 607 defines the nature of religious life as "a consecration of the whole person" manifesting "the marvelous marriage established by God as a sign of the world to come." The next two paragraphs specify the essentials of religious life as distinct from secular institutes. Religious pronounce public vows, live a fraternal life in common, and are separated from the world. By this deliberate withdrawal from the world, religious lose what is known as the *secular* condition.[42] Antonio Queralt closely links the fact that religious renounce the world to the Council's declaration that "the religious state belongs inseparably to the life and holiness of the Church".[43]

Secular institutes are characterized by a secular apostolate in the world, and by a life consecrated by the full profession of the evangelical counsels through sacred bonds—vows, promises, or oaths, as defined in their constitutions.[44] What is the nature of the vows professed by members of secular institutes? Although they may be pronounced publicly, the vows taken in secular institutes are not accepted "in the name of the Church." Some authors, however, argue they must be public because they have some official character in the Church. The commissioners actually debated if a third category of vows should be introduced—public, private, and what secular institutes do—but it was determined that this question could not be adequately answered at that time.[45] The nature of the bond still remains uncertain.

Canon 711 introduces another enigma. The canon states that "consecration as a member of a secular institute does not change the member's proper canonical status." Tomas Rincón-Pérez reflects, "It is not easy for canonical doctrine to decipher the precise scope and meaning of this precept."[46] One would expect at least that members of secular institutes would comprise a *consecrated state* with particular rights and obligations, distinct from the lay state. If members of secular institutes remain lay persons in the world, is consecration by means of the profession of the evangelical counsels a special vocation in the Church?[47]

Power of the Superior in Institutes of Consecrated Life
and Societies of Apostolic Life

Nature of the Power

Canon 596 describes the power of a superior—in religious and secular institutes and in societies of apostolic life—as that which is "defined in the universal law and in the constitutions." The Code of 1917 called the power of religious superiors *dominative,* a private power of a private entity. C. 596 only speaks of "that power." Why could the commissioners not define what "that power" is? At the fifth session of the commission, Bidagor formulated a question that was at the heart of the commissioners' dilemma: "Could the power of jurisdiction extend to the laity and even to women?"[48] He answered immediately that according to the present law, it could not, "but this doctrine is not a source of peace."[49] The question Bidagor raised touched upon what Joseph Cardinal Ratzinger called one of the thorniest legal and constitutional problems in all the history of the Church.[50] The question of the origin and exercise of power within the Church marked the underlying doctrinal debate throughout the sessions of the Pontifical Commission for the Revision of the Code. Left unresolved, the related questions regarding lay jurisdiction and the power of the lay religious superior could only remain clouded in controversy.

This uncertainty resulted in certain norms in the Code of 1983 that either are contradictory or have unclear and puzzling terminology.[51] For example, canon 129 states that those who are in sacred orders are capable of the power of governance, while the laity may *cooperate* in such power, and c. 274§1 states "only clerics can obtain offices the exercise of which requires the power of . . . governance." The debates over the formulations of these canons are outside the scope of this chapter but they help explain why in c. 596§1 the nature of the power of the religious superior was left deliberately vague. One consultor proposed that the power of superiors be termed "ecclesiastical power," "for it is derived from ecclesiastical power."[52] M. Said, the relator of the sub-commission, responded that while the possibility of lay jurisdiction had been discussed many times, it was not within the competence of the commission to render a decision on its merits. Furthermore, another consultor objected, the addition of the word "ecclesiastical" would seem to equate the power of superiors with the hierarchical power of governing.[53]

Despite this response, a commentary in the *New Commentary on the Code of Canon Law* by the Canon Law Society of America written by R. McDermott states:

> Superiors and chapters of institutes of consecrated life and societies of apostolic life possess *ecclesiastical power of governance* within the limits of universal and proper law. This ecclesiastical power is public authority given by the Church and carried out in its name.[54]

This inclusion is particularly curious since the earlier edition of the same *Commentary* included the response of the consultor quoted above and states that the issue "will continue to be studied and discussed until greater clarity is achieved."[55] That clarity has not yet been achieved, which makes such commentaries misleading to the general reader.

The commissioners were duly cautious and deliberately imprecise in the formulation of c. 596§1. Aware of the ongoing canonical debate regarding lay jurisdiction, they preferred to leave the power of non-clerical superiors vague. Although J. L. Gutiérrez finds it disconcerting that a power without a precise nature would be introduced into a legal body, the alternatives might have been worse.[56]

It is not possible in this chapter to explore all the meanings given to the term "jurisdiction," nor all the factors involved in proposing that the Code does seem to grant certain jurisdictional powers to the lay religious superior.[57] If jurisdiction is taken to mean the power to effect a change in the status of another, it does appear that this power is given to the lay religious superior in the following cases: first, in granting an indult of exclaustration to a perpetually professed member of the institute; second, in giving an indult of departure to a member in temporary vows in an institute of pontifical right; and third, in issuing a decree of dismissal.[58] However, it must be noted that if a superior of a religious institute can exercise the power of jurisdiction, there is an essential difference between this jurisdiction and that which is proper to the ordained priesthood. This distinction of jurisdictional power was not considered in *Women and Jurisdiction, An*

Unfolding Reality, the LCWR Study of Selected Church Leadership Roles.[59] In a press release announcing this book, Beal comments that this study "shows that while scholars have been busy debating whether lay people can exercise jurisdiction in the Church, lay people have been busy exercising jurisdiction."[60] *Women and Jurisdiction* is a challenge to the Church to overcome "its delay in taking practical steps to appoint women to leadership roles that involve the power of governance."[61] Such comments reinforce the necessity for a clearer statement by the Church regarding the power of non-ordained superiors.

A proposed resolution of lay jurisdiction for religious superiors is a consideration of this power being transmitted by means of delegated power or habitual faculties, whereby the title to the power remains with the hierarchical authority delegating the religious.[62] The nature of habitual faculties makes it a particularly apt means for this transfer of power. Habitual faculties are granted to a person, not for personal reasons, but by reason of the office he/she holds. As such, habitual faculties pertain to and remain with the successors in the office.[63] At the moment of the approbation of a religious institute, when the society is granted juridical personality in the Church, power is granted to the religious superior to carry out the obligations enumerated for religious superiors in the universal law and in the proper law of the institute—namely, the constitutions. Not all the acts of a religious superior require habitual faculties, but certain ones, as noted above, do. The power granted to the superior remains in the office and is transmitted to his/her successor, making it reasonable to conclude that habitual faculties could provide for the transmission of those jurisdictional powers necessary for religious superiors.

A definitive answer regarding the nature and origin of the power of the lay religious superior has not yet been given by the Church. Because of the close bond that exists between the power of sacred orders and that of ecclesiastical governance, it seems particularly important that if non-ordained religious superiors are seen to hold jurisdictional powers, the transfer of this power be clearly differentiated from that of ordination.

Personal Authority

In the United States in the aftermath of the Council, there was a trend to put forward *group leadership, fellowship authority,* and government by *consensus.* In 1969 Sister Mary Francis Borgia, O.S.F., informed the Annual Congress of the Canon Law Society of America: "The primary authority in religious life is fellowship authority. . . . The designation of a local superior in the small (and even larger) group is disappearing."[64] A proposal submitted to the Pontifical Commission in 1968 by the Conference of Major Religious Superiors of Women's Institutes, which would later be known as the Leadership Conference of Women Religious (LCWR) in the United States, substituted collegial authority for the personal authority of a superior: "Within every religious institute the highest authority shall rest within a collegial body (such as a general chapter) which is representative of the membership of the institute."[65] Actually a general chapter is only periodic, occurring every six years for many religious institutes; it does not substitute for the ordinary governance of a superior general and her council.

Numerous letters and decrees from the Sacred Congregation of Religious and Secular Institutes from the time of the Council to the promulgation of the *Code* reiterated the need for personal authority in all religious institutes. The response to one religious institute's request to be governed by a council, a board of directors, or another such group, was: "The office of superior cannot be dispensed with in the government of local houses."[66] Forbidding the replacement of a local superior by a local coordinator, the congregation explained: "a superior is not merely a 'first among equals' but is one to whom obedience is owed as a person who holds the place of God."[67] This directive was further expounded upon in a letter in April 1970:

> The relationships between religious and superiors are such as to be unobtainable except in dealing with an individual person duly invested with authority. Such personal relationships could hardly be realized where a senate, an assembly, or any other group of this kind replaced the superior. In addition, we cannot lose sight of the role of the superior as spiritual leader and not as a simple administrator.[68]

The decree, *Experimenta circa,* issued by the congregation in February 1972, reminded religious that purely democratic forms of government were not acceptable; a superior must exercise personal authority and not merely act as an executor.[69] A letter of the Congregation to superiors general in July of the same year stated that while revised constitutions should include the necessity for consultation and collaboration, "the obligation and the right of the superior to exercise prudently the role of personal authority should be respected."[70] Again, in a private letter on August 11, 1973, the Congregation said that the expression, "total collegial rule with a local superior chosen by the group" was unclear and not in accord with the decree of February 2, 1972, *Perfectae caritatis,* no. 14, and *Evangelica testificatio,* no. 25.[71] These directives often were not heeded.[72]

Does total collegial government have authenticity in a religious institute? There is no evidence that this group could accept vows *in the name of the Church.* What power does such collegial authority have? These questions cause a deeper reflection on the source of authority within religious institutes. The revised *Code* designates a religious community as one living in a "lawfully constituted house, under the authority of a superior."[73] Canon 618 states that the power of a religious superior comes "from God through the ministry of the Church." Many American religious communities, seeking to be liberated from Rome's control, claim the authority of the institute comes from the members. Such a stance is a step backward to private, dominative power. Solely private power is possible for an institute which separates itself from the Holy See in response to a perceived attack on its autonomy and self-determination.[74]

While the Church insists on the personal authority of a superior, it does not regulate only one model for the practice of obedience in all religious institutes. The recent document *The Service of Authority and Obedience* recognizes that "the way of listening to and living authority and obedience has changed both in the Church and in society."[75] The reasons given by the CICLSAL are:

> the coming to awareness of the *value of the individual person,* with his or her vocation, and intellectual, affective and spiritual gifts, with his or her freedom and rational abilities; the centrality of the *spirituality of communion,* with the valuing of the instruments that help one to live it; a different and less individualistic way of understanding mission, in the *sharing* of all

members of the People of God, with the resulting forms of concrete collaboration.[76]

The preceding chapters have developed the post-Conciliar
understanding of the vow of obedience emphasizing the dignity
of the human person and encouraging the formative
dialogue through which a sister comes to know herself in
mature freedom. Nevertheless, it is the obligation of the superi-
or to ensure that the desire for *self-realization* does not hinder
the common life and mission of the institute.

As personal authority has been under attack or rejected by
some religious institutes, a similar account could be cited
regarding a diminishment of life in common, abandonment of
corporate apostolates in favor of personal pursuits, and individ-
ualized forms of prayer substituting for common prayer. The
following section will consider the ecclesial documents issued
after the *Code of Canon Law, 1983,* particularly as they address
the unresolved questions regarding the government of religious
institutes and the nature of religious consecration.

ECCLESIAL DOCUMENTS
AFTER THE *CODE OF CANON LAW*, 1983

*Essential Elements in the Church's Teaching on Religious Life
as Applied to Institutes Dedicated to Works of the
Apostolate, May 31, 1983*

The period of experimentation had resulted in so many
changes in religious institutes in the United States that many
bishops requested direction from John Paul II in order that they
could guide the renewal process in the light of the revised Code.
The instruction, *Essential Elements in the Church's Teaching on
Religious Life as Applied to Institutes Dedicated to Works of the
Apostolate (Essential Elements),* from the Sacred Congregation for
Religious and Secular Institutes (SCRSI), was sent as an enclosure in a letter addressed to all the bishops of the United States
on June 22, 1983.[77] The initial paragraphs explain its purpose: to
respond to requests from religious superiors, chapters, and bishops for directives in assessing the recent past and looking toward
the future. No new doctrine or law is to be presented, but rather

"a clear statement of the Church's teaching regarding religious life at a moment which is particularly significant and opportune."[78] Furthermore, it was noted, *Essential Elements* marked the end of the period of experimentation mandated by *Ecclesiae sanctae II*. In this document the elements that form a religious institute are clearly identified; lacking these essential elements, religious life "loses its identity."[79] In order to facilitate acceptance of this instruction, in his letter of introduction the Holy Father announced his appointment of Archbishop John Quinn to head a special commission of bishops mandated to implement a program of assistance for both individual bishops and the episcopal conference of the United States.

Essential Elements was received by some religious and bishops with tremendous relief and gratitude. After the years of experimentation, religious could rest in the explanation this instruction offered as it presented the norms on religious life. The instruction placed ecclesial documents and the *Code of Canon Law* within their spiritual and theological context.[80] Moreover, the document called for a deeper collaboration between religious and their bishops, thereby anticipating "a new spirit of trust and charity."[81] Others, however, were enraged by what they considered "Roman interventionism" without prior consultation.[82] These strong reactions were voiced by those who perceived *Essential Elements* as both unilateral and discriminatory, a singling out of religious in the United States and a return to a pre-Vatican monastic style of life.[83] These responses belie both historical facts as well as the fundamental foundation of religious life.

Perhaps because of this opposition from those institutes which had implemented radical reforms during the time of experimentation, Archbishop Quinn suggested that *Essential Elements* could be interpreted analogously.[84] One could question this approach to interpretation in the light both of the expressed purpose of the document as "a clear statement of the Church's teaching regarding religious life." and of the Holy Father's own introduction of it as a "document on the salient points of the Church's teaching on religious life."[85]

Essential Elements is called an instruction and, as such, it set out the provisions of the *Code* and developed the manner in which it was to be put into effect. Distilling from many ecclesial documents, *Essential Elements* offered a "comprehensive synthesis of the Church's provisions," and, in so doing, it addressed two of the pressing issues regarding religious institutes: the origin and ecclesial nature of religious life and the transmission of power to the superior.[86]

Affirming that "religious life has its own place in relation to the divine and hierarchical structure of the Church,"[87] *Essential Elements* continued to describe that relationship:

> The Church does more than bring an institute into being. She accompanies, guides, corrects and encourages it in its fidelity to its founding gift (see *LG* 45) for it is a living element in her own life and growth. She receives the vows made in the institute as vows of religion with ecclesial consequences, involving a consecration made by God Himself through her mediation. She gives to the institute a public sharing in her own mission, both concrete and corporate (see *LG* 17; *AG* 40). She confers on the institute, in accordance with her own common law and with the constitutions that she has approved, the religious authority necessary for the life of vowed obedience. In short, the Church continues to mediate the consecratory action of God in a specific way, recognizing and fostering this particular form of consecrated life.[88]

In this paragraph, *Essential Elements* precisely identifies the ecclesial nature of religious life in its origin, growth, mission, and government. A few paragraphs later it clarifies that the Church confers the religious authority necessary "at the time of establishing each institute and by the approving of its constitutions."[89] Moreover, it clearly states that authority does not derive from the members nor is it shared. "It is invested in the person of the superior."[90]

This section of *Essential Elements* on religious government was singled out for extensive opposition. Granfield characterized the description of religious authority as a "monarchical model," a "papal paradigm," a model "that may have served the church well in the past" but is not appropriate now and should be replaced with a "democratic model."[91] Sister D. Vidulich called "the 1983 SCRIS *Essential Elements* . . . a feeble recall to a lukewarm monastic style completely divorced from Vatican II theology."[92] Sister Lora Ann Quinonez, LCWR Executive Director in 1983, reported that at their 1983 assembly, forty-three members publicly repudiated

> the characterization of religious life in *Essential Elements* as
> alien to the experience of American sisters . . . it is an attempt
> to quell what Rome sees as rebellion; it is an anonymous docu-
> ment, produced in secret; its fuzzy, ambiguous legal force
> leaves the door wide open for unchecked administrative
> abuse.[93]

Besides expressing dissatisfaction with the Church, this statement was presented as progressive. These sisters saw religious life as apart from the Church; however, this is actually an antiquated approach. Much of the criticism following the promulgation of *Essential Elements* hearkens back to an earlier time in which religious life was seen as parallel to and even independent from the life and holiness of the Church herself.

Essential Elements provided the theological context for a comprehensive review of canonical norms regarding religious life and, as such, it stirred tremendous controversy among those religious who had hoped for a more radical permanent change in the structure of religious life. Because of the theological and juridical precision offered by *Essential Elements,* it is unfortunate that it has only been translated into a few languages.[94]

"To Men and Women Religious on their Consecration in the Light of the Mystery of Redemption," Redemptionis Donum

In March of 1984, Pope John Paul II issued his apostolic exhortation *Redemptionis donum*.[95] This brief document offers the theological underpinnings for the ecclesial dimension of religious life, setting profession of the evangelical counsels solidly in the "economy of the Redemption."[96] The covenant of spousal love, "spousal because it is redemptive," which characterizes religious profession was said to be "a special gift of God to the Church."[97] It is not solely for the good of an individual, or a community, but "constitutes a special possession of the whole People of God."[98] Therefore, "deep, very deep must be the bond which links it to the Church."[99]

Redemptionis donum elaborates upon the explanation of religious profession given in *Essential Elements*: profession is "deeply rooted in baptismal consecration and a fuller expression of it."[100] *Redemptionis donum* continues: "Religious profession creates a new bond between the person and the One and Triune God, in Jesus Christ."[101] The profession of the vows to

practice the evangelical counsels of chastity, poverty, and obedience is the expression of this total consecration to God and
the means that leads to its achievement.

While not directly addressing the power of the religious
superior, *Redemptionis donum* places the vow of obedience in a
profound theological perspective. Submission to God's law is a
condition of all Christian life, but in the "state of perfection the
vow of obedience establishes . . . the duty of a particular reference to Christ, 'obedient unto death.'"[102] In fulfilling the vow of
obedience, religious strive to follow Christ's readiness to do His
Father's will even to the cross. In this way, religious participate
in the economy of Redemption.[103] It is this reality that inspires
submission to legitimate superiors who hold the place of God.[104]
This submission, in turn, exemplifies an interior freedom born
of mature self-surrender and an intense response of faith.[105]

Redemptionis donum is a call to meditate on the vocation to
religious life in the light of the mystery of Redemption. As such,
it broadened the theological framework for the essential elements of religious life, as outlined by the Sacred Congregation
one year earlier. At the same time, this document did not
address the issues left unresolved from the documents of
Vatican II and the *Code of Canon Law*. While the document is
addressed to religious, the words "consecrated person(s)"
appear nineteen times; the document fell short of describing
the distinction of religious consecration, which creates a new
bond, and the consecration by members of secular institutes.

"The Church, In the Word of God Celebrates the Mysteries
of Christ for the Salvation of the World,"
Final Report of the 1985 Extraordinary Synod

The Final Report of the 1985 Extraordinary Synod addressed
the lights and shadows of post-Conciliar renewal. The central
and fundamental idea of the Council, according to the report,
was the ecclesiology of communion.[106] Communion is founded
on union with Peter and his successors, not on a secularized
and democratic model. Communion demands submission to
"one faith, one baptism, one Lord" (Eph 4:5). While it is true, the
report concluded, that "the one and unique spirit works with
many and varied spiritual gifts and charisma (1 Cor 12:4ff) . . .

the pluralism of fundamentally opposed positions . . . leads to dissolution, destruction and the loss of identity."[107] Such loss of religious identity was said to be not the fault of Vatican II, but a result of a "partial and selective reading of the council, as well as [from] a superficial interpretation of its doctrine."[108]

Reflections on the Report through the
Experience of Religious Institutes in the United States

This loss of identity referred to by the Synod has affected many religious institutes in the United States. According to *The Official Catholic Directory*, in 1967 there were 176,671 women religious in the United States. Today, in 2008, there are 63,032.[109] What caused this extreme decline? The long period of experimentation already discussed was one factor. Also "The Sisters' Survey," undertaken by the Conference of Major Superiors of Women (CMSW, later to be called the LCWR), has been called "the most significant factor for the observable systematic deconstruction of juridical structures in institutes of women religious in America and for the undeniable progressive polarization of American women religious themselves."[110] "The Sisters' Survey" was undertaken without the knowledge of the Vatican and was published despite the Magisterium's avowed disapproval.[111] The questions posed by the survey reflected the beliefs of those who created it and, in this way, the study became a basis for shaping the direction of renewal.[112] For example, it is rather surprising to see how the vow of obedience is defined in "The Sisters' Survey:" "a promise to listen to the community as it speaks through many voices."[113] Even the meaning of law becomes relativistic: "All authentic law is by its very nature flexible and can be changed by the community in which it is operative."[114] Only a handful of examples are needed to convey the attitude present in "The Sister's Survey." Unfortunately, many religious were led astray by the false belief that they should disregard the authentic teachings of the Church and any legitimate authority, in the name of renewal. This directive of leadership implicated many women religious who had not chosen this alienation from the Church. Inevitably, as described by the 1985 Synod Report, this disregard led some religious communities to a loss of identity. "The Sisters' Survey" is cited here solely as an example of the misinterpretation of the ecclesial documents that led to defiance of the authority of the universal Church.

In some cases this alienation led some religious institutes to threaten to go *non-canonical,* to abandon their canonically recognized status. It is interesting that in some cases, the same religious who desire jurisdictional power do not wish to be associated with the ecclesiastical structure of the Church. Thomas Doyle, O.P., states that

> one often hears the threat to go *non-canonical* in reaction to the canonical requirement that certain basic elements of religious life be included in an institute's constitutions. In such cases open dialogue with the SCRIS on disputed points is necessary to prevent precipitous action. Such a dialogue must be predicated on what is best for the Church and not simply on what is good for some members of the community at this point in history. In remembering that religious are part of the church and not *the* Church, they should respond to the will of the Holy See with fidelity, knowing that the supreme authority is guided by the same Spirit that infused the Apostles.[115]

Doyle explains the consequences if the Holy See were to rescind the canonical status of a religious institute. First, the institute would no longer be a juridical person. Since the temporal goods of the institute belong not to the collective membership but to the juridic person, the Holy See would have the obligation to dispose of the goods.[116] Second, the vows of the members would continue unless the members asked for dispensation or transfer to another institute. Furthermore, there would be other complex civil problems regarding exemption from income taxes, civil incorporation, and accreditation and approbation of works. Doyle's article concludes with the words of John Paul II to the American Bishops in 1983:

> May everyone realize that the greatest misunderstanding of the charism of religious, indeed the greatest offense to their dignity and their person, would come from those who might try to situate their life or mission outside its ecclesial context. Religious are betrayed by anyone who would attempt to have them embrace teaching against the magisterium of the Church, who conceived them by her love and gave them birth in her liberating truth.[117]

Alienation from the Vatican, however, was not the experience of all religious institutes within the United States. Some communities sought to deepen their communion with the Church and to follow the teaching of the Magisterium. Following a Vatican meeting in March 1989 regarding American religious, James Cardinal Hickey reported that the LCWR did not represent the views of all religious institutes in the United States. Shortly after, Cardinal Hickey was appointed as official delegate of the Holy See to those institutes of active religious who embraced "a shared commitment to consecrated life as set forth by Vatican II."[118] On June 13, 1992, the Congregation for Institutes of Consecrated Life and Societies of Apostolic Life (CICLSAL) approved a second organization for major superiors of women in the United States, called the Council of Major Superiors of Women Religious (CMSWR). The Statutes of the CMSWR explain the purpose of the council:

> . . . to establish an effective collaboration among those major superiors who desire it, for fulfilling the nature, purpose, spirit, character and sound traditions of their particular institutes as sanctioned by competent ecclesiastical authority (c. 578), and as encompassing all the documents of the Second Vatican Council as well as post-conciliar documents on consecrated life. . . .

The CMSWR is a means of support to major superiors of institutes

> who stress community-lived profession of the vows and the transcendent nature of the consecrated life, . . . who look to the Magisterium, to the spirit of their founders/foundresses and to their wholesome traditions in determining future directions, . . . who view the role of the superior as fundamental to religious obedience based on faith.[119]

The light and shadow of renewal in religious institutes in the United States show the necessity for a clear understanding of the relationship between religious life and the Magisterium. The relationship is not the same as that of associations of the faithful or of secular institutes. As part of the "life and holiness" of the Church, religious are privileged to have the Holy Father as their highest superior and to have the assurance of being able to live daily vowed obedience.[120] Within this filial relationship of obedience, religious discover their true identity. This reality is more keenly experienced by each religious superior, whose autonomy is balanced by submission to the teachings of the Church, and whose power and authority spring from that source. The following document from the Congregation for Institutes of Consecrated Life and Societies of Apostolic Life offers profound insight into the evolution of the place of religious life in the Church.

"Fraternal Life in Community,"
Congregavit Nos in Unum Christi Amor

Fraternal Life in Community, issued by the Congregation for Institutes of Consecrated Life and Societies of Apostolic Life on February 2, 1994, offers criteria of discernment for fraternal life in common, upon which depends "the effectiveness of religious life."[121] Reflecting on "the renewed vision of religious community," the document singles out "the development of ecclesiology" as the prime factor for the "evolution of our understanding of religious life."[122] As the Church reflects upon herself, religious life is seen as part of her own "life and holiness."[123] *Fraternal Life* goes even farther in saying that religious life is at the heart of the Church's mystery of communion.[124] In paragraph 10, *Fraternal Life* quotes from an earlier document, *Religious and Human Promotion* "As 'experts in communion, religious are, therefore, called to be an ecclesial community in the Church and in the world, witnesses and architects of the plan for unity which is the crowning point of human history in God's design.'"[125]

With forthrightness the document examines the positive aspects of renewal that result in greater community participation and less rigid and formalistic lifestyles.[126] It also acknowledges the danger inherent in communities which have chosen to live with no one in charge or where all decisions are made collegially.[127] While these changes may be an attempt at collegiality, the document recalls that true fraternity cannot be a fruit of human effort alone. It is a gift of God, "a gift that comes from obedience to the Word of God, and also, in religious life, to the authority who reminds us of that Word and relates it to specific situations."[128] The presence of authority is not detrimental to fraternity, but rather "authority has as its main task building in unity the brothers and sisters of a fraternal community."[129] Faith alone allows us to understand this mystery of obedience, through which the obedience of the New Man brought salvation (see Romans 5:19).[130]

Fraternal Life in Community is directed to religious institutes who seek to improve the quality of their fraternal life. It also offers "reasons for reflection" for those who distanced themselves from the true understanding of community.[131] In 1999 Sister Doris Gottemoeller lamented the non-reception of this document by many in the United States. "The inability or unwillingness to answer the questions of what community living means today and what our common obligation or commitment is weakens our credibility internally and externally." Gottemoeller expressed her desire to "begin the conversation again."[132]

Fraternal Life in Community emphasized a critical distinction between religious and secular institutes. It is important to ponder whether the fraternal aspect of religious life, the call of religious to be "experts in communion" under the true authority of a religious superior, is at the heart of the distinction between religious consecration and secular consecration. Many of the documents on religious life that follow develop this mystery and the responsibility of religious to live the spirituality of communion.

The Synod on Consecrated Life

The concern of the bishops of the world for the reality of consecrated life became evident in their choice of the topic for the 1994 Synod.[133] As the Holy Father explained, following upon Synods for the Christian family (1980), the laity (1987), and the priesthood (1990), the Synod on Consecrated Life was to be the *kairos* moment for the integration of the conciliar texts.[134] There were "four great moments" of the Synod process: the *Lineamenta,* the *Instrumentum laboris,* the actual meetings of the Synod, and the post-synodal apostolic exhortation *Vita consecrata.*[135]

The *Lineamenta,* presented in November, 1992, was, as its Latin name describes, an outline of or general presentation on consecrated life with questions to promote further reflection. A *Lineamenta* has no magisterial authority; it is solely for the purpose of stimulating discussion. Nevertheless, the *Lineamenta* depends upon previous ecclesial documents. One section, titled "The Consecrated Life in the Church Communion," reflected upon religious as "experts in communion" by not only being with and in the Church, but "in feeling themselves to be the Church, identifying themselves with her." [136] The authenticity of this relationship is proved in the obedience rendered to "the Petrine ministry," in "loving communion and obedience to the Roman Pontiff," to the pastors of the Church, to the nature of one's institute, and to one's proper superior.[137]

This brief section on Church communion—which alone contains twenty-nine references to the canons of the 1983 *Code* and various Vatican documents—aroused tremendous controversy. It was considered by some to be a "return to the past" and criticized for its "defective legalistic ecclesiology," coming from a "rigid authoritarian perspective."[138] As a result, this section was extensively revised in the subsequent *Instrumentum laboris.* Those who opposed the *Lineamenta*'s section on ecclesial communion considered the expanded version in the *Instrumentum laboris* "less preceptorial and minatory in tone."[139]

Even the mild tone of the *Instrumentum laboris* did not win the approval of everyone. In an address to the Leadership Conference of Women Religious in August 1994, then president Sister Doris Gottemoeller spoke about the "ecclesial identity issue." She asked: "How significant is public membership and participation in the Church to our identity as apostolic women religious?"[140] While generations of sisters have wanted recognition, Gottemoeller continued, "How can we justify this continued commitment to public identification with the Church?"[141] This remark typifies other comments prevalent in the United States and denotes an effort to separate religious life from the Church herself. Yet, apart from the Church there is no religious life. Religious do not *choose to participate* in the Church; they *are part* of the Church. This message of the *Instrumentum laboris* would be developed in myriad ways by some participants in the 1994 Synod of Bishops, and it would be challenged by others.

As an immediate preparation for the Synod on Consecrated Life, Pope John Paul II offered a series of addresses during his general audiences. In his September 28, 1994, audience, John Paul II reiterated that while religious life does not belong to the hierarchal structure of the Church, it does "belong unquestionably to her life and holiness."[142] As a consequence, he continued, it is an "unshakable truth" that "this state of life will endure as an essential element of the Church's holiness."[143] In another address on October 12, 1994, John Paul II disagreed with those who consider the state of consecrated life as a purely human institution "that arose from the initiative of Christians who wanted to live the Gospel more deeply." While Jesus did not establish any religious communities, John Paul II explained, Jesus both wanted and established "the state of consecrated life in its overall value and essential elements."[144]

Pope John Paul II thus affirmed the divine origin of consecrated life, although it must be noted that he spoke of "the state of consecrated life" rather than religious life. This terminology causes some confusion, which was perpetuated in the post-synodal apostolic exhortation *Vita consecrata.*

Seventeen months after the closing of the Synod, Pope John Paul II promulgated *Vita consecrata,* which has been called the second Magna Carta on consecrated life. This exhortation is dedicated not only to religious, but to all those consecrated through the profession of the evangelical counsels—monastics, hermits, contemplatives, apostolic religious, secular institutes, and in anticipation of new forms of consecrated life—as well as for societies of apostolic life. *Vita consecrata* offers a profound interpretation of *Lumen gentium* 44 and states:

> This means that the consecrated life, present in the Church from the beginning, can never fail to be one of her essential and characteristic elements, for it expresses her very nature.[145]

Moreover, it continues:

> The idea of a Church made up only of sacred ministers and lay people does not therefore conform to the intentions of her divine Founder, as revealed to us by the Gospels and the other writings of the New Testament.[146]

Consecrated life is not separate, but will always be part of the Church. The Synod Fathers had expressed the desire for all the members of mixed religious institutes—those envisaged as a brotherhood with lay religious and priests—to have equal rights and obligations, with the exception of those which stem from sacred orders. Pope John Paul II did not accept this proposition. Rather, he announced the establishment of a commission to study the various questions involved.[147] John Paul II deliberately avoided addressing the question of lay jurisdiction, despite the request of the Synod Fathers. It is uncertain whether the commission was established.

It is interesting to note that *Vita consecrata* uses the quotation from *Religious and Human Promotion* on religious being *experts of communion,* but it substitutes "consecrated persons" for "religious":

> Consecrated persons are asked to be true experts of communion and to practice the spirituality of communion as "witnesses and architects of the plan for unity which is the crowning point of human history in God's design."[148]

It is unclear if this was an oversight or if the Holy Father really intended this quote to refer to all forms of consecrated life, even those that do not live a life in common. The instruction from the CICLSAL in 2002, *Starting Afresh from Christ,* again applies the quotation from *Vita consecrata* to all in consecrated life.[149] The instruction from the same Congregation in 2008, *At the Service of Authority and Obedience,* refers in general to the spirituality of communion "as the spiritual climate of the Church at the beginning of the Third Millennium," and entrusts this "as an active and exemplary task of religious life at all levels."[150] From the context it appears that the term *religious life,* as used in that sentence, means the mystery of the Church as communion. These instructions refer in general to consecrated life without specifying a unique role for consecrated religious. Therefore, the instructions do not resolve the questions regarding the origin of religious life, its differentiation from secular institutes, and the nature of the power of the superior.

CONCLUSION

After a consideration of the ecclesial documents promulgated after the 1983 *Code of Canon Law,* it can be seen that *Essential Elements* and *Vita consecrata* came closest in defining the divine origin of consecrated life. *Fraternal Life* hinted at a major distinction between religious and secular consecration when it called religious to witness to the spirituality of communion, but future documents obscured this understanding. There remains a need for the Holy See to clarify the uniqueness of each form of consecrated life and the nature of the power of the religious superior. Pope John Paul II said in *Vita consecrata* that a commission would be formed to study this question. As far as can be ascertained, this commission, if formed, has not resolved the issue of lay jurisdiction in religious institutes. The publication of books such as *Women and Jurisdiction* indicate a strong need for this question be addressed.

The Second Vatican Council firmly established the ecclesial dimension of religious life and, at the same time, opened a debate on the nature of religious consecration that has not yet ended. This book, written by sisters belonging to different religious institutes in the United States, seeks to revisit the vision of religious life, rooted in the rich tradition of the Church and the further unfolding of ecclesiology in the twentieth century. Religious in the United States depend upon the guidance of the Magisterium to rediscover the uniqueness of religious consecration as different from secular consecration in order to develop in continuity with the past a renewed theology of religious life.

NOTES

FOREWORD

1. *Perfectae caritatis*, October 28, 1965.
2. *"Faciem tuam, Domine, requiram."*
3. Instruction, "The Service of Authority and Obedience," May 11, 2008, no. 3.

INTRODUCTION

1. John Paul II, "Homily," May 9, 2001. Cited in Statutes CMSWR, 2 fn.
2. Schroeder, *Canons and Decrees,* 25th Session, 220–221.
3. *Normae,* I, VIII, no. 101, 1113.
4. Veermersch, 759.
5. Pius XII, "States of Perfection," 37–38.
6. Pius XII, "Allocution to Superiors General," 153.

ACKNOWLEDGMENTS

1. John Paul II, "Homily," 2 nf.

CHAPTER 1

1. Cf. Allen and O'Brien, "Appropriate Renewal," 253–254.
2. John Paul II, *Christifideles laici*, 10.
3. Ibid., 11.
4. Ibid., 12.
5. Cf. Tillard, *The Mystery of Religious Life*, 61.
6. Saint Augustine, *Sermo 13 de Tempore*, quoted in *Liturgy of the Hours Volume 1*, 541.
7. Ibid.
8. Cf. Cantalamessa, *Sober Intoxication of the Holy Spirit*, 41–47.
9. Ibid., 15. The section goes on to state: "The secular character of the lay faithful is not therefore to be defined only in a sociological sense, but most especially in a theological sense. The term *secular* must be understood in light of the act of God the creator and redeemer, who has handed over the world to women and men, so that they may participate in the work of creation, free creation from the influence of sin and sanctify themselves in marriage or the celibate life, in a family, in a profession, and in the various activities of society."
10. John Paul II, *Vita consecrata*, 16, see also 31.
11. Canon 573.
12. Canon 713.
13. *Catechism of the Catholic Church (CCC)*, 925.
14. Sacred Congregation for Religious and Secular Institutes (SCRSI), *Essential Elements*, 6.
15. John Paul II, Audience, Rome, 1994. The passage continues: "In a similar way, it can be said that the profession of the evangelical counsels further develops the consecration received in the Sacrament of Confirmation. It is a new gift of the Holy Spirit, conferred for the sake of an active Christian life in a closer bond of collaboration and service to the Church in order to produce, through the evangelical counsels, new fruits of holiness and apostleship in addition to the demands of the consecration received in Confirmation. The Sacrament of Confirmation—and the character of Christian soldiering and Christian apostleship that it entails—is also at the root of the consecrated life."
16. Ibid.

17. John Paul II, *Vita consecrata*, 30.
18. Gambari, *Religious Life*, 91.
19. John Paul II, *Redemptionis donum*, 7. See also *CCC*, 1214, 1239.
20. Cf. Tillard, *Religious Life*, 80–84: "What is the baptismal perfection to which religious life constantly tends? First and essentially, it is the impregnation in us and the sealing of us with the Pasch of the Lord Jesus in its two inseparable moments of death and resurrection. . . . But this is not primarily a 'conquest' by strength of arm, a mobilization of all one's energies for the reproduction of an external model that is transcendent and actually always inaccessible. It is rather a mystery that is completely interior. It is a mustering of oneself in order to permit one to be gradually fashioned by the paschal power of the Lord who wishes to 'assimilate' us to Himself, to make us become Him, to lead us to an ever more realistic and total communion in His death-resurrection. Baptism and subsequently the eucharist have sown in us, as it were, a paschal seed that seeks to overcome us. Christ wishes to imitate Himself in us. . . . If to sanctify oneself means essentially to 'reproduce' Christ in oneself, this is not a matter of copying an external model but of an imitation through 'active communion' with the Lord who seeks to assimilate us to Himself. Radically, 'to imitate Christ' is to permit oneself to be penetrated by the power of His Pasch. . . . It is then a death that is an invitation as the death and dissolution of a grain of wheat are an invitation of the ripened ear. The more there grows in us the detachment from everything that shuts us within ourselves and that thus prevents us from giving ourselves to God, the more and to the same measure is there inscribed in the void the image of the Lord Jesus rising up from the death and pervaded by the glory of the Father."
21. John Paul II, *Vita consecrata*, 76.
22. John Paul II, *Redemptionis donum*, 3.
23. John Paul II, *Vita consecrata*, 14.
24. Because of the uniqueness of each vocation, the means of conversion are also specific to each person. One can become reliant on feelings or external signs and miss the critical moment of responding to God's call. The response is always to that which is deeper, and it involves sacrifice.
25. Benedict XVI, Address, Rome, 2007. The full passage states: "Your Gospel witness, to be truly effective, must stem from a response without reserve to the initiative of God who has consecrated you to Him with a special act of love. . . . Those who are chosen by God for the consecrated life make this spiritual longing their own in a definitive way. In it, in fact, they have one expectation: the Kingdom of God—that God reign in our will, in our hearts, in the world. In them burns a unique thirst for love that can only be quenched by the Eternal One alone."
26. John Paul II, *Vita consecrata*, 18. "Those who let themselves be seized by this love cannot help abandoning everything to follow him" (cf. Mt 1:16–20; 2:14; 10:21, 28).
27. Cabasilas, *Life in Christ*, quoted in Ratzinger, *On the Way*, 35.
28. SCRSI, *Essential Elements*, norms.
29. John Paul II, *Vita consecrata*, 18. See chapter 3 of this book in which Sr. Mary Dominic develops Saint Thomas's understanding of the act of religious consecration as comparable to that of a holocaust.
30. John Paul II, Audience, Rome, 1994.
31. Benedict XVI, Address, Cologne, 2005.
32. SCRSI, *Essential Elements*, 5.
33. Benedict XVI, *Spe salvi*, 27.
34. Cole and Conner, *Christian Totality*, 37–38.
35. Paul VI, *Evangelica testificatio*, 7.
36. Paul VI, *Perfectae caritatis*, 5.
37. Gambari, 88.
38. SCRSI, *Essential Elements*, 8.
39. Paul VI, *Evangelica testificatio*, 33: "The importance of the surroundings in which one lives should not be underestimated either in relation to the habitual orientation of the whole person—so complex and

divided—in the direction of God's call, or in relation to the spiritual integration of the person's tendencies. Does not the heart often allow itself to cling to what is passing?"

40. Cole and Conner, 53. See also Paul VI, *Evangelica testificatio*, 34: "In the present disarray, it is especially necessary for religious to give witness as persons whose vital striving to attain their goal—the living God—has effectively created unity and openness in the depth and steadfastness of their life in God. This is accomplished by the integration of all their faculties, the purification of their thoughts, and the spiritualization of their senses."

41. *CCC*, 925.

42. Canon 607, #1.

43. Canon 607, #2–3.

44. SCRSI, *Essential Elements*, 10. "The very nature of religious vocation involves a public witness to Christ and to the Church. Religious profession is made by vows which the Church receives as public. A stable form of community life . . . manifests in a visible way the covenant and communion which religious life expresses. A certain separation from family and from professional life at the time a person enters the novitiate speaks powerfully of the absoluteness of God. . . . A further aspect of the public nature of religious consecration is that the apostolate of religious is in some sense always corporate. Religious presence is visible, affecting ways of acting, attire, and style of life."

45. Ibid., 1317.

46. Ibid., 32–37.

47. Ibid.,18–22.

48. Ibid., 10, 34.

49. Ibid., 23–27.

50. Cf. Paul VI, *Ordo professionis religiosae*. This is to be distinguished from members of secular institutes who profess to live the evangelical counsels by "sacred" bonds, promises, or in some cases by vow to their institutes, that are not public in nature; and from members of societies of apostolic life who establish "some" bond or promise with their society less radical than vows or sacred promises and may or may not embrace the evangelical counsels (see canons 607, 712, 731).

51. Gambari, 94. See also 101: "The position of religious in the Church has its own configuration, placing them in a category juridically distinct from that of the laity and of the clergy."

52. Paul VI, *Lumen gentium*, 43; Paul VI, *Evangelica testificatio*, 37: John Paul II, *Redemptionis donum*, 4; John Paul II, *Vita consecrata*, 35. (Cf. Thomas Aquinas, *Summa theologiae* II–II q. 184, a. 5, ad 2; II–II q. 186, a. 2, ad 1).

53. Schleck, *The Theology of Vocations*, 98, quoting Thomas Aquinas, II–II, q. 184, a.4.

54. Gambari, 42. Due to misunderstandings about the meaning of the term *way* or *state* of perfection, it has fallen out of common usage. However, John Paul II used the term in both *Redemptionis donum* #4 and *Vita consecrata* #35. In the latter, way or state of perfection is defined in terms of the effective wealth of means that are proper to this form of evangelical life, combined with the "particular commitment" of those who occupy such a state.

55. Gambari, 107.

56. Paul VI, *Lumen gentium*, 44.

57. Canon 607.

58. John Paul II, *Redemptionis donum*, 8.

59. See Cole and Conner, "Consecrated Life," *Religious Life Magazine*, March/April 2007, 19–20. We are grateful for the canonical analysis provided by Sister Joseph Marie, on this point.

60. Canon 1191; *CCC*, 2102.

61. Schleck, 336, referring to St. Thomas Aquinas, III, Q. 65, a.1.

62. Cole and Conner, 36, quoting John Paul II, "While conjugal love goes to Christ the Bridegroom through a human union, virginal love goes directly to the person of Christ through an immediate union with him without intermediaries: a truly complete and decisive spiritual espousal."

63. Schleck, 338. The passage continues: "It is an event in and through which something proper to eternity, to our first meeting with Christ in heaven takes place by way of anticipation here on earth. . . . Indeed, in a sense it would be unfitting for there to be a sacramental sign because the heavenly nature of this vocation and way of life would be somewhat diminished and it would be brought into the realm of earthly states and realities."

64. Ibid., 339. See also Tillard, 20: "Religious life is a presence of the eschatological kingdom. . . . It is at the front of the advancing Church, the point where the dynamism toward the Parousia attains its maximum intensity and where the thrust of the kingdom toward universality is felt to its fullest."

65. Tillard, 55–56. See also *Vita consecrata,* 20: "The first duty of the consecrated life is to make visible the marvels wrought by God in the frail humanity of those who are called. They bear witness to these marvels not so much in works as by the eloquent language of a transfigured life, capable of amazing the world. To people's astonishment, they respond by proclaiming the wonders of grace accomplished by the Lord in those whom he loves. . . .The consecrated life thus becomes one of the tangible seals which the Trinity impresses upon history, so that people can sense with longing the attraction of divine beauty."

66. John Paul II, *Vita consecrata,* 72.

67. Benedict XVI, *Spe salvi,* 31.

68. John Paul II, *Vita consecrata,* 25. For young people called out of a world "sensitive to the language of signs" to the radicality of religious consecration, only the great traditions in religious life that incorporate the past century's growth in the knowledge of the human sciences promise the possibility of an adequate and authentic response of love to the call to religious consecration.

69. Cole and Conner, 248.

70. Congregation for Institutes of Consecrated Life and Societies of Apostolic Life (CICLSAL), *Fraternal Life in Community*, 8.

71. Ibid., 9.

72. CICLSAL, "Jubilee of the Consecrated Life," appendix I.B.

73. Cf. *CCC,* 1324; Paul VI, *Lumen gentium,* 11.

74. The necessity to be formed in the common life suggests the importance for structures of support within religious life that provide for the realization of human potentials necessary for the mature participation and contribution of members to the common striving of a community. Common life is a particular means for communion with God, necessitating life-long formation and formative dialogue. In recent years, writings regarding the dignity of the human person and recognition of the service of obedience and authority have contributed to an awareness of the necessity to develop continually common life.

75. CICLSAL, *Fraternal Life in Community*, 54: "Along with sending them to preach the Gospel to every creature (Mt. 28:19–20), the Lord sent his disciples to live together 'so that the world may believe' that Jesus is the one sent by the Father and that we owe him the full assent of faith (Jn. 17:21). The sign of fraternity is then of the greatest importance because it is the sign that points to the divine origin of the Christian message and has the power to open hearts to faith. For this reason, 'the effectiveness of religious life depends on the quality of the fraternal life in common.'"

76. In the past fifty years, the community of persons in marriage and family life has been under serious attack. Our culture increasingly esteems wealth and power and idealizes self and pleasure over loving commitments, interdependence in relationship, and the value of sacrifice. The result has been the institutionalization of the phenomenon of separation as a response to difficulties encountered in living out what we understand as the blessing of God-given community. Witness the prevalence of divorce, widespread use of contraception in marriage, and fears that drive us to the killing of the most vulnerable among us. These highlight only a few of the most notable attacks on the communion of persons in our culture.

77. John Paul II, *Vita consecrata,* 46.

78. Benedict XVI, *Deus caritas Est,* 39. The full passage reads: "Faith, which sees the love of God revealed in the pierced heart of Jesus on the Cross, gives rise to love. Love is the light—and in the end, the only light—that can always illuminate a world grown dim and give us the courage needed to keep living and

working. Love is possible, and we are able to practice it because we are created in the image of God. To experience love and in this way to cause the light of God to enter into the world—this is the invitation I would like to extend with the present Encyclical."

79. Canon 607.

80. This is in contrast to those living the evangelical counsels in secular institutes whose way of life is to be lived as a hidden leaven sanctifying the world from within.

81. Canon 608; 667; 669.

82. Benedict XVI, *Angelus,* Lourdes, 2008.

83. John Paul II, *Evangelium vitae,* 83. The section continues: "It is the outlook of those who see life in its deeper meaning, who grasp its utter gratuitousness, its beauty and its invitation to freedom and responsibility. It is the outlook of those who do not presume to take possession of reality but instead accept it as a gift, discovering in all things the reflection of the Creator and seeing in every person his living image (cf. Gen. 1:27; Ps. 8:5). This outlook does not give in to discouragement when confronted by those who are sick, suffering, outcast, or at death's door. Instead, in all these situations it feels challenged to find meaning, and precisely in these circumstances it is open to perceiving in the face of every human person a call to encounter, dialogue and solidarity."

84. Cf. Gambari 396–410. "It is especially in regard to this 'way of living, of praying, and of working' that Vatican II calls for *aggiornamento* (cf. *Perfectae caritatis* 3–4); while instead, renewal aims at developing the very content of religious life," 398.

85. SCRSI, *Essential Elements,* 25; Paul VI, *Perfectae caritatis,* 8; John Paul II, *Redemptionis donum,* 15.

86. Ibid. The section goes on to state: "They must see that the institute is at once faithful to its traditional mission in the Church and open to new ways of undertaking it. Works need to be renewed and revitalized, but this has to be done always in fidelity to the institute's approved apostolate and in collaboration with the respective ecclesiastical authorities. Such renewal will be marked by the four great loyalties emphasized in the document, *Religious and Human Promotion*: 'fidelity to humanity and to our times; fidelity to Christ and to the Gospel; fidelity to the Church and its mission in the world; fidelity to religious life and to the charism of the institute' (*Religious and Human Promotion* 13)."

87. Ibid., 26.

88. Ratzinger, *Salt of the Earth,* 269.

89. Clarke, *St. Thérèse of Lisieux,* 57.

CHAPTER 2

1. Flor Peeters is an esteemed twentieth-century Flemish composer and adviser to Vatican Council II. *Ipsi Sum:* musical composition often sung at profession of the vows.

2. Clare of Assisi, First Letter to Agnes of Prague, *Clare of Assisi Early Documents,* #8.

3. Martin, *The Feminist Question,* 224.

4. Ibid., 263.

5. Origen, *Commentary on the Song of Songs II,* 134.

6. Congregation for Divine Worship, *Rite of Consecration of Virgins.*

7. John Paul II, *Mulieris dignitatem,* 22.

8. Augustine, *De doctrina Christiana,* 15–122.

9. Bonaventure, 1259–1260a: 302b, *Itinerarium* 2.11. "*Sunt vestigia simulacra et spectacula nobis ad contuendum Deum proposita et signa divinitus data; quae, inquam, sunt exemplaria vel potius exemplata, proposita mentibus adhuc rudibus et sensibilibus, ut per sensibilia, quae vident, transferantur ad intelligibilia, quae non vident, tanquam per signa ad signata.*" See also Bonaventure 1254a: *De sci. Chr.,* q. 4, concl., and ad 16; 1273a: *Hexaëmeron,* Coll. 2, n.9; 1254–57: *Christus unus Omn. Magister,* n. 17.

10. Hellman, *Divine and Created Order in Bonaventure's Theology,* 15.

11. Abbott, *Lumen gentium,* #1.

12. John Paul II, *Theology of the Body,* 76.
13. "But every sign consists in the three-cornered *relation itself* connecting the sign at one and the same time to the mind and to the object signified." Deely, *Four Ages of Understanding*, 219.
14. Ibid., 442.
15. Ibid., 585.
16. Bonaventure, *Breviloquium,* V, 211a. Cf. Miller, Sister Paula Jean, *Marriage: The Sacrament of Divine-Human Communion, A Commentary on St. Bonaventure's Breviloquium,* 1996.
17. John Paul II, *Mulieris dignitatem*, #20.
18. Deely, 585.
19. Genesis 2:21–24, John 19:34, Ephesians 5:32. These texts inspired the patristic notion of the integral nature of the Church as a marital covenant with God.
20. John Paul II, *Mulieris dignitatem*, #20.
21. Pius XII, *Sacra virginitas,* #31. "The greatest glory of virgins is undoubtedly to be the living images of the perfect integrity of the union between the Church and her divine Spouse. For this society founded by Christ it is a profound joy that virgins should be the marvelous sign of its sanctity and fecundity."
22. Ibid., #30.
23. John Paul II, *Theology of the Body,* 269.
24. Schleck, *The Theology of Vocations,* 130.
25. Ibid., 131.
26. Pardilla, *Christ's Way of Life,* 79–80.
27. Song of Songs 4:12 "She is a garden enclosed, my sister, my promised bride; a garden enclosed, a sealed fountain."
28. Ratzinger, "Letter on the Collaboration of Men and Women," #9.
29. Isaiah 54:5 "For your Maker is your husband, the Lord of hosts is his name; the Holy One of Israel is your Redeemer, the God of the whole earth he is called."
30. John Paul II, *Mulieris dignitatem*, #26.
31. John Paul II, *Theology of the Body,* 314.
32. Ratzinger, *Called to Communion,* 39.
33. For a detailed development of the complementarity of missions, see author's *Members of One Body, Prophets, Priests, Kings, An Ecclesiology of Mission* (New York: Alba House), 1999.
34. Grygiel, *Virginity and Marriage, Two Expressions of the Spousal Sovereignty of Man,* 5.
35. Ibid., 9.
36. John Paul II, *Theology of the Body,* 279.
37. John Paul II, *Mulieris dignitatem*, #21.
38. Ambrose, *De virginibus,* 7 PL XVI: 272.
39. Augustine, *De sancta virginitate,* PL XL: 55.
40. John Chrysostom, *De virginitate,* PG XLVIII: 80.
41. John Paul II, *Theology of the Body,* 267; 285; 281; 282.
42. Fulgentius, *Epist*.3, c. 4, n.6; PL LXV.
43. Schleck, 339.
44. *Lucae,* 15:34 (VII, 395b). "*Istius deosculationis origo est in Verbo incarnate, in quo est unio summi amoris et connexionis duplicis naturae, per quam Deus no osculatur, et no Deum deosculamur.*"
45. *II Sent.,* d.29, a.2, q.2 (II, 702a). "*De gratia per quam fit matrimonium inter Deum et animam.*"
46. *Breviloquium,* Pars V, c.1 (V, 252a). "*Ipsa nihilominus est donum, per quod anima perficitur et efficitur sponsa Christi, filia Patris aeterni et templum Spiritus sancti.*"
47. *De triplici via,* c.1, n.213 (VIII, 6b). "*Tertio, quod dedit Spiritum sanctum insignaculum acceptationis, in privilegium adoptionis, in anulum desponsationis. Fecit enim animam christianam suam amicam, suam filiam, suam sponsam.*"

48. *Breviloquium,* Pars V, c. 1 (V, 253a).

49. *Sermones detempore,* "In nativitate Domini," Sermo I (IX, 108b). *De primo, Genesis secundo: "Erunt duo in carne una," scilicet Deus et homo. Istud commercium fuit contractum per carnis assumtionem; unde dicere possumus illud Genesis secundo: "Hoc nunc os ex ossibus meis et caro de carne mea."*

50. *Tractatus de plantatione paradisi,* n.15 (V, 578b). *"Ut post sextam diem collocetur in paradisi, in quo per contemplationem quiescens et dormiens, ad spiritualis connubii perducatur arcanum, ubi vere absconduntur, tanquam thesauri sapientiae et scientiae, copiae multiformes atque spirituales et inaestimabiles deliciae paradisi."*

51. *Soliloquium,* c.2, n.16 (VIII, 50b–51a). *"Et tandem quieta et somnolenta, recumbens in amplexibus divinis, cum laeva Sponsi sponsam sub capite amicabiliter sustentat, et dextera Dilecti dilectam familiariter amplexatur."*

52. *Legenda maior,* (VIII, 505a).

53. Pegis, "St. Bonaventure, St. Francis and Philosophy," 3.

54. *Legenda maior,* VIII, c.9.1 (VIII, 530a).

55. *Breviloquium,* Pars IV, c.1 (V, 241b).

56. *Vita mystica,* c. 4, n.3 (VIII, 167a).

57. *De perfectione vitae ad sorores,* I.1 (VIII.8).

58. John Paul II, *Redemptionis donum,* #2.

59. Ibid. #3.

60. Ratzinger, *Donum vitae,* #41.

61. *Congregavit nos in unum Christi amor,* #10.

62. John Paul II, *Redemptionis donum,* #5.

63. Ibid.

64. Ibid., #7.

65. *Congregavit nos,* #3.

66. Ibid., #10; emphasis added.

67. John Paul II, *Redemptionis donum,* #7.

68. Ibid., #8.

69. Ibid.

70. Ibid.

71. Ibid.

72. Ibid., #9.

73. John Paul II, *Theology of the Body,* 292.

74. John Paul II, *Redemptionis donum,* #10.

75. Ibid., #13.

76. Ibid., #5.

77. John Paul II, *Vita consecrata,* #3.

78. Ibid., #16.

79. Ibid., #40.

80. Ibid., #18.

81. Ibid., #34.

82. Ibid., #18.

83. Ibid., #35, emphasis added.

84. Ibid., #18, emphasis added.

85. Ibid., #72.

86. Ibid., #19.

87. Ibid., emphasis added.
88. Ibid., #20, emphasis added.
89. Ibid., #105.
90. Ibid., #36.
91. Ibid., #103.
92. John Paul II, *Mulieris dignitatem*, #20.
93. Ibid., #25.
94. Ibid., #21.
95. Stein, *Woman*, 62.

CHAPTER 3

1. *Lumen gentium*, 44.
2. John Paul II, *Vita consecrata*, 14.
3. Ibid.,16.
4. Montalembert, *Monks of the West*, 171.
5. Emily F. Bowden, *The Fathers of the Desert*, 52, 54, 61.
6. Festugière, *La Première Vie grecque de saint Pachôme [Vita Prima]*, quoted in Rousseau, *Pachomius*, 100–101.
7. Montalembert, *Monks of the West*, 337.
8. *Religious Sisters*, 11–12.
9. Thomas Aquinas, *Summa theologiae* II–II, Q. 186 a.7.
10. *Lumen gentium*, 39.
11. Ibid., 44.
12. Ibid.
13. Ibid., 46.
14. John Paul II, *Vita consecrata*, 16.
15. John Paul II, *Redemptionis donum*, 9.
16. *Lumen gentium*, 44.
17. Canon 573.
18. Canon 607§2.
19. Thomas Aquinas, *Summa theologiae* II–II, Q. 88, a. 6.
20. Ibid.
21. Ibid., Q. 184, a. 5; Q. 186 a. 1.
22. Ibid., Q 81, a. 6; Q. 186 a. 6.
23. *Lumen gentium*, 42.
24. Thomas Aquinas, *Summa theologiae* II–II Q. 88 a.6, c.
25. *Lumen gentium*, 44.
26. Ibid., 45.
27. Gambari, *Journey Toward Renewal*, 68.
28. *Lumen gentium*, 44.
29. Ibid., 43.
30. Ibid.
31. Ibid., 45.
32. John Paul II, *Redemptionis donum*, 8.
33. *Catechism of the Catholic Church*, 2332.
34. John Paul II, *Original Unity*, 43.
35. Ibid., 139.

36. John Paul II, *Redemptionis donum*, 11.

37. *Perfectae caritatis*, 12.

38. John Paul II, *Original Unity*, 43.

39. Paul VI, *Sacerdotalis caelibatus*, 50.

40. Ibid., 24.

41. John Paul II, *Redemptionis donum*, 11.

42. *Perfectae caritatis*, 12.

43. Ibid.

44. Paul VI, *Evangelica testificatio*, 13.

45. *Perfectae caritatis*, 12.

46. Paul VI, *Evangelica testificatio*, 15.

47. Cf. ibid., 13.

48. Ibid.

49. *Perfectae caritatis*, 12.

50. *Lumen gentium*, 42, quoted in Paul VI, *Evangelica testificatio*, 14.

51. John Paul II, *Vita consecrata*, 15.

52. Roland de Vaux, *Les Institutions de l'Ancien Testament*, 342, quoted in Lucien 53. Legrand, *The Biblical Doctrine of Virginity*, 82–83.

53. Cf. *Perfectae caritatis*, 12.

54. Canon 599.

55. Canon 607§1.

56. John Paul II, *Vita consecrata*, 26.

57. Ibid., 21.

58. Fribourg, Fribourg, and Miller, eds. *Analytical Lexicon of the Greek New Testament*, s.v. "kleronomos."

59. Pinckaers, *The Pursuit of Happiness God's Way*, 49.

60. Gambari, *Religious Life*, 284.

61. Sacred Congregation for Religious and Secular Institutes, *Essential Elements*, 16.

62. Canon 668§1–5.

63. *Perfectae caritatis*, 13.

64. Legrand, *The Biblical Doctrine of Virginity*, 62

65. St. Catherine of Siena, *Le lettere di santa Catarina da Siena*, Letter 29.

66. Hans Urs von Balthasar, *the Christian State of Life*, 154.

67. Thomas Aquinas, *Summa theologiae* II–II, Q. 186, a.3.

68. Ibid., a. 3, c.

69. Canon 600.

70. *Perfectae caritatis*, 13.

71. Ibid., emphasis added.

72. Paul VI, *Evangelica testificatio*, 19.

73. Ibid., 22.

74. Ibid., 22, 18.

75. Ibid., 18.

76. John Paul II, *Vita consecrata*, 90.

77. Ibid.

78. *Perfectae caritatis*, 13.

79. Paul VI, *Evangelica testificatio*, 21.

80. Ibid.

81. *Perfectae caritatis*, 14.

82. Paul VI, *Evangelica testificatio,* 29.

83. Ibid., 23.

84. Ibid., 27.

85. Ibid., 24.

86. John Paul II, *Redemptionis donum,* 13.

87. Ferdinand Valentine, *Religious Obedience,* 46.

88. Thomas Aquinas, *Adoro te domine.* ca. 1224–1274; tr. by Gerard Manley Hopkins, S.J., 1844–1899. Music: Chant, Mode V; Paris Processionale, 1697.

89. Congregation for Institutes of Consecrated Life and Societies of Apostolic Life, *Faciem tuam,* 19.

90. *Perfectae caritatis,* 14.

91. Ibid., 146, emphasis added; Schneiders, *New Wineskins,* 141, 151.

92. Quoted in Cole & Conner, *Christian Totality,* 155.

93. *Lumen gentium,* 43, quoted in Paul VI, *Evangelica testificatio,* 27; *Perfectae caritatis,* 14, quoted in Paul VI, *Evangelica testificatio,* 27, emphasis added.

94. *Lumen gentium,* 46.

95. *Perfectae caritatis,* 14.

96. Ibid.

97. Ibid., 15.

98. Ibid.,14.

99. Congregation for Institutes of Consecrated Life and Societies of Apostolic Life, *Fraternal Life in Community,* 44.

100. Ibid.

101. John Paul II, *Vita consecrata,* 92.

102. *Perfectae caritatis,* 14.

103. John Paul II, *Vita consecrata,* 43.

104. Congregation for Institutes of Consecrated Life and Societies of Apostolic Life, *Fraternal Life in Community,* 48.

105. Ibid.

106. Cf. *Catechism of the Catholic Church,* 470, which points out that "The Son of God . . . communicates to his humanity his own personal mode of existence in the Trinity. In his soul as in his body, Christ thus expresses humanly the divine ways of the Trinity."

107. John Paul II, *Vita consecrata,* 16.

108. Ibid., 21.

109. Ibid., 16.

110. Ibid, 21.

111. Cole and Conner, *Christian Totality*, 147.

CHAPTER 4

1. Congregation for the Doctrine of the Faith, *Letter to the Bishops of the Catholic Church on Some Aspects of the Church Understood as Communion,* 19. See also 1: "A deeper appreciation of the fact that the Church is a Communion is, indeed, a task of special importance. . . ." For John Paul II's discussions of the Second Vatican Council and *communio,* see Karol Wojtyla, *Sources of Renewal* (New York: Collins, 1980), 4.3, 133–54.

2. Ibid., 3.

3. CICL, *Fraternal Life in Community*, 10. Emphasis added.

4. John Paul II, *Vita consecrata,* 46.

5. CICL, *Starting Afresh from Christ,* 28.

6.   Ibid.

7.   Ibid.

8.   CICL, *Fraternal Life in Community*, 58.

9.   See Lonergan, "The Unity of Man," 538–42.

10. Lonergan, "Human Development," in *Insight*, 494. Other philosophers who make a similar kind of argument include M. A. Krapiec, O.P., Edith Stein, O.C.D., and Msgr. Robert Sokolowski.

11. See the false alternative expressed by Chittister, "Remember the Vision; Embracing the Dream," p. 4 and 5: "Vatican II . . . was a vision of participation in decision-making, or community rather than hierarchical monarchy."

12. See the feminist overload and polarization in Ibid.: "If we proclaim ourselves to be ecclesial women we must ask if what we mean by this is that we will do what the men of the church tells us to do or that we will do what the people of the church need to have us to do." See also Schneiders overt feminist ideology in interpreting various vocations in the Church, "Self Determination and Self- Direction," 163: "No doubt it was the new and positive approach to the world which first exposed many women religious to a new cultural movement that would change their lives: feminism. Religious began to analyze the patriarchal structures of the church and to repudiate male domination of their own life and that of others."

13. Plato describes pure democrats as "devotees of equality," see Hamilton and Cairns, *Republic, The Collected Dialogues of Plato Including the Letters*, Book VIII, 1292a 11 and 23–24. Aristotle distinguishes between five different kinds of democracy in *Politics* 1291b30–1293a30. The pure democracy tends to produce demagogues, "where the laws are not supreme, there demagogues spring up. . . . The demagogues make the decrees of the people override the laws, by referring all things to the popular assembly."

14. For contemporary description of different kinds of democracies, see Yves Simon, *Philosophy of Democratic Government* (Notre Dame, University of Notre Dame Press, 1993); James P. Kelly, III, ed., *Christianity, Democracy, and the American Ideal: A Jacques Maritain Reader* (Manchester, New Hampshire: Sophia Institute Press, 2004); and for a consideration of the values and laws associated with different kinds of states see Edith Stein, *An Investigation Concerning the State* (Washington DC: ICS Publications, 2006).

15. SCRSI, *Essential Elements*, 49. See also, Chapter 9: Government, nos. 49–52.

16. Ibid., 51. See also, *The Service of Authority and Obedience*, #3: "Finally one must not forget that consecrated life commonly sees, in the 'synodal' figure of the general chapter (or of analogous gatherings), the supreme authority of the institute, to which all the members beginning with the superiors, must make reference."

17. Gambari, *Renewal in Religious Life,* 83–84. See also, "Manner or System of Government," 78–79.

18. For developments and difficulties in governing structures related to "A new concept of the human person [which] emerged in the immediate wake of the Council" and "New governing structures [which] emerged from revised constitutions. . . ," see CICL, *Fraternal Life in Community*, 5d and e.

19. Schneiders, in *Finding the Treasure*, 62, again using falsely exaggerated categories describes it this way: "*Evolution*: A life form evolves as its constitutive coordinates develop, that is, as they change or are reformulated in a process of mutual and reciprocal modification in response to the stimuli of the environment. For example, as the understanding by contemporary women Religious of the relationship between leaders and members changed, under the influence of changes in both the theological and cultural environment of the Church, from divine-right monarchy to egalitarian and collegial interaction, major changes occurred in the way ministries were selected. As ministries were selected differently, changes occurred in how living situations were determined, which led to a diversification in the understanding of community life. Uniform common life shared only by members of the same congregation who lived together in a common dwelling ceased to be the only conceivable realization of community. This has led to new relationships among members of various congregations and with laypeople, which has contributed to the present reexamination of issues of membership."

20. See Ibid., 54–55, where Schneiders argues by setting up an artificial middle option between two false alternatives that her evolutionary model "falls nicely" between two other opposing models: (1) "an ontological Platonic and essentialist model" and (2) "a mechanical, aggregational health club model."

21. Pitts discussion of *Faciem tuam* in this book, chapter 3, p. 35 [manuscript].

22. John Paul II, *Vita consecrata*, 43.

23. See CICL, *The Service of Authority and Obedience*, especially #20.

24. See this artificial understanding of vows in Farley, *Beginning, Keeping, Changing Personal Commitments*, 23. The Cover of this Book has a different set of subtitles: *Making, Keeping, Breaking Personal Commitments.* Farley argues this point about relations of love and friendship: "Explicit, expressed commitments to love someone are not just prime cases for understanding what it means to make a commitment. They are also particularly clear cases for understanding what free choice can do when it comes to influencing within ourselves a human emotion like love. Presumably, the point of making a commitment to love is to do what all commitments aim to do: set up a relationship in which we are obligated to a word given as a pledge—obligated to keep on loving as we have promised into the future. Here, then, are all the questions we have previously seen of whether or not a choice now for the future can be effective in any way; and whether, insofar as such a choice is effective, it contradicts and undermines the love it intends to preserve."

25. See this contrary position in Ibid., 24: "This kind of love has always had a reputation for fleetingness. That is why it was considered necessary—if some such relationships were to continue—to stabilize them by moving them into institutional frameworks like the traditional institution of marriage or a vowed and regulated life in community. Today, however, in our society, not even this strategy offers the strong supportive base that seems needed. Institutions no longer 'carry themselves.' It tends to be the case, rather, each loving relationship and each specific commitment must 'carry the institution.' Can commitment as such, however, really promise a future to love?"

26. For this suggestion see, for example, Ibid., 90: "That is, if what makes it impossible to go on in a commitment-relationship is the particular framework that structures the relationship, then restructuring—even radical restructuring—may restore possibility. 'Framework' has many levels of meaning, of course. There is the level at which, for example, 'marriage' and 'religious congregation' and 'friendship,' are frameworks that structure our relationships into generic forms.*"*

27. Ibid., 113. After listing six different formulations of the meaning of God's covenant, Farley basically undermines the possibility of covenant when she states: "Each of these statements needs careful consideration, since each represents a claim that is not only complex but in some way debatable."

28. See Ibid., 98, where the false understanding of the source of vocation as coming from human beings rather than from God is presupposed: "Why do we tie our commitments to love with commitments to certain frameworks for love (frameworks like marriage, religious community, special causes and projects)? . . . [W]e commit ourselves to love at least partly because we want to stabilize our loves in the midst of the fickleness of our feelings. We want to give our loves a future by embodying them in a framework that makes ongoing demands upon us, that keeps us together and with one another and attentive and awake, that allows us to share our lives and to grow as we collaborate in mutual concern and mutual enterprise."

29. See Farley, *Personal Commitments*, 138, where she obliquely refers to Whitehead in chapter 4, note 3.

30. See Greeve Davaney, *Feminism and Process Thought*, 3, introduction, "The vision of reality developed by Alfred North Whitehead and proponents of the process school of thought offers a metaphysical system based on an understanding of the self. . . . For Whitehead all our conceptions must start with experiencing subjects. Whitehead understands these experiencing subjects as units or momentary instances of process and analyzes them under two broad aspects—as subjects for themselves in the immediacy of their own experience and as objects available to contribute to subsequent experiencing subjects."

31. See Ibid., 1–2, for some important aspects of this association. "Interchange between feminism and process thought is significant because both make common assertions and share fundamental presuppositions. Both thoroughly reject traditional Western ways of conceiving of self, world, and God. Both assert that Western humanity has primarily understood the world dualistically and [as a] patterned reality hierarchically."

32. See, for example, Ibid., 3: "Women are presently reclaiming our right to self-definition and, indeed, our right to contribute to the definition of reality itself. . . ."
33. Even though Lonergan very well understood the importance of conjugate and central forms, which give a stable identity for processes, and for the cycles of progress and decline (See *Insight*, 538–44 and 251–61); Schneiders, erroneously suggests that Bernard Lonergan's description of "historical-mindedness" promoted this process view of religious reality. In her words: "What Bernard Lonergan has called 'historical-mindedness' is the result of the period of experimentation. Change is not a path to some future state of stability. The stable state is change. While this terrifies Vatican officials, it energizes the religious who have taken responsibility for determining their own forms of life" in "Self-Determination and Self-Direction," 166.
34. John Paul II, *Vita consecrata*, 41.
35. CICL, *Fraternal Life in Community*, 58.
36. John Paul II. *Novo millennio ineunte*, 58.
37. John Paul II, *Redemptoris Mater*, 25–37.
38. Ibid., 26, 49. See also, "As the People of God, the Church makes her pilgrim way towards eternity through faith, in the midst of all the peoples and nations, beginning from the day of Pentecost. *Christ's Mother* . . . constantly 'precedes' *the Church* in her *journey* through human history."
39. Ibid., 28.
40. Ibid., 41
41. *Perfectae caritatis,* 1.
42. CCC, can. 607. See also SCRSI, *Essential Elements*, norms 4 and 14.
43. Suenens, *The Nun in the World*, 54.
44. Ibid., 53.
45. Ibid., 55. See also, 112.
46. Sacred Congregation for Religious and Secular Institutes (SCRSI), *Directives for the Mutual Relations between Bishops and Religious in the Church,* 2.
47. John Paul II, *Vita consecrata,* 30.
48. Ibid., 17.
49. Schneiders, *Finding the Treasure, Religious Life in a New Millennium*, 107.
50. Ibid., 108.
51. SCRSI, *Essential Elements,* 18.
852 Ibid., 18.
53. CICL, *Fraternal Life in Community*, 2.
54. See Schneiders, "Self-Determination and Self-Direction in Religious Communities," 153–178. Basing her analysis on the work of Edward Kilmartin, she polarizes and exaggerates alternate models: "In short, at the basis of the official understanding of religious life is a christomonistic ecclesiology that legitimates a divine-right monarchy model of the church. We will examine this ecclesiology later in contrast to the pneumatological ecclesiology that grounds the self-understanding of contemporary religious as self-determining agents in the church., 159. See also, "Conflicting Ecclesiologies," 166–69.
55. John Paul II, *Vita consecrata,* 17.
56. Ibid., 3. See also, Congregation for Institutes of Consecrated Life (CICL), *Fraternal Life in Community,* 2.
57. See CICL, *Directives on Formation in Religious Institutes,* 27.
58. The 1983 Code of Canon Law "specifies . . . [that] 'life in common' . . . consists of 'living in one's own lawfully constituted religious house' and in 'leading a common life' through fidelity to the same norms, taking part in common acts, and collaboration in common services," CICL, *Fraternal Life in Community*, 3; as "'experts in communion' religious are, therefore, called to be an ecclesial community in the community in the Church and in the world . . . ," Ibid., 10.
59. John Paul II, *Vita consecrata,* 66; and CICL, *Starting Afresh from Christ,* 18.

60. See Padilla, *Christ's Way of Life at the Center of Formation for Religious Life*, 5–8 and 377.

61. See Ibid., "The Instruction [*Potissimum Institutioni*] . . . presents Christ as the educator of the disciples, who were called to follow him (cf. *PL* 19; 29), and it presents the following as a journey with different stages (cf. *PL* 19; 29) . . . As the Instruction notes, Jesus was not content to call the disciples, but he educated them patiently during his public life, and also after his resurrection (cf. *PL* 19). . . . Consequently those responsible for formation must learn from Jesus how to arouse an attitude of total docility to the Father and practice the pedagogy of fortitude and patience. . . . They should initiate novices to a real experience of the paschal mystery of Christ (cf. *PL* 47), showing them that the paschal mystery is, as it were, the heart of all formative programmes (cf. pl 29). . . ," 267–68.

62. John Paul II, *Vita consecrata*, 41.

63. CICL, *Starting Afresh from Christ*, 15, referring back to John Paul II, *Vita consecrata*, 55.

64. CICL, *Fraternal Life in Community*, 43.

65. John Paul II, *Vita consecrata*, 36.

66. Ibid., 68.

67. Ibid.

68. Gambari, *Renewal in Religious Life*, 333. See also all of chapter 10: 331–51.

69. Ibid., 335.

70. Ibid., 350–51.

71. CICL, *Fraternal Life in Community*, 3, referring to can. 602.

72. See, for example, the concluding paragraph of McDonough, "The Council as Catalyst," 386–404: "In four decades of trying to achieve an *accommodate renovatio*, many communities of American Catholic sisters appear to have unconsciously but enthusiastically adapted themselves into impending oblivion, while some other communities of American Catholic sisters appear to have consciously and steadfastly remained basically unrenewed. And, in this ongoing process, the genuine challenge of Vatican Council II for religious life as a gift to the church—and to the waiting world—remains as yet overwhelmingly unrealized. Or so it seems to me."

73. Consider, for example, the following emotionally loaded words of Schneiders in "Self-Determination and Self-Direction," 162: "Small wonder that when CRSI, in 'Essential Elements,' serenely declared that the period of experimentation was now over and that religious were to put on their habits and repair to their convents, there to take up again a Tridentine lifestyle of cloister and institutional apostolates largely laid down for them by ecclesiastical authority, the declaration was met with astonished disbelief and generally ignored."

74. John Paul II, *Vita consecrata*, 41.

75. SCRSI, *Essential Elements*, 20. Cf. 48. See also norm 10 and CICL. *Fraternal Life in Community*, 14. For a discussion of how the virtue of charity forms the lives of religious striving for perfection, see Schleck, *The Theology of Vocations*, 89–99.

76. Unfortunately, some religious were poorly advised after the Second Vatican Council to abandon the practice of praying the Liturgy of the Divine Office and daily participation in the Eucharist as the center for their communal life. As is evident from the following passage from Schneiders, "Self-Determination and Self-Direction," 163: "[Women religious] surrendered community prayers that fulfilled obligations but had little effect on life and accepted instead the challenge to discover personal and communal forms of prayer that would make them new persons for a new world."

77. CICL, *Starting Afresh from Christ*, #26, referring to John Paul II, *Vita consecrata*, 18 and 95. The relation between the Eucharist and the love among the Divine Persons in the Holy Trinity is expressed in Pope Benedict XVI's encyclical letter *Deus caritas est* and his post-synodal apostolic exhortation *Sacramentum caritatis*. While these two documents were addressed to the whole Church, they also have special application to the spirituality of communion for religious.

78. Wojtyla, *Sources of Renewal*, 138.

79. John Paul II, *Vita consecrata*, 31. Emphasis added. See also, Padilla, *Christ's Way of Life,* 275: "Also in the new millennium the full force of the conciliar teaching on the Church as communion must be preserved. However, ecclesial communion is not a monolithic communion or a chaotic communion, but a communion that offers the beauty of order. . . . One does not build authentic ecclesial communion and real ecclesial collaboration by suffocating or watering down the identity and spiritual characteristics of her different members. Bishops, laity and consecrated persons must be faithful to their own ecclesial identity. This fidelity is the only dynamism that can renew and strengthen the relations of love and respect that should reign among the different members of the People of God. Consistency with the spiritual commitments of one's own programme of life is the firm foundation on which genuine 'spirituality of communion' (n. 28; VC 51) is built."

80. See the following exaggerated feminist distortion of the gift of the ordained priesthood, "The inappropriateness, to say nothing of the sheer affront, of having to introduce an outsider to preside at the most intimate community gatherings became increasingly evident. And for women it was exacerbated by the necessity of the outsider being male. The symbolic subordination and enforced sacramental dependence were galling to increasing numbers." In Schneiders, *Selling All*, 389.

81. Benedict XVI, Message for the 44th World Day of Prayer for Vocations, 4–5.

82. CICL, *Starting Afresh from Christ*, 26, referring to John Paul II, *Vita consecrata*, 51.

83. Honorius *Solet annuere*. See also Allen and O' Brian, "The Decree on the Appropriate Renewal of Religious Life—*Perfectae caritatis,"* 251–270.

84. Tanner, *Decrees of the Ecumenical Councils,* 776.

85. Leo XIII, *Gravissimas,* 487.

86. SCRSI, *Essential Elements*, norm 12. See also norm 9: "For religious, community life is lived in a house lawfully erected under the authority of a superior designated by law (can. 608)."

87. See the false understanding of the meaning of an essential characteristic as univocal Platonic essence and the subsequent reduction of an analogical essential element to an accidental aspect of religious community in Schneiders' argument in *Finding the Treasure*, 55, that "a life form, such as a Religious congregation, contrary to what is sometimes implied in Vatican documents, is not a Platonic essence composed of 'essential elements,' that is realized in substantially identical but accidentally different ways in different historical situations. Her footnote no. 8 to this passage states: "This is the impression created by the document issued by the Vatican Sacred Congregation for Religious and Secular Institutes on June 22, 1983 (dated May 31, 1983) titled *Essential Elements in Church Teaching on Religious Life. . . .*"

88. CICL, *Fraternal Life in Community*, 10. Emphasis added.

89. Ibid., 59a–b.

90. McDonough, "Canonical Counsel: Categories of Consecrated Life," 302–303.

91. Demonstrating her lack of understanding of authentic dynamic interaction between canonical constitutions, ecclesial congregations, and religious institutes, Sandra Schneiders encouraged women religious to adopt the "strategies [of] non-reception of official law, and the development of customs contrary to law . . ." in "Self-Determination and Self-Direction," 171.

92. Gambari, *Renewal in Religious Life*, 236.

93. Ibid., 246–247.

94. See Schneiders' attempt to undermine by oversimplifying Church teaching in *Selling All, 309:* "Lurking in the background of most discussions are two contradictory, and largely unexamined, premises. First is the assumption, fostered by tradition, Canon Law, Vatican literature, and the rhetoric of even revised rules, that common life, mitigated perhaps by certain necessities but essentially intact, is the normative form of community from which any deviation is an (ideally temporary) 'exception.'"

95. Ibid., 371. See also her false conflation of some poor practices of individual or communities in the past with fundamentally good elements in community life: ". . . most renewed congregations have abandoned this [Post-Tridentine model of intentional communities] as fundamentally unhealthy, and few are inclined to resuscitate it even though there is considerable pressure from ecclesiastical authority to do so. The

coerciveness, authoritarianism, ideological rigidity and thought control, shaming and shunning techniques for formation and social control . . . are fortunately a part of the past that seems definitely outgrown."

96. See, for example Ibid., 316, (and final two chapters) where the author attempts to separate artificially community life and apostolate, to conclude that: ". . . classical common life is not, theologically, the necessary or ideal embodiment of community for mobile ministerial Religious"; again in Schneiders' (*Selling All*, 317) own words we see the fallacy of false alternatives: "I am proposing . . . abandoning the term *common life* because of the historical baggage it carries, especially its negative connotations of total institution, uniformity, and authoritarianism, as well as its positive connection with the monastic lifeform."

97. Ibid., 309. Schneiders describes their thinking in false alternatives this way: "In other words, if it were possible (which, most would admit, it is not), all members of the congregation should and would be living a perhaps updated but basically traditional version of common life. Second is the gut-level conviction of most Religious that returning to common life would be personally and ministerally counterproductive, and so . . . they have no desire or intention of doing so."

98. See *Perfectae caritatis* and Allen, M. Prudence, and O'Brien, M. Judith, *The Decree on the Appropriate Renewal of Religious Life, Perfectae caritatis*, in Matthew L. Lamb and Matthew Levering, eds., *Vatican II: Renewal Within Tradition* (Oxford: University Press, 2008), chapter 12: 251–270.

99. CICL, *Starting Afresh from Christ*, 18.

100. *Fraternal Life in Community*, 59e. The passage continues: "The consequences of this have certainly not been positive; they lead us to ask serious questions about the appropriateness of continuing along this path, and suggest the need to undertake a path of rediscovering the intimate bond between community and mission, in order creatively to overcome unilateral tendencies, which invariably impoverish the rich reality of religious life."

101. Ibid., 65, referring back to SCRSI, *Essential Elements* III, 12.

102. Ibid. The passage continues: "Superiors and religious are invited to reflect seriously on this sorrowful outcome and, consequently, on the importance of resuming with vigour the practice of fraternal life in common." See also John Paul II, *Vita consecrata*, 67, for a description of how formation must have a communal dimension.

103. Ibid., 8.

104. Ibid., 45.

105. Ibid., referring in note 61 to SCRSI, *Essential Elements*, 18, and CICL, *Directives for the Mutual Relations*, 11–12.

106. Ibid., 13.

107. Ibid., 11.

108. John Paul II, *Vita consecrata*, 51. See also, Pardilla, *Christ's Way of Life*, 370: "Jan Cardinal Schotte, called *Vita consecrata* the "*magna charta* of consecrated life" because "its basis is Trinitarian and Christological, filled with the spirit of communion and founded on the paschal mystery. . . . This document has become the *magna charta* for an effective renewal of the consecrated life."

109. CICL, *Starting Afresh from Christ*, 28.

110. CICL, *The Service of Authority and Obedience*, 16.

111. Wojtyla, *The Acting Person*, 271.

112. See CICL, *Fraternal Life in Community*, 39. See also, CICL, *Starting Afresh in Christ*, 12, for two examples of this principle applied to religious communities.

113. Wojtyla, *The Acting Person*, 285.

114. Flannery, *Pastoral Constitution on the Church in the Modern World*, 32.

115. Compare this expansive description of post Vatican II solidarity in the whole body of Christ as an eschatological sign of a vibrant religious community in communion with the other vocations in the church, with the following narrow view of solidarity in Sandra Schneider's article "Self-determination and Self-direction," 164: "Deprived of the ascribed status that went with strange clothes and stranger practices, women religious had to earn, by deeds, the respect and love of fellow Christians. And in that earning, they have experienced a new

solidarity with the rest of the laity, a solidarity in commitment to the transformation of the world and a solidarity in oppression with the church."

116. Wojtyla, *The Acting Person*, 285.

117. van den Berg, "St. Benedicta's Thoughts on Community," 22.

118. Wojtyla, *The Acting Person*, 290.

119. CICL, *Fraternal Life in Community*, 32.

120. *Starting Afresh from Christ*, 29.

121. Wojtyla, *The Acting Person*, 287.

122. John Paul II, *Vita consecrata*, 74. Emphasis added. This principle is stated in the inverse in *Fraternal Life in Community*, 32: "Without dialogue and attentive listening, community members run the risk of living juxtaposed or parallel lives, a far cry from the ideal of fraternity."

123. Paul VI, *Ecclesiam suam*, 64.

124. Ibid., 82.

125. John Paul II, *Ut unum sint*, 28, referring back to *Gaudium et spes*, 24, and Paul VI, *Lumen gentium*, 13.

126. Ibid., 29–32.

127. Ibid., 33–36. See also, *Novo millennio ineunte*, 54–56.

128. Kasper, "Communion through Dialogue," 24.

129. Ibid., 25.

130. CICL, *The Service of Authority and Obedience*, 20b.

131. CICL, *The Service of Authority and Obedience*, 14b, referring to *Code of Canon Law*, 601.

132. Kasper, "Communion through Dialogue," 34.

133. Ibid.

134. Aristotle, *Nicomachean Ethics*, 6–12.

135. Aelred, *Spiritual Friendship*, Book III, 79, 111. "This is that extraordinary and great happiness which we await, with God himself acting and diffusing, between himself and his creatures whom he has uplifted, among the very degrees and orders which he has distinguished, among the individual souls whom he has chosen, so much friendship and charity, that thus each loves another as he does himself; and that, by this means, just as each one rejoices in his own, so does he rejoice in the good fortune of another, and thus the happiness of each one individually is the happiness of all, and the universality of all happiness is the possession of each individual. There one finds no hiding of thoughts, no dissembling of affection. This is true and eternal friendship, which begins in this life and is perfected in the next, which here belongs to the few where few are good, but there belongs to all where all are good."

136. Thomas Aquinas, *Summa theologica*, vol. III, part I–II, Q. 23.

137. John Paul II, *Vita consecrata*, 39.

138. Ibid., 64.

139. Ibid., 84.

140. Ibid., 94, referring back to Vatican Council II, *Dei Verbum*, 2.

141. Paul VI, *Evanglica testificatio*, 39.

142. SCRSI, *Essential Elements*, 19.

143. See John Paul II, *Novo Millennio Ineunte at the close of the Great Jubilee of the year 2000*, "A spirituality of communion indicates above all the heart's contemplation of the mystery of the Trinity dwelling in us, and whose light we must also be able to see shining on the face of brothers and sisters around us. . . . This makes us able to share their joys and sufferings, to sense their desires and attend to their needs, to offer them deep and genuine friendship," 43.

144. CICL, *Fraternal Life in Community*, 37.

145. Ibid., 37

146. CICL, *Starting Afresh from Christ*, 29.

147. John Paul II, *Vita consecrata*, 92.
148. CICL, *Fraternal Life in Community*, 41.
149. Ibid., 54. See also, 55–56.
150. Ibid., 2b.
151. Congregation for Catholic Education, *Educating Together in Catholic Schools*, 14.
152. Plenaria of the Sacred Congregation for Religious and for Secular Institutes, *Religious and Human Promotion*, 24. See also 12b, 4 where religious are called to be *"gospel experts."*
153. CICL, *Fraternal Life in Community,* 2b. See also, John Paul II, Apostolic Exhortation *Redemptionis donum, To Religious on Their Consecration in the Light of the Mystery of the Redemption, 15*, "For the sake of this light with which you must 'shine before men,' of great importance among you is the witness of mutual love, linked to the fraternal spirit of each community, for the Lord has said: 'By this all men will know that you are my disciples, if you have love for one another,'"15.

CHAPTER 5

1. Vatican II Council, *Perfectae caritatis*, 8.
2. Ibid. Also see Code of Canon Law, cc. 673 and 675.
3. See *Catechism of the Catholic Church*, 457.
4. Giussani, *At the Origin of the Christian Claim*, 53.
5. See Vatican II Council, *Lumen gentium*, 5.
6. International Theological Commission, *Texts and Documents*, 309–310. Emphasis added.
7. See Thomas Aquinas, *Summa theologiae*, I, q. 43, a. 2, reply to objection 3.
8. Of course, the term *dogma* is used in the pejorative sense here to highlight the problem of its degeneration into a merely formulaic category. No dogma is simply this.
9. See Scola, *The Nuptial Mystery*, 72–73, 222–229.
10. See Augustine, *The Trinity*, Book XV, 424.
11. Ibid., Book VI, 209.
12. Thomas Aquinas, *Summa theologiae*, I, q. 28, a. 2.
13. See José Granados, "Toward a Theology of the Suffering Body," 553.
14. See Scola, 106.
15. See John Paul II, *Memory and Identity*, 54–55.
16. See Alexander Schmemann, *For the Life of the World*, 14.
17. Thomas Acquinas, *Summa theologiae*, I, q. 28, a. 2.
18. *Dives in misericordia*, 1.
19. "Letters from the Front," *Fraternity and Mission*, 3.
20. See Vatican II Council, *Lumen gentium*, 2–4, 9.
21. Ibid.
22. See Ratzinger, "The Ecclesiology of the Constitution *Lumen gentium*," 141, 149.
23. See de Lubac, *Catholicism*, and Ratzinger, *What it Means to be a Christian*.
24. *Catechism of the Catholic Church (CCC)*, 778.
25. de Lubac, *The Splendor of the Church*, 44.
26. See Paul VI, *Ecclesiam suam*, 64.
27. See John Paul II, *Christifideles laici*, 32.
28. *CCC*, 2126.
29. Ibid., 397.
30. Batut, "The Refusal to Grasp," 9–10.

31. See Kenneth L. Schmitz, *The Gift: Creation*, 48. See also Walker, "The Poverty of Liberal Economics," 19–50; 474, footnote 11.
32. Schmitz, 73–74.
33. Ibid., 69–70.
34. See Vatican Council II, *Gaudium et spes*, 24.
35. Congress on Vocations in Europe, *New Vocations for a New Europe*, 11.
36. Ibid.
37. See Giussani, *The Religious Sense*.
38. *CCC*, 1617.
39. Ibid., 2028.
40. See ibid, 1263.
41. This understanding dominates the thought of St. Paul (1 Cor. 7:32–38). Also see Ambrose, *On Virgins*; Augustine, *Holy Virginity*; and John Paul II, *Vita consecrata*, 18.
42. John Paul II *Redemptionis donum*, 7.
43. John Paul II, *Vita consecrata*, 30.
44. Vatican II Council, *Ad gentes*, 18.
45. See Vatican II Council, *Lumen gentium*, 43–47; John Paul II, *Vita consecrata*, 29.
46. John Paul II, *Redemptionis donum*, 8.
47. Ibid., 9.
48. Ibid., 8. Emphasis added.
49. Ibid., 4.
50. Vatican II Council, *Gaudium et spes*, 24.
51. John Paul II, *Salvifici doloris*, 5.
52. Ibid., 1.
53. Ibid., 18.
54. Ibid., 26.
55. Ibid., 27.
56. Benedict XVI, *Deus caritas est*, 31.
57. Benedict XVI, *Address to Catholic Educators*, 17 April 2008.
58. Ibid.
59. Congregation for Catholic Education, *Reflection and Guidelines on Consecrated Persons and Their Mission in Schools*, 20.
60. Ibid., 24.
61. Ibid., 20.
62. Paul VI, *Evangelica testificatio*, 52.
63. John Paul II, *Redemptionis donum*, 7. This phenomenon also has a pneumatological dimension: "The mission of the Spirit hereby becomes the object of Christian experience. Thus is unfolded the mystery of the Godhead: after the Son, the Word and Wisdom of God, the Spirit is in turn manifested as a divine person entering into the history of men whom He transforms interiorly into the image of the Son of God." Léon–Dufour, ed., *Dictionary of Biblical Theology*, 368.
64. John Paul II, *Vita consecrata*, 14.
65. Ibid., 75.
66. Ibid., 15.
67. Ibid., 16. Emphasis added.
68. Ibid., 109.

CONCLUSION

1. Aquinas, *Summa theologica (ST)* II–II, Q. 183, a. 2; *Lumen gentium,* 44.
2. Ihnatowicz, "Consecrated Life in Ecclesiology."
3. John XXIII, "Opening Speech to the Council," 787.
4. Ibid., 791.
5. G. Philips, "Dogmatic Constitution," 105.
6. Wulf, "Dogmatic Constitution on Church," 122; see also Beyer, "Life Consecrated," 71.
7. See Wulf, "Introductory Remarks," 254–56.
8. Paul VI, "Secular Institutes."
9. See Beyer, "Life Consecrated," 65.
10. *Renovationis causam* I, 2.
11. *Perfectae caritatis,* 11.
12. Ihnatowicz, "Consecrated Life in Ecclesiology"; see Schleck, *The Theology of Vocations,* 87–88.
13. See *Lumen gentium,* 12.
14. Ibid., 44.
15. Bea, "Intervention," in Fogliasso, *Il decreto,* 46.
16. *Lumen gentium,* 44.
17. See Fogliasso, *Il decreto,"* 13–68; Wulf, "Decree on the Appropriate Renewal," 302–32.
18. *Perfectae caritatis,* 1.
19. Ibid., 11.
20. See *Perfectae caritatis,* 2.
21. See Carey, *Sisters in Crisis,* Chapter 2: "Ready for Renewal."
22. Norgren, "A Response," *Documents of Vatican II,* 484.
23. See McEleney, "Religious Life," 464.
24. *Ecclesiae sanctae,* II–I 6.
25. Ibid.
26. A special general chapter was to be convened within two or three years (*Ecclesiae sanctae II* no. 3). It could be divided into two distinct periods, separated by not more than a year. The experiments proposed could be prolonged until the next ordinary general chapter, which would have the faculty to continue them further but not beyond the chapter immediately following (*Ecclesiae sanctae II* no. 6).
27. See *Ecclesiae sanctae,* II–I 2.
28. *Perfectae caritatis,* 4.
29. "Inevitably there were a fair number of misjudgments in the procedure followed, but above all in the evaluation of the results of such consultations. The fault lay less with the institutes themselves than with certain sociologists or psychologists who were acting as their technical advisers in this delicate process." Dortel-Claudot, "The Task of Revising the Constitutions," 96.
30. *Ecclesiae sanctae,* II Intro.
31. Ibid., II–I 6; II–I 3, 8.
32. Frison, "Renewal of Religious," 76.
33. "The Final Report," 445, n. 4.
34. Frison, "Renewal of Religious," 45.
35. Ibid., 45
36. Carey, *Sisters in Crisis,* 114.
37. Coursey, "Theology of Religious Authority," 453–454.
38. Paul VI, "Congress of Canonists," 341.

39. *Communicationes* 2 (1970): 169–170; *Communicationes* 7 (1975): 89, VI. Marcuzzi examines the advantages and disadvantages of the various titles proposed. Marcuzzi, "Natura della potestà," 775. See also A. Gutiérrez, "De nomine quo apte," 37–59, 143–50, 225–32.

40. Bandera, "Eclesiologia de la vida religiosa," 577–602, quoted by Rincón-Pérez, ""Institutes of Consecrated Life," 1463.

41. See Beyer, "Life Consecrated," 78; *Communicationes* 13 (1981), 401–4.

42. J. Beyer considers the "secularity" considered by the Council that is proper to "laymen" or "nonconsecrated" is different from the "secularity" that characterizes secular institutes. "More precision in the terminology can be desired," according to Queralt, "Value of 'Religious' Consecration," 62, footnote 56.

43. *Lumen gentium*, 44; Queralt, "Value of 'Religious' Consecration," 43.

44. C. 709; c. 712.

45. Rincón-Pérez, "Institutes of Consecrated Life," 1918.

46. Ibid., 1912. In an attempt to clarify this enigma one commentator states, "the secular consecrated, in effect, do not change their canonical state, but at the same time, their canonical status is special, that of consecration." Another commentator explains that this canon only refers to the non-loss of the secular condition, which religious do forfeit.

47. DePaolis, "The Identity of the Consecrated Life," 98.

48. *Communicationes* 25 (1993): 260–61.

49. C. 118 CIC '17; *Communicationes* 25 (1993): 261.

50. See Ratzinger, "Announcements and Prefatory Notes," 300.

51. Castillo Lara said that the consultors in the Plenary of the Pontifical Commission for the Revision of the Code in October, 1981, chose "a formula of compromise." *Communicationes* 15 (1984): 259–60. Provost says, "The 1983 code is a work of compromise, as was the Second Vatican Council it is intended to implement. The code does not represent us with a fully coherent system, whether in the consistent usage of terms or in the application of a single, well-developed theory of government. More than its predecessor, the new code is a combination of practical decisions, traditional structures, and competing theories, sometimes laid side-by-side without an effort to compose their differences." Provost, "The Participation," 417. See also McDonough, "Laity and the Inner Working of the Church," *The Jurist* 47 (1987): 235; Celeghin, "Sacra Potestas," 185, n. 58; Ghirlanda, "De natura, origine," 120–34.

52. *Communicationes* 11 (1970): 306.

53. Ibid.

54. McDermott, "Institutes of Consecrated Life," in *New Commentary*, 761.

55. Holland, "Commentary on c. 596,"463–64.

56. See J. L. Gutiérrez, "Dalla potestà," 99.

57. See Schaumber, "Power of Jurisdiction."

58. C. 686§1; c. 688§2; c. 699§1.

59. In stating the complexity of the unresolved issues the book states: "this study assumes the *de jure* capacity of women to participate in the exercise of jurisdiction." Mulney and others, *Women and Jurisdiction*, 6.

60. Beal, Press Release, March 8, 2002, for Mulney, *Women and Jurisdiction*, Coriden also takes a similar position. He argues that women have jurisdiction in the Church; therefore, the law must be changed to match the reality. Coriden, "Lay Persons," especially 336, 345.

61. Mulney, *Women and Jurisdiction*, 7.

62. See Schaumber, "Power of Jurisdiction." In juridical doctrine, little attention has been given habitual faculties. See Arrieta, *Governance Structures*, 36. The Code simply states that the juridical regime is the same as that established for delegated power (c. 132). Habitual faculties confers the capacity to realize certain acts in a valid or licit manner.

63. See canon 132§2.

64. Rothluebber, "Experiments in Religious Renewal," 124–25.

65. Conference of Major Religious Superiors of Women's Institutes in the United States of America, *Proposed Norms,* 16–17.

66. SCRSI, "Private Letter," October 5, 1969.

67. SCRSI, "Private letter," (1972), 954. In an interview on Vatican Radio in the same year, Jean Cardinal Danielou, in describing the "decadence in religious life," referred to "group dynamics [that] are substituted for religious obedience." Danielou, "Interview," October 23, 1972, 474.

68. SCRSI, "Private Letter," April 1970, 160.

69. See SCRSI, "Decretum circa regimins," 393–394. This would become a font for c. 596 CIC '83.

70. SCRSI, "Private letter," July 10, 1972, 479.

71. SCRSI, "Private letter," August 11, 1973, 342.

72. Only a few will be cited: Schneiders spoke of "conflicting ecclesiologies:" "The leaders of women's religious life in this country have come to explicit awareness within the last few years that the underlying conflict between, on the one hand, Vatican officialdom in its attempt to dictate the parameters and control the practice of religious life and, on the other, women religious in their claim to self-determination and adult responsibility is not only a clash between medieval patriarchs and modern democrats, but, more deeply, a clash between two incompatible ecclesiologies." Schneiders, "Self-determination," 166. "We seem to have come a long way in religious life. In a very few years we have moved from the concept of the will of God in a superior's pronouncements to the will of God in a 'discerned decision.'" Reese, and Roy, "Discernment as Muddling Through," 82.

73. C. 608.

74. See Schneiders, "Self-Determination."

75. *The Service of Authority and Obedience,* 3.

76. Ibid.

77. The date of the letter from the Holy Father was April 3, 1983. *Essential Elements* bears the date of May 31, 1983.

78. *Essential Elements,* 2.

79. Ibid., 4.

80. See Holland, "Code and *Essential Elements*"; C. Honsberger, "Commentary on 'Essential Elements."

81. J. Quinn, address to "Institute on Religious Life," quoted by Holland, "Code and *Essential Elements,*" 337.

82. Ibid; one of the major complaints against *Essential Elements,* as voiced by women religious of the Union of Superiors General when they met with the Holy Father in June and July, 1983, was that they were not involved in its preparation. "Women Religious Meet," 485.

83. "The 1983 SCRIS *Essential Elements* is a feeble recall to a lukewarm monastic style completely divorced from Vatican II theology." Vidulich, "Finding a Founder"; Caspary, "Preconciliar Mold," 17.

84. Quinn, "Pastoral Service to Religious," 428.

85. *Essential Elements* 2; John Paul II, "Letter to Bishops," 1983, 178.

86. *Essential Elements* III.

87. Ibid., 38.

88. Ibid., 42.

89. Ibid., 49; Holland explains that the act of the chapter which elects the general superior, designates the person to exercise authority, but does not confer the authority. Holland, "Internal Governance," 41.

90. Ibid., 49.

91. Granfield, "Changes in Religious Life," 121.

92. Vidulich, "Finding a Founder," 170.

93. Quinonez and Turner, *American Catholic Sisters,* 62, 87.

94. SCRSI translated *Essential Elements* into Italian, French, and Spanish. Those translations are available on the Vatican website. *Essential Elements* was translated into German by the Episcopal Conference in Germany, but that translation is currently out of print.

95. John Paul II, *Redemptionis donum*.

96. Ibid., 13.

97. Ibid., 8; 14.

98. Ibid., 14.

99. Ibid., 15.

100. Ibid., 7, *Essential Elements* 5ff.

101. *Redemptionis donum*, 7.

102. It is interesting to note that many of the ecclesial documents after 1983 do not hesitate to return to the traditional concept of religious life as a "state of perfection."

103. See *Redemptionis donum*, 13.

104. See *Perfectae caritatis*, 14; *Redemptionis donum*, 13.

105. See *Redemptionis donum*, 13.

106. Report, II, C, 1.

107. Ibid., C. 2.

108. Report I, 4.

109. *The Official Catholic Directory*, 1968 and 2003.

110. McDonough, "Juridical Deconstruction," 336. See also McDermott, "*Novus habitus mentis*," 267–87.

111. Bernard Ransing to Sister Emmanuella, April 23, 1967, quoted in Carey, *Sisters in Crisis*, 117. The SCRSI stated that the responsibility for renewal was with each individual institute, the autonomy of which could be jeopardized if survey results were made public.

112. See Neal, *From Nuns to Sisters*, 5. Neal admits that elements of the "Sisters' Survey" went beyond information gathering and assessment and helped create changes in the structures of religious institutes involved in the study. See also Carey, *Sisters in Crisis*, especially chapter 7: "The Many Faces of Indoctrination."

113. Neal, "The Sisters' Survey," quoted in Carey, *Sisters in Crisis*, 113.

114. Ibid., 114.

115. Doyle, "Canonical Status of Religious Institutes," 624.

116. See cc. 584, 1256.

117. John Paul II, "Address to American Bishops," September 19, 1983, unpublished, quoted by Doyle, 364.

118. Council of Major Superiors of Women Religious (CMSWR), "Mission Statement," Washington, D.C., 2002.

119. CMSWR, "Statutes." It is interesting to compare this purpose with the stated purpose of the LCWR as accessed on their website on September 14, 2008: "the scope of the conference's concerns is broad and includes: collaborating in Catholic church and societal efforts that influence systemic change; studying significant trends and issues within the church and society; utilizing our corporate voice in solidarity with people who experience any form of violence or oppression; creating and offering resource materials on religious leadership skills."

120. *Lumen gentium*, 44; c. 590§2.

121. See *Congregavit nos*, 6; Ibid., 71.

122. Ibid., 2.

123. *Lumen gentium*, 44.

124. See *Congregavit nos*, 2.

125. *Congregavit nos*, 10.

126. See *Congregavit nos*, 47.

127. Ibid., 48.

128. Ibid., 48.

129. *Congregavit nos,* 50.

130. See *Congregavit nos,* 53; *Essential Elements,* 49; *Perfectae caritatis,* 14.

131. *Congregavit nos,* 6.

132. Gottemoeller, "Beginning the Conversation," 137–39.

133. See Schotte, "Toward the Synod," 29–42.

134. See John Paul II, "Start of the 1994 Synod," 307.

135. Schotte, "Toward the Synod," 38.

136. *Religious and Human Promotion,* 24; *Lineamenta,* 35.

137. *Lineamenta,* 36; 39.

138. O'Riordan, "Synod on the Consecrated Life," 79; McDermott, "The Fruits of Consultation," 185. Both see also McDermott, "*Lineamenta.*"

139. O'Riordan, "The Synod on the Consecrated Life," 79.

140. Gottemoeller, "Apostolic Religious Life," 254.

141. Ibid.

142. *Lumen gentium,* 44.

143. John Paul II, "General Audience," September 28, 1994.

147. Ibid., 61.

BIBLIOGRAPHY

Abbot, Walter M., ed. *The Documents of Vatican II*. New York: Corpus Books, 1966.

Aelred of Rievaulx. *Spiritual Friendship*. Kalamazoo, MI: Cistercian Publications, 1977.

Allen, M. Prudence, R.S.M., and Judith M. O'Brien, R.S.M. "The Decree on the Appropriate Renewal of Religious Life, *Perfectae Caritatis*." In *Vatican II: Renewal within Tradition*. Edited by Matthew L. Lamb and Matthew Levering. New York: Oxford University Press, 2008: 253–54.

Ambrose. "*De virginibus*." In *Patrologiae Cursus Completus*. Edited by J. P. Migne. Series Latina 7 (PL) XVI. Parisiis: Garnier Fratres Editores, 1844–1855.

―――. *On Virgins*. Translated by Boniface Ramsey. New York: Routledge, 1997.

Aquinas, Thomas. *Adoro te devote*, ca. 1224–1274. Translated by Gerard Manley Hopkins, S.J. 1844–1899. Music: Chant, Mode V; Paris Processionale, 1697.

―――. *Summa Theologica*. Translated by Fathers of the English Dominican Province. New York: Benziger Brothers, Inc., 1947.

―――. *Summa Theologica*. Translated by Fathers of the English Dominican Province. 5 vols. Westminster, MD: Christian Classics, 1981.

Aristotle. *Nicomachean Ethics: The Basic Works of Aristotle*. Edited by Richard McKeon. New York: Random House, 1941.

Arrieta, Juan Ignatius. *Governance Structures within the Catholic Church*. Montreál: Wilson & Lafleur Ltée, 2000.

Augustine, Charles. *Commentary on Canon Law*. St. Louis, MO: B. Herder Co., 1919.

Augustine of Hippo. *De sancta virginitate*. In *Patrologiae Cursus Completus*. Edited by J. P. Migne. Series Latina (PL) XL, c. 55. Parisiis: Garnier Fratres Editores, 1844–1855.

―――. *Holy Virginity*. Translated by Ray Kearney. Hyde Park, NY: New City Press, 1999.

―――. *Sancti Aurelii Augustini Hipponensis episcopi opera omnia, opera et studio monachorum ordinis Sancti Benedicti e congreatione*. Edited by S. Mauri. Parisina altera, emendata et aucta. Paris: Gaume Fratres, 1836. (Cited as follows: *De doctrina christiana libri quattuor*. In *Patrologiae Cursus Completus*. Edited by J. P. Migne, Series Latina (PL), XXXIV, c. 15–122.)

―――. *Sermo 13 de tempore: PL 39*, 1097–1098. From the *Liturgy of the Hours Volume 1*. New York: Catholic Book Publishing Co., 1975.

Balthasar, Hans Urs von. *The Christian State of Life*. San Francisco: Ignatius Press, 1983.

Batut, Jean-Pierre. "The Refusal to Grasp." *Communio International Catholic Review* 24 (1997): 9–10.

Benedict, Saint. *The Rule of Saint Benedict*. Edited by Timothy Fry. Collegeville, MN: The Liturgical Press, 1981.

Benedict XVI. "Address, Cologne, August 18, 2005." Available at: http://www.vatican.va/holy_father/benedict_xvi/speeches/2005/august/documents/hf_ benxvi_spe_20050818_youth-celebration_en.html.

―――. "Address, Rome, February 2, 2007." Available at: http://www.vatican.va/holy_father/benedict_xvi/speeches/2007/february/documents/hf_benxvi_spe_2007 0202_festa-presentazione_en.html.

―――. "Address to Catholic Educators." Washington, DC, 2008.

―――. "Angelus, Lourdes, September 14, 2008." Available at: http://www.vatican.va/holy_father/ benedict_xvi/angelus/2008/documents/hf_ben-xvi_ang_20080914_lourdes_en.html.

―――. *Deus caritas est*. Encyclical letter. Rome: December 25, 2005.

————. "Message for the 44th World Day of Prayer for Vocations, 29th April 2007." Available at: www.vatican.va/holy_father/benedict_xvi/messages/vocations/documents/hf_benxvi_mes_20071203_xlv-vocations_en.html.

————. *Spe salvi.* Encyclical letter. Rome: November 30, 2007.

Beyer, Jean. *Il diritto della vita consacrata.* Translated by Achille Palazzini. Milan: Editrice Àncora, 1989.

————. "Life Consecrated by the Evangelical Counsels." In *Vatican II, Assessment and Perspectives.* Vol. 3. Edited by Rene Latourelle. New York: Paulist Press, 1989: 64–89.

Bonaventure of Bagnoregio. *Opera omnia.* Edited by Studio et cura PP. Collegii a S. Bonaventura ad plurimos codices mss. Emendate, anecdotis aucta, prolegomenis scholiis notisque illustrata, Quaracchi, 1882–1902. 10 volumes in-folio.

Boni, A. *Gli istituti religiosi e la loro potestà di governo.* Rome: Pontificium Athenaeum Antonianum, 1989.

Bowden, Emily F. *The Fathers of the Desert: Vol.1.* London: Burns and Oates, 1907.

Brown, Brendan Francis. "The Canonical Juristic Personality." Ph.D. diss., Catholic University of America, 1927.

Camisasca, Massimo. "Letters from the Front." *Fraternity and Mission* 9, no. 4 (2006): 3.

Cantalamessa, Raniero, O.F.M., Cap. *Sober Intoxication of the Holy Spirit.* Cincinnati, OH: Servant Books, 2005.

Catechism of the Catholic Church. 2nd ed. Citta del Vaticano: Libreria Editrice Vaticana, 1997.

Carey, Ann. *Sisters in Crisis.* Huntington, IN: Our Sunday Visitor, 1997.

Caspary, A. "Are Sisters being asked to fit a preconciliar mold after 20 years of renewal?" *National Catholic Reporter* (March 2, 1984): 17.

Catherine of Siena. "Letter 29." In *Le lettere di santa Catarina da Siena.* Edited by Niccolo Tommaseo. Florence: 1860. Quoted in *The Way of the Cross* (see below).

Celeghin, Adriano. *Origine e natura della potestà sacra posizioni postconciliari.* Brescia: Editrice Morcelliana, 1987.

Chittister, Joan D., O.S.B. "Remember the Vision: Embracing the Dream. Keynote address at the meeting of the Leadership Council Women Religious, August 19, 2006." Available at: www.lcwr.org/lcwrannual assembly/KeynoteChittister.htm.

Clare of Assisi. "First Letter to Agnes of Prague, #8." In *Clare of Assisi Early Documents.* Edited by Regis Armstrong and translated by Saint Bonaventure. New York: Franciscan Institute Publications, 1993.

Code of Canon Law. Citta del Vaticano: Libreria Editrice Vaticana, 1983.

Cole, Basil, O.P., and Paul Conner, O.P. *Christian Totality.* Staten Island, New York: Alba House, 1997.

————. "Consecrated Life," *Religious Life Magazine* (March/April 2007): 19–20.

Conference of Major Religious Superiors of Women's Institutes in the United States of America. *Proposed Norms for Consideration in the Revision of the Canons Concerning Religious as submitted to the Pontifical Commission on Revision of the Code of Canon Law.* Washington, D.C.: CMSW National Secretariat, 1968.

Congregation for Catholic Education. *Reflection and Guidelines on Consecrated Persons and Their Mission in Schools.* Rome: Vatican Press, 2002.

Congregation for Divine Worship. *Rite of Consecration of Virgins.* Rome: Vatican Press, 1970.

Congregation of Institutes of Consecrated Life and Societies of Apostolic Life. *Essential Elements in the Church's Teaching on Religious Life as Applied to Institutes Dedicated to Works of the Apostolate.* Vatican City: 31 May 1983.

————. *Congregavit nos in unum Christi amor.* Rome: Vatican Press, 1984.

————. "Fraternal Life in Community/*Congregavit nos in unum Christi amor,* February 2, 1994." *L'Osservatore Romano* (February 20, 1994): inserto tabloid, I–XV.

————. *Instruction: Starting Afresh from Christ.* May 19, 2002. Vatican City: Libreria Editrice Vaticana, 2002.

————. *Instruction, The Service of Authority and Obedience, Faciem tuam, Domine, requiram.* May 11, 2008. Vatican City. Available at: www.vatican.va/roman_curia/congregations/ccscrlife/documents/rc_con_ccscrlife_doc_20080511_auto rita-obbedienza_en.html.

————. *Vita consecrata.* Rome: March 25, 1996.

Congress on Vocations in Europe. *New Vocations for a New Europe.* Rome: Vatican, 1997.

Coriden, James A. "Lay Persons and the Power of Governance." *The Jurist* 59 (1999): 335–347.

Council of Major Superiors of Women Religious in the United States of America. "Mission Statement." Washington, D.C.: 2002.

————. "Statutes." Washington, D.C.: 1995.

Coursey, R. "Problems in the Theology of Religious Authority." *RfR* 28 (1969): 452–457.

Danielou, Jean Cardinal. "Interview on Vatican Radio, October 23, 1972." *Origins* 30 (1973): 474.

de Lubac, Henri. *Catholicism.* Translated by Elizabeth Englund and Lancelot C. Sheppard. San Francisco: Ignatius Press, 1988.

————. *The Splendor of the Church.* Translated by Michael Mason. San Francisco: Ignatius Press, 1986.

De Paolis, Velasio. "The Identity of the Consecrated Life." *Consecrated Life* 22: 90–125.

de Vaux, Roland. *Les institutions de l'Ancien Testament: Vol. II.* Paris, 1960. Quoted in Lucien Legrand (see page 238).

Deely, John. *Four Ages of Understanding.* Ontario, Canada: University of Toronto Press, 2001.

Deutsch, Bernard F. "Jurisdiction of Pastors in the External Forum." Ph.D. diss., Catholic University of America, 1957.

Dortel-Claudot, Michael. "The Task of Revising the Constitutions of the Institutes of Consecrated Life as Called for by Vatican II." In *Vatican II, Assessment and Perspectives.* Vol. 3. Edited by Rene Latourelle. New York: Paulist Press, 1989: 90–130.

Dossat, Y. "Waldenses." *New Catholic Encyclopedia* (1967): 770–771.

Doyle, "The Canonical Status of Religious Institutes" *Angelicum* 63 (1986): 616–638.

Farley, Margaret A. *Beginning, Keeping, Changing Personal Commitments.* San Francisco: Harper and Row, 1986.

Farrell, Benjamin. "The Rights and Duties of the Local Ordinary Regarding Congregations of Women Religious of Pontifical Approval." Ph.D. diss., Catholic University of America, 1941.

Ferraris, Lucius. "Regulares." *Prompta bibliotheca* 6 (1861): col. 1054.

Festugière. *La première vie grecque de saint Pachôme, introduction critique et traduction.* Vol. 4, part 2 of *Les Moines d'Orient.* Paris: Editions du Cerf, 1965. Quoted in Philip Rousseau (see page 241).

Flannery, Austin, O.P., ed. *Pastoral Constitution on the Church in the Modern World: Gaudium et spes* (December 7, 1965). In *Vatican Council II, Vol. 1: The Conciliar and Post Conciliar Documents.* New Port, NY: Costello Publishing Company, 1998.

Fogliasso, Emilio. *"Il decreto 'Perfectae caritatis.'" Sul rinnovamento della vita religiosa,* 2d. ed. Turin: Elle Di CI, 1968.

Fribourg, Timothy, Barbara Fribourg, and Neva F. Miller, eds. *Analytical Lexicon of the Greek New Testament.* Grand Rapids, MI: Baker Books, 2000.

Frison, Basil. "Renewal of Religious." *Studia Canonica* 1 (1967): 45–78.

Fuertes, J. B. *"De potestate dominativa in religionibus non exemptis." CpR* 34 (1953): 198–209; 274–279; 341–346.

Fulgentius. "Epist. 3, c. 4, n.6." In *Patrologiae Cursus Completus.* Edited by J. P. Migne. Series Latina (PL) LXV. Parisiis: Garnier Fratres Editores, 1844–1855.

Gambari, Elio, S.M.M. *Journey Toward Renewal.* Boston: St. Paul Editions, 1968.

———. *Religious Life According to Vatican II and the New Code of Canon Law.* Boston: St. Paul Editions, 1986.

———. *Renewal in Religious Life.* Translated by Daughters of St. Paul. Boston: St. Paul Editions, 1967.

Ghirlanda, Gianfranco. *"De natura, origine et exercitio potestatis regiminis iuxta novum Codicem."* *Periodica* 74 (1985): 109–164.

Giussani, Luigi. *At the Origin of the Christian Claim.* Translated by Viviane Hewitt. Montreal: McGill-Queens University Press, 1998.

———. *The Religious Sense.* Translated by John Zucchi. Montreal: McGill-Queen's University Press, 1997.

Gottemoeller, Doris. "Apostolic Religious Life: Ecclesial Identity and Mission." *Origins* 24 (1994): 252–256.

———. "Community Living: Beginning the Conversation." *RfR* (March–April 1999): 137–216.

Granados, José. "Toward a Theology of the Suffering Body." *Communio International Catholic Review* 33 (2006): 553.

Granfield, P. "Changes in Religious Life: Freedom, Responsibility, Community." *America* 151 (1984): 120–123.

Greeve Davaney, Sheila, ed. *Feminism and Process Thought: The Harvard Divinity School/Claremont Center for Process Studies Symposium Papers.* New York: The Edwin Mellen Press, 1981.

Gregory IX. "Decretales." In *Emanuelis Turneysen.* 1783.

Grygiel, Stanislaw. "Virginity and Marriage: Two Expressions of the Spousal Sovereignty of Man." Unpublished paper.

Gutiérrez, Anastasio. *"De nomine quo apte designentur instituta quae consilia evangelica amplectuntur."* *CpR* 56 (1975): 37–59, 143–150, 225–232.

Gutiérrez, Jose Luis. *"Dalla potestà dominativa alla giurisdizione."* *Ephemerides Iuris Canonici* 39 (1983): 74–103.

Hamilton, Edith, and Huntington Cairns, eds. *Republic: The Collected Dialogues of Plato Including the Letters.* Princeton University Press, 1969.

Hellman, J. A. Wayne. *Divine and Created Order in Bonaventure's Theology.* St. Bonaventure, New York: Franciscan Institute, 2001.

Holland, Sharon. "Commentary on c. 596." In *The Code of Canon Law: A Text and Commentary.* Washington, D.C.: CLSA, 1985: 463–464.

———. "Internal Governance in Consecrated Life." *Proceedings of the Forty-Fifth Annual Convention of the Canon Law Society of America in San Francisco, CA, October 10–13, 1983.* Washington, D.C.: CLSA (1984): 37–48.

———. "The Code & Essential Elements." *The Jurist* 44 (1984): 304–338.

Honorius III. *"Solet annuere:* On the Rule of the Friars Minor (1223)." In *Bullarum Diplomatum et Privilegiorum Sanctorum Romanorum Pontificum.* Vol. 3. Translated by Luigi Tomassetti and Francesdo Gaude. 1958. English translation available at: http://www.papalencyclicals.net/Hon03/regulae.htm.

Honsberger, Claudia. "A Commentary on 'Essential Elements.'" *The Homiletic & Pastoral Review* (December 1984): 19–27.

Hughes, Philip. *The Church in Crisis: A History of the General Councils.* Garden City: Hanover House, 1961.

Iannone, Filippo. *Il capitolo generale.* Rome: Edizioni Dehoniane, 1988.

Ihnatowicz, J. A., S.T.D. "Consecrated Life in the Ecclesiology of Vatican II." Available at: http://www.ewtn.com/library/PRIESTS/FR91203.TXT.

International Theological Commission. *Texts and Documents: 1969–1985.* Edited by Michael Sharkey. San Francisco: Ignatius Press, 1989.

Jarrell, Lynn Marie. "The Development of Legal Structures for Women Religious Between 1500 and 1900: A
     Study of Selected Institutes of Religious Life for Women." Ph.D. diss., Catholic University of America,
     1985.

John Chrysostom. *De virginitate*. In *Patrologiae Cursus Completus*. Edited by J. P. Migne. Series Graeca, 80,
     (PG) XLVIII. Parisiis: Garnier Fratres Editores, 1857–91.

John XXIII. "Gaudet Mater ecclesia, opening address of the Second Vatican Council, October 11, 1962." *AAS* 54
     (1962): 786–796.

John Paul II. *"Apostolic exhortation Redemptionis donum."* *AAS* 76 (March 25, 1984): 513–546.

———. "Audience, Rome, October 26, 1994." Available at:
     http://www.vatican.va/holy_father/john_paul_ii/audiences/alpha/data/aud19941026en.html.

———. *Christifideles laici*. Post-Synodal Apostolic Exhortation on the Laity. Rome, December 30, 1988.

———. *Dives in misericordia*. Rome: Vatican, 1980.

———. *Evangelium vitae*. Encyclical letter. Rome, March 25, 1995.

———. "General Audience, September 28, 1994." *Insegnamenti* 17, no. 2 (1994): 402–406.

———. "General Audience, October 12, 1994." *L'Osservatore Romano, English edition* 42 (1994): 15.

———. "Homily, May 9, 2001." *Mass for the Beatification of Sister Maria Adeodata Pisani and others,
     Malta*. Cited in *Statutes CMSWR* (2001): 2 fn.

———. "Letter of His Holiness John Paul II to the Bishops of the United States, April 3, 1983." In
     Enchiridion Vaticanum (1983–1985): 164–179.

———. *Mulieris dignitatem*. Vatican City: Vatican Polyglot Press, 1988.

———. *Memory and Identity*. New York: Rizzoli International Publications Inc., 2005.

———. *Novo Millennio Ineunte at the close of the Great Jubilee of the year 2000*. Rome: Vatican, January
     6, 2007.

———. *Original Unity: Catechesis on the Book of Genesis*. Boston: St. Paul Editions, 1981.

———. *Redemptor hominis*. Rome: Vatican, 1979.

———. *Redemptoris mater: Mother of the Redeemer On the Blessed Virgin Mary in the Life of the Pilgrim
     Church*. Rome: Vatican, 1987

———. *Salvifici doloris*. Rome: Vatican, 1984.

———. *Sources of Renewal*. New York: Collins, 1979.

———. *The Acting Person*. Dordrecht: D. Reidel, 1979.

———. "The Start of the 1994 Synod of Bishops." *Origins* 24 (1994): 305–308.

———. *Theology of the Body*. Boston: Pauline Books and Media, 1997.

———. *Ut unum sint: On Commitment to Ecumenism*. Rome: Vatican, 1995.

———. *Vita consecrata*. Post-Synodal Apostolic Exhortation on the Consecrated Life and Its Mission in the
     Church and in the World. 25 March 1996.

Kasper, Walter. "Communion through Dialogue." In *A Spirituality of Communion through Dialogue*:
     *Proceedings of the Council of Major Superiors of Women Religious National Assembly (October 6–9,
     2006)*: 19–35.

Larraona, Arcadius. *"Commentarium–Partem secundum libri II Codicis quae est: de Religiosis."* *CpR* 1
     (1920): 171–177.

Leage, R. W. *Roman Private Law, Founded on the Institutes of Gaius and Justinian*. Edited by C. H. Ziegler.
     London: St. Martin's, 1930.

Legrand, Lucien. *The Biblical Doctrine of Virginity*. New York: Sheed & Ward, 1963.

Leo XIII. *Gravissimas (May 16, 1901)*. *Acta Leonis XIII*, 21: 79–81. English text: "On Religious Orders in
     Portugal," *The Papal Encyclicals*.

Leon-Dufour, Xavier, ed. *Dictionary of Biblical Theology*. Ijamsville, Maryland: The Word Among Us Press, 2000.

Lonergan, Bernard, S.J.. *Insight: A Study of Human Understanding*. Ontario, Canada: University of Toronto Press, 1992.

Manning, Joseph Leroy. "The Free Conferral of Offices." Ph.D. diss., Catholic University of America, 1945.

Marcuzzi, Pierre G. *"Considerazioni sulla natura della potestà degli istituti di vita consacrata."* *Salesianum* 46 (1984): 773–786.

Martin, Francis. *The Feminist Question*. Grand Rapids, MI: William B. Eerdman's Publishing, 1994.

McDermott, Rose. "Consecrated Life and its Role in the Church and in the World: The Lineamenta for the 1994 Synod of Bishops." *The Jurist* 53 (1993): 239–262.

———. "Consecrated Life and the *Novus Habitus Mentis*." *The Jurist* 56 (1996): 267–287.

———. "Institutes of Consecrated Life and Societies of Apostolic Life." In *New Commentary on the Code of Canon Law*. Washington, D.C.: CLSA, 2000: 741–749.

———. "The Fruits of Consultation: The 1994 Synod's *Instrumentum Laboris*." *RfR* 53 (1994): 180–191.

McDonough, Elizabeth. "Canonical Counsel: Categories of Consecrated Life." *Review for Religious* 50, no. 2 (March/April 1991): 300–306.

———. "Juridical Deconstruction of Religious Institutes." *Studia Canonica* 26 (1992): 307–341.

———. "Laity and the Inner Working of the Church." *The Jurist* 47 (1987): 228–245.

———. "The Council as Catalyst." *Review for Religious* 64, no. 4 (2005): 386–404.

McEleney, John J. "Religious Life." In *Documents of Vatican II*. New York: Corpus Books, 1966: 462–465.

Montalembert, Charles Forbes René. *Monks of the West*. Boston, 1860.

Munley, Anne, Rosemary Smith, Helen Garvey, Lois MacGillivray, and Mary Milligan. *Women and Jurisdiction*. Silver Springs, MD: Leadership Conference of Women Religious, 2001.

Neal, Mary Augusta. *From Nuns to Sisters*. Mystic, CT: Twenty-Third Publications, 1990.

Norgren, William A. "A Response." In *Documents of Vatican II*. New York: Corpus Books, 1966: 483–485.

O'Brien, Joseph D. *The Exemption of Religious in Church Law*. Milwaukee: Bruce Publishing, 1943.

O'Connor, James I. "Dominative Power of Religious Superiors." *The Jurist* 21 (1961): 1–26.

Official Catholic Directory. New Providence, NJ: P. J. Kenedy & Sons, 1968, 2008.

Origen. *Commentary on the Song of Songs II*. In *Patrologiae Cursus Completus*. Edited by J. P. Migne. Series Graeca, (PG) XIII:134. Paris, Garnier Fratres Editores, 1857–1868.

O'Riordan, Sean. "The Synod on the Consecrated Life." *The Furrow* 46 (1995): 78–86.

Orth, Clement Raymond. "The Approbation of Religious Institutes." Ph.D. diss., Catholic University of America, 1931.

Padilla, Angel. *Christ's Way of Life at the Center of Formation for Religious Life: The Biblical and Theological Perspective of Formation*. Rome: Rogate, 2005.

Paul VI. "Address to the International Congress of Canonists, May 25, 1968." *AAS* 60: 341.

———. "Address to the Participants in the International Congress of Secular Institutes, September 20, 1972." Available only in Italian at: www.vatican.va/holy_father/paul_vi/speeches/1972/september/documents/hf_p-vi_spe_19720920_istituti-secolari_it.html.

———. "Apostolic letter *motu proprio Ecclesiae sanctae*, August 6, 1966." *AAS* 58 (1966): 757–787.

———. *"Ecclesiam suam*: Encyclical On the Church." Available at: http://www.vatican.va/holy_father/paul_vi/encyclicals/documents/hf_pvi_enc_06081964_ecclesiam_en.html.

————. *Evanglica Testificatio on the Renewal of the Religious Life*. Rome: Vatican, 1971.

————. *Lumen Gentium: Dogmatic Constitution on the Church*. Second Vatican Council. 21 Nov. 1964.

————. *Ordo professionis religiosae*. Rome: February 2, 1970.

————. *Perfectae caritatis:* Decree on the Adaptation and Renewal of Religious Life. Proclaimed by Paul VI. 28 October 1965.

————. *Sacerdotalis caelibatus:* Encyclical on the Celibacy of the Priest. 24 June 1967.

Pegis, Anton. "St. Bonaventure, St. Francis and Philosophy." *Medieval Studies* 15 (1953).

Peirce, Charles Sanders. *The Collected Papers of Charles Sanders Peirce*. Vols. I–VI: edited by Charles Hartshorne and Paul Weiss (Cambridge, MA: Harvard University Press, 1931–1935); Vols. VII–VIII: edited by Arthur W. Burks (same publisher, 1958); all eight vols. in electronic form: edited by John Deely (Charlottesville, VA: Intelex Corporation, 1994). Dating within the CP is based on the Burks Bibliography at the end of CP 8. The abbreviation followed by volume and paragraph numbers with a period between follows the standard CP reference form.

Percival, Henry R., ed. "The Seven Ecumenical Councils." In *Nicene and Post-Nicene Fathers*. Vol. 14, 2nd Series. New York: Charles Scribner's Sons, 1900.

Philips, Gérard. "Dogmatic Constitution on the Church." In *Commentary on the Documents of Vatican II*. Vol. 1. Edited by Herbert Vorgrimler. New York: Herder & Herder, 1989: 105–137.

Pinckaers, Servais, O.P. *The Pursuit of Happiness—God's Way: Living the Beatitudes*. New York: Alba House, 1998.

Pius XII. "Address to the Members of the First Congress on the States of Perfection, December 8, 1950." *AAS* 43 (1951): 26–36.

————. "Allocution to Superiors General, February 11, 1958." *AAS* 50 (1958): 153–161.

————. "Apostolic constitution Provida Mater Ecclesia, February 2, 1947." *AAS* 39 (1947): 114–124.

————. "Encyclical letter *Sacra virginitas*, March 25, 1954." *AAS* 46 (1954): 161–191.

Pontifical Council for the Interpretation of Legislative Texts. *Communicationes.*

Provost, James. "The Participation of the Laity in the Governance of the Church." *Studia Canonica* 17 (1983): 417–448.

Queralt, Antonio. "The Value of 'Religious' Consecration According to Vatican II." In *Vatican II, Assessment and Perspectives*. Vol. 3. Edited by Rene Latourelle. New York: Paulist Press, 1989: 27–63.

Quinn. "Bishop's Pastoral Service to Religious." *Origins* 13 (1983): 428.

Quinonez, Lora Ann and Mary Daniel Turner. *The Transformation of American Catholic Sisters*. Philadelphia: Temple University Press, 1992.

Ragazzini, Severino M. *La potestà nella Chiesa*. Rome: Desclée, 1963.

Ratzinger, Joseph. "Announcements and Prefatory Notes of Explanation (concerning *the Nota praevia explicativa* of the Constitution on the Church)." In *Commentary on the Documents of Vatican II*. Vol. 1. Edited by Herbert Vorgrimler. New York: Herder & Herder, 1967: 297–305.

————. *On the Way to Jesus Christ*. San Francisco: Ignatius Press, 2005. Quoting Nicholas Cabasilas. *Life in Christ*. St. Vladimir's Seminary Press, 1974.

————. *Called to Communion: Understanding the Church Today*. Translated by Adrian Walker. San Francisco: Ignatius Press, 1996.

————. *Donum vitae*. Rome: Congregation for the Doctrine of the Faith, 1987.

————. "Letter to the Bishops of the Catholic Church on the Collaboration of Men and Women in the Church and in the World." Rome: Congregation for the Faith, 2006.

————. *Salt of the Earth: The Church at the End of the Millennium—An Interview with Peter Seewald*. San Francisco: Ignatius Press, 1997.

————. "The Ecclesiology of the Constitution *Lumen Gentium*." In *Pilgrim Fellowship of Faith: The Church as Communion*. Edited by Stephan Otto Horn and Vinzenz Pfnür. San Francisco: Ignatius Press, 2005.

————. *What It Means to be a Christian*. Translated by Henry Taylor. San Francisco: Ignatius Press, 2006.

Reese, Thomas and Paul Roy. "Discernment as Muddling Through." *The Jurist* 38 (1978): 82–117.

Religious Sisters. English version of *Directoire des superieures* and *Les adaptations de la vie religieuse*. Westminster, MD: The Newman Press, 1962.

Rincón Perez, Tomas. "Institutes of Consecrated Life and Societies of Apostolic Life." In *Annotated Code of Canon Law*. Edited by E. Caparros, M. Thériault, and J. Thorn. Montréal: Wilson & Lafleur Limitée, 1993: 409–492.

Rothluebber, Francis Borgia. "Recent Experiments in Religious Renewal." From *Proceedings of the Thirty-First Annual Convention of the Canon Law Society of America in Cleveland, Ohio, October 20–23 1969*. Washington, D.C.: CLSA, 1970: 122–128.

Rousseau, Philip. *Pachomius: The Making of a Community in Fourth-Century Egypt*. Berkeley: University of California Press, 1985.

————. *Widening the Dialogue*. Ottawa: Canadian Religious Conference, and Washington: Leadership Conference of Women Religious, 1974.

Sacred Congregation for Bishops and Regulars. "*Congregationis presbyterorum saecularium*, September 16, 1864." *Fontes* 4, no. 1993. (1926): 985–990.

————. "*Normae secundum quas sacra congregatio episcoporum et regularium procedere solet in approbandis novis institutis votorum simplicium*, June 28, 1901." In *Timotheus Schaefer, De Religiosis ad normam codicis Iuris canonici, 4d ed*. Rome: Typis Polyglottis Vaticanis, 1947: 1102–1135.

Sacred Congregation for Religious and Secular Institutes. "*Decretum circa regimins ordinarii rationem et religiosi saecularizati accessum ad officia et beneficia ecclesiastica*, February 2, 1972." *AAS* 64 (1972): 393–394.

————. *Essential Elements in the Church's Teaching on Religious Life as Applied to Institutes Dedicated to Works of the Apostolate*. Rome, May 31, 1983.

————. "Private Letter, October 5, 1969." Prot. N. 1678/69.

————. "Private letter, April, 1970." *RfR* 34 (1975): 160.

————. "Private letter." *RfR* 31 (1972): 954.

————. "Private letter, July 10, 1972." *CLD* 7: 477–483.

————. "Private letter, August 11, 1973." *CLD* 8: 342.

————. "Religious and Human Promotion, April 25–28, 1978." Boston: St. Paul's, n.d.

Sägmüller, Johannes Baptist. "Exemption." In *Catholic Encyclopedia* (1901): 706–707.

Said, Mark. "The Present State of the Reform of the Code Concerning the Section 'De Institutis Perfectionis.'" *Studia Canonica* 8 (1974): 213–235.

Santos, Eutimio Sastre. "*Il posto della costituzione Conditae a Christo, 8 Dicembre 1900, nella storia giuridica dello stato religioso*." *Informationes* 26 (2000): 110–139.

St. Thérèse of Lisieux: Her Last Conversations. Translated by John Clarke, O.C.D. Washington, D.C.: ICS Publications, 1977.

Schaefer, Timotheus. *De religiosis, 4d ed*. Rome: Typis Polyglottis Vaticanis, 1947.

Schaumber, Sr. Mary Nika (Monica). "The Evolution of the Power of Jurisdiction in the Lay Religious Superior in the Ecclesial Documents of the Twentieth Century." Ph.D. diss., Pontifical University of the Holy Cross, 2003.

Schmemann, Alexander. *For the Life of the World*. Crestwood: St. Vladimir's Seminary Press, 1973.

Schmitz, Kenneth L. *The Gift: Creation*. Milwaukee: Marquette University Press, 1982.

Schneiders, Sandra, I.H.M. *Finding the Treasure: Religious Life in a New Millennium*. Vol. 1. Mahwah, NJ: Paulist Press, 2000.

————. *New Wineskins*. Mahwah, NJ: Paulist Press, 1986.

————. "Self-Determination and Self-Direction in Religious Communities." In, *Women in the Church I.* Edited by Madonna Kolbenschlag. Washington, D.C.: The Pastoral Press, 1987.

————. *Selling All: Commitment, Consecrated Celibacy, and Community in Catholic Religious Life. Religious Life in a New Millennium*, Volume Two. Mahwah, NJ: Paulist Press, 2001.

Schleck, Charles A. *The Theology of Vocations*. Milwaukee: Bruce Publishing, 1963.

Schotte, Jan Cardinal. "The Consecrated Life in the Church and World: Toward the Synod." *RfR* 53 (1994): 29–42.

Schroeder, Henry J., ed. *Canons and Decrees of the Council of Trent*. St. Louis: B. Herder Books, 1941.

Schumacher, Evelyn Ann. *An Undivided Heart: Pope John Paul II on the Deeper Realities of the Consecrated Life*. Chicago: Institute on Religious Life, 2002.

Scola, Angelo. *The Nuptial Mystery*. Translated by Michelle K. Borras. Grand Rapids: William B. Eerdmans Publishing Company, 2005.

Stein, Edith. *Woman*. Translated by Freda Mary Oben. Washington: Institute of Carmelite Studies, 1987.

Suenens, Leon Joseph. *The Nun in the World: Religious and the Apostolate*. Westminster, MD: The Newman Press, 1963.

Synod of Bishops. "The Church, in the Word of God, Celebrates the Mysteries of Christ for the Salvation of the World: The Final Report of the 1985 Extraordinary Synod." *Origins* 15 (1985): 444–450.

Tanner, Norman P., , S.J., ed. *Decrees of the Ecumenical Councils*. London: Sheed and Ward and Georgetown Press, 1990.

Tillard, J. M. R., O.P. *The Mystery of Religious Life*. Herder Book Co.: St. Louis, 1967.

Valentine, Ferdinand, O.P. *Religious Obedience: A Practical Exposition for Religious Sisters*. Westminster, MD: Newman Press, 1950.

van den Berg, Regina M., F.S.G.M. "St. Benedicta's Thoughts on Community." From *Proceedings of the Tenth National Assembly of the Council of Major Superiors of Women Religious in the United States of America, Theme: Fraternal Life in Community*. Washington DC: CMSWR, 2001: 11–43. Refers to Edith Stein. "Individual and Community." In *Philosophy of Psychology and the Humanities*. Washington, D.C.: ICS Publications, 2001" 279–84.

Vatican II Council. *Ad gentes*. Rome: Vatican, 1965.

————. *Gaudium et spes*. Rome: Vatican, 1965.

————. *Lumen gentium*. Rome: Vatican, 1964.

————. *Perfectae caritatis*. Rome: Vatican, 1965.

Vermeersch, A. "Nuns." In *Catholic Encyclopedia* (1939): 164–168.

————. "Religious Life." *Catholic Encyclopedia* 12 (1911): 748–762.

Vidulich, Dorothy. "Finding a Founder." In *Midwives of the Future*. Edited by Ann Patrick Ware. Kansas City, MO: Leaven Press, 1985: 161–171.

Walker, Adrian. "The Poverty of Liberal Economics." In *Wealth, Poverty & Human Destiny*. Edited by Doug Bandow and David L. Schindler. Wilmington: ISI Books, 2003.

Way of the Cross with Saint Catherine of Siena, The. Translated by Sr. Mary of the Trinity, O.P. Rome: National Center of Catherinian Studies, 1985.

Weber, N.A. "Waldenses." *Catholic Encyclopedia* 15 (1912): 527-530.

"Women Religious Meet with the Pope to Discuss Their Life." *Origins* 13 (1983): 482–486.

Wulf, Friedrich. "Dogmatic Constitution on the Church." In *Commentary on the Documents of Vatican II*. Vol. 1. Edited by Herbert Vorgrimler. New York: Herder & Herder, 1967: 105–137.

————. "Introductory Remarks on Chapters 6 & 7." In *Commentary on the Documents of Vatican II*. Vol. 1. Edited by Herbert Vorgrimler. New York: Herder & Herder, 1967: 253–260.

CONTRIBUTORS

Mother Agnes Mary Donovan, S.V., was one of the first members of the Sisters of Life, which was founded in 1991 by John Cardinal O'Connor, the late Archbishop of New York. Prior to that she was a professor of clinical psychology at Columbia University and worked in the areas of family intervention, mother/child relationships, and special needs children. This background prepared her for ministry with the Sisters of Life and she is regularly called on across the country to speak on the order's primary focus: the protection of the sacredness of human life.

Sister Mary Elizabeth Wusinich, S.V., is a member of the Sisters of Life, a new religious institute founded in 1991 by Cardinal John O'Connor. She holds a BA in Theology from the Fransiscan University of Steubenville, Ohio. She has served in her religious community's formation program as postulant director and novice director. Currently she is the Director of the Family Life/Respect Life Office for the Archdiocese of New York.

Sister Paula Jean Miller, F.S.E., is a member of the Franciscan Sisters of the Eucharist, whose motherhouse is in Meriden, Connecticut. She is director of Catholic studies and professor of theology at the University of St. Thomas in Houston, Texas. She holds a PhD in Sacred Theology from the John Paul II Institute for Studies on Marriage and Family in Washington, DC.

Sister Mary Dominic Pitts, O.P., is a member of the Dominican Sisters of St. Cecilia in Nashville, Tennessee and is an instructor in theology and English at Aquinas College. She holds a BA in English, an MA in biblical studies, and a PhD in linguistics. During her dissertation work she went to Queen's University, Belfast, Northern Ireland; it was there that she converted to Catholicism.

Sister Mary Prudence Allen, R.S.M., is a member of the Religious Sisters of Mercy in Alma, Michigan. She holds a PhD in philosophy, and is a professort at St. John Vianney Theological Seminary in Denver, Colorado and a Distinguished Professor Emeritus at Concordia University, Montreal. Her multi-volume work titled *The Concept of Woman* is published by Eerdmans and her scholarly articles have appeared in such publications as *American Catholic Philosophical Quarterly*, *Homiletic and Pastoral Review*, *Seminary Journal*, *International Philosophical Quarterly*, and *Maritain Studies*.

Sister M. Maximilia Um, F.S.G.M., was born in Seoul, South Korea, in 1973. At the age of two she and her family immigrated to Toronto, Canada. Immediately following completion of her BA in theology, Sr. M. Maximilia entered the Congregation of the Sisters of St. Francis of the Martyr St. George in Alton, Illinois. Since that time she has earned an MTS in marriage and family and is currently pursuing a JCL at Catholic University of America.

Sister Mary Judith O'Brien, R.S.M., is a member of the Religious Sisters of Mercy, Alma, Michigan. She received her doctorate in canon law from the Pontifical Gregorian University in Rome. She is currently Vice-Chancellor of the Diocese of Saginaw in Michigan. With Sister Mary Prudence Allen, R.S.M., she co-authored the chapter "The Decree on the Appropriate Renewal of Religious Life, Perfectae Caritatis," in *Vatican II: Renewal Within Tradition* (Oxford University Press).

Sister Mary Nika Schaumber, R.S.M., is a member of the Religious Sisters of Mercy, Alma, Michigan. She received her doctorate in canon law from the University of the Holy Cross, Santa Croce, in Rome. Her dissertation, "The Evolution of the Power of Jurisdiction of the Lay Religious Superior in the Ecclesial Documents of the Twentieth Century," is published in the *Series Canonica* of the same university. She currently is on staff in the Department of Religion at Saint Francis Health System in Tulsa, Oklahoma.

The Council of Major Superiors of Women Religious in the USA (CMSWR), in union with the Holy Father and assisted by the Bishops of the United States, wish to support one another mutually in preserving the gift of their respective vocations and in progressing "still more in the life in which God has called them . . ." (LG n. 47). The specific purpose of the Council is to provide a realistically viable and mutually helpful forum for participation, education, and dialogue on the shared patrimony of the Church's teachings on matters central to the mystery and reality of religious life as integral to the life and holiness of the Church.

Other Titles of Interest

Aquinas 101
A Basic Introduction to the Thought of
Saint Thomas Aquinas
Francis Selman

This brief, engaging, and readable summary of the influential thought of St. Thomas Aquinas takes complex, confusing topics and thoughtfully, yet clearly, summarizes the legacy of one of the Catholic Church's greatest minds.
ISBN: 9780870612435 / 224 pages / $15.95

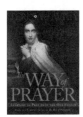

The Way of Prayer
Learning to Pray with the Our Father
Teresa of Avila

Edited and translated by William Doheny

This simple guide on how to pray offers today's Christians—whether novices or veterans—sensible insight on the practice of prayer and meditation. Readable, personal, and practical, Teresa's commentary is a wonderful way to discover the passion and the wisdom of this beloved woman mystic.
ISBN: 9780870612466 / 192 pages / $12.95

Visits to the Most Holy Sacrament and to Most Holy Mary
The Classic Text Translated and with a
Spiritual Commentary by Dennis Billy, C.Ss.R.
Alphonsus de Liguori

The first complete and faithful English translation from its original Italian of *Visits to the Most Holy Sacrament and to Most Holy Mary*, a devotional classic by St. Alphonsus de Liguori.
ISBN: 9780870612442 / 160 pages / $15.95

Behold Your Mother
Priests Speak about Mary
Edited by Stephen J. Rossetti

Nine esteemed priests, including Benedict J. Groeschel, C.F.R., and Gerald O'Collins, S.J., share how their devotion to the Blessed Mother has supported their life and ministry. *Behold Your Mother* seeks to renew this devotional practice for younger clergy, those with years of priestly life, and the laity.
ISBN: 9781594710285 / 160 pages / $14.95

ave maria press®

Available from your local bookstore or from
ave maria press / Notre Dame, IN 46556
www.avemariapress.com / Ph: 800-282-1865
A Ministry of the Indiana Province of Holy Cross

Prices and availability subject to change.

Promo Code: F0A011090000